Farthest Reach

OREGON AND WASHINGTON

by

NANCY WILSON ROSS

WESTWINDS
PRESS®

Farthest Reach: Oregon and Washington was first published in the United States by Alfred A. Knopf, Inc., New York in 1941. Published by WestWinds Press®, an imprint of Graphics Arts Books®, Portland, Oregon, in 2015 with new typography and design, but without the original fold-out map and photographs.

Library of Congress Cataloging-in-Publication Data

Ross, Nancy Wilson, 1901-1986
  Farthest reach : Oregon and Washington / Nancy Wilson Ross.
    pages cm
  Originally published: 1941.
  Includes bibliographical references.
  ISBN 978-1-941821-43-5 (pbk.)
  ISBN 978-1-941821-61-9 (e-book)
  ISBN 978-1-941821-79-4 (hardbound)
  1. Oregon—Description and travel. 2. Washington (State)—Description and travel. I. Title.
  F881.R67 2015
  917.9504—dc23
                    2014043261

Front cover illustration: iStock.com/© kristyewing
Design: Vicki Knapton

Published by WestWinds Press®
An imprint of

GRAPHIC ARTS
BOOKS®

P.O. Box 56118
Portland, Oregon 97238-6118
503-254-5591
www.graphicartsbooks.com

Contents
....

Admission and Acknowledgments

I want to begin this book by admitting freely that it is a personal interpretation of a part of America which I love, which I knew as a child in the intimate way that only children can know a country, and which I revisited and chose again for a home as an adult who had seen a good slice of the globe in between.

It is impossible with a book of this nature to be definitive, or in any sense complete. But I should like the book to accomplish two things: give the outsider a feeling of the unique flavor of this particular part of America, and give the insider a heightened sense of what he has here, what it came from, and what he can do with it if he once comes to see it in its full potentiality.

This is not a book for students, because students are very well taken care of with excellent libraries in Oregon and Washington dealing exclusively with Northwest material. I know how good these libraries are because I have made use of them and found their staffs cooperative and helpful. I have had, indeed, cooperation and help from so many people that I dare not start on a list of those to whom I am indebted, and shall have to take this opportunity of thanking them in general for special favors which have been granted to me in assembling this material.

SECTION I

The Last Playground

CHAPTER I

What Is the
Pacific Northwest?

No matter how one arrives at the geographic boundaries for the Pacific Northwest they are apt to be, in the end, personal and arbitrary. When I choose to treat under this title only the two states of Oregon and Washington, omitting Montana and Idaho, I am well aware that I cut myself off from valuable and interesting material. In particular I lose the Panhandle of Idaho, which so nearly became a part of Washington at one time, and which is today so much a part of that "Inland Empire" over which the city of Spokane unquestionably rules. The omission of northern Idaho and western Montana also deprives me of much romantic and picturesque early mining history, and prevents reportage on a section rich in that democratic heartiness and frontier sociability which still belong to Cow Country. In considering also the vital indigenous and potential resources of the Northwest I shall miss the contribution of the two states to the east, usually included in resource surveys of this section of America.

The geographic characteristics shared by the two seacoast states are: a wet green seaboard, a backbone of mountains roughly dividing the land in half, and a high and arid inland area. Oregon and Washington have produced ways of life that have manifest likenesses and significant differences as a direct result of the effect of similar landscape and climate. Without frontage on the Pacific Ocean, Montana and Idaho would share only the eastern, dry, or Cow Country qualities of this land and its folk; and so sadly I omit them, saluting in passing their rare natural beauties and their tangy frontier flavor.

There is, in the Pacific Northwest, something no other part of America possesses in quite the same degree: a freshness and promise, as though the future hadn't yet quite run out of the hourglass, as one so often feels it has along the Eastern seaboard and in the Old South, and even in many parts of the Middle West. This feeling has been packed into two enticing and nostalgic phrases: the Last Frontier, the Last Evergreen Playground. The search for this special blend of promise and answer brings yearly to the Northwest a tide of new tourists and emigrants hoping to recapture some fading dream around a campfire in sight of a snowcap, or to wrest a better way of life out of a land still in the process of "opening up."

The sense of expansion and growth arises in part from the fact that so much of local history has taken place within the memory of living man. There are old men still alive—and full of vital juices in their eighties and nineties—who were among the first whites in their district. There is certainly still plenty of untracked forest; many peaks that haven't been climbed or measured; miles of "view" without house or human; many a lonely anchorage for exploring boats. The Past and the Present do seem almost to meet in this land—so near is that which was to that which is. Even young people on the west coast can remember the Great Trees and the Paul Bunyans who chopped them down; those Scotch and Irish yarners, fiddlers, and singers, and the later silent giants out of Scandinavia, who helped turn stretches of this green country into burned-off wastes, growing fireweed, and the delicious wild blackberry. Old Indians crowding the hundred mark can still be found—by those who know where to look—willing to tell tales and dream their haunting myths out loud. Chinook jargon, that speech by which "Bostons," King George Men, and Indians conversed and traded in the old days, lingers with flavorsome effect in the speech of old-timers; soft words like "cultus," "skookum," "wa-wa," "klahowya." Indian ways of cooking dominate white feasts in the summertime; clams baked under seaweed on the beach; *salmon sluitum* on picnics of the pioneers. Not long in their graves are those credited with bringing to this country the first honey bees, the first dandelions (for medicine), the first fruit trees. Even damask roses from the mission gardens of the first French fathers on the coast can be found in a few old yards; and the great masses of yellow Scotch broom that glorify the spring countryside were said to have been brought by the early French sisters. Later comers to the land of promise brought the cows and chickens, the stoves, wagons, pianos, and mirrors, and all the rest of the large and small things by which a comfortable life is lived.

No single book could possibly encompass all the stories within a single story which would constitute an adequate chronicle of the Pacific Northwest.

Lumber and Fisheries, Shipping and Mines, Horse and Cattle ranching, Reclamation by Irrigation—each could make a saga many-sided and dramatic.

The inland country has its yarns of vigilantes and outlaws where cattle rustling was a popular pastime and where men paid for drinks in gold dust. The coast keeps pace with its stories of the wild waterfront days, of shanghaiing and smuggling around all the islands, Puget Sound, and the Strait of Juan de Fuca.

There are the tales of the days before there were roads and the rivers carried the life from the coast inland; the era of steamboating on the Columbia in the heyday of the mining boom to the east when the handsome sternwheelers and side-wheelers laboriously breasted the current, carrying prospectors and adventurers, outlaws and harlots, upriver to their assorted destinies. And back behind the steamboat to the earliest days when sailing vessels were the only connection with the world outside the wilderness; when the Sandwich Islands were the nearest source of supplies and Canton was more accessible than Boston.

There is the story of the coming of the railroads, with all their attendant scandals and crises. The steel rails pushed slowly westward through desert and mountain, dust and snow, bringing with them a flock of speculators and agents, promise-makers and promise-breakers to give the railroads a bad name in the Far West from which they have never recovered. The turning wheels carried the seed of "Jim Hill mustard" across the Rockies, and for many a town, with its hope of becoming a prosperous "terminus" finally destroyed, this was to be the only gold the railroads ever brought.

It is due in large part to the railroads that the Chinaman added his brief color to the Northwest scene. The Chinese were brought in as cheap labor, and when the railroads had been built, or abandoned, they went on into placer mining, into laundries and truck gardens and into many kitchens, until the citizens decided that their low wage scale was a growing menace and rose to push them out. But it wasn't long ago that their blue coolie suits and sandals, wide-brimmed straw hats and baskets of vegetables on poles, were a familiar picture in the streets. On holidays they sailed their bright paper kites to the envy of the same children who sang after their impassive yellow faces:

Ching Chong Chinaman, sitting on a rail,
Along came a blackbird and pulled off his tail.

The tail was the queue, of course, and the Chinamen suffered silent martyrdom over their long black braids. Drunks could never resist pulling them, and when feeling against the Chinese rose high, masked men went so far as to enter shops and hold up stages to cut off this sacred appendage as a warning that its owner was not wanted in the country (although without it a Chinaman dared not return to his native land). Only a scattering of the old Chinese are left. Most of the family servants have gone back to China to die as all good Celestials hope to do. Some few remain—cantankerous and loyal, temperamental and profane—performing their culinary miracles with chicken, pork, and green vegetables.

Women are often heard to complain of the shortsightedness that deprived them of an easy solution to the servant problem on this coast. Certainly the hardworking Northwest woman would make a book by herself, beginning with the Indian "wives" who helped white men to endure frontier privations and who must have suffered in their own way when the whites and the reds began to fight for dominance and they stood helpless between two worlds. The first white women in the Far West were missionary wives—with the exception of Jane Barnes, an adventurous London barmaid who created havoc among Indians as well as whites with her costumes and her carryings-on during a brief stay at Fort Vancouver in 1814. The missionary women seem to have all been exceptional characters; Eliza Spalding and Mary Walker enduring martyrdom no less real than that of the beautiful blonde Narcissa Whitman whom the Indians murdered outright. Missionary wives had at least a Cause to work for, but there were hundreds of other women who came west during the forties on through the fifties, sixties, seventies, and even into the eighties, against their will and better judgment, leaving behind all comforts and going into seemingly endless privations and want because their men had caught the virulent "Oregon fever." These were the women who bore their children along the line of march, saw their favorite possessions abandoned in the wayside dust as overloaded oxen gave out, buried their dead and drove the wagons over the graves so the Indians might not find them, coming after months of endurance to the trail's end only to find hardships and discomfort more vital than any they had experienced so far. These earliest women made possible the famous trip of Asa Shinn Mercer from the West Coast to the East in the sixties to bring back a cargo of New England virgins, and later Civil War widows, to fill the frontier's most desperate need—good wives for the white men. They provided the necessary respectable background for "Mercer's girls" to come to.

An over-romantic and too fulsome treatment of the pioneer has led many people in the Northwest to a sharp reaction which—with equal stupidity—allows no good word to be said for these hardy early emigrants from the east. The novel *Honey in the Horn*, although it outraged and angered many descendants of pioneers, who are apt to ask sourly what the Pulitzer Prize stands for anyway if it can be given to such a book, certainly came to many of the less beglamored residents of the Northwest as a distinctly astringent relief. Truth, however, is apt to lie between extremes, and certainly the proper approach to the pioneers of early Oregon—despite current tastes in literary modes—does not lie through an Okies of 1840 angle any more than it lies through a transplanting of Virginia cavaliers and their ladies. The early Oregon pioneers were American folk; the same kinds of people and in just about the same proportion of races and types as the settlers of the Eastern seaboard and the Middle West.

The complete story of the Pacific Northwest Indian—treated not alone as ethnological subject but as human being—has never been told, and it would make a fascinating chronicle, rich and varied and full of strongly developed personalities. The Northwest Indian pantheon contains names worthy of a place alongside King Philip, Black Hawk, or Tecumseh. First of all there is the remarkable Young Joseph of the Nez Percés, who conducted an unwilling campaign against the whites to retain the beautiful Wallowa Valley, ancestral home of his people. Joseph's retreat of over one thousand miles hampered by women and children, and his superb last stand, are ranked as masterpieces of military strategy. Then there is Leschi whom the whites hanged for wanting to keep the Nisqually plains for Indian horseracing and the streams for Indian fishing; a story on which violent sides have been taken—both Ezra Meeker, the old pioneer, and the contemporary writer of fiction, Archie Binns, finding Leschi less guilty than Governor Stevens. There's Captain Jack of the Modocs who waged a war in the Dantesque landscape of the southern Oregon lava beds; Lawyer and Moses, Kamiakin and Seattle, and the Duke of York from Port Townsend who affected a high silk hat, had two wives known as Jenny Lind and Queen Victoria, and whose engaging character was blackened—perhaps unfairly—by Theodore Winthrop, the young Bostonian whose *The Canoe and The Saddle* is a Far Western classic of the early days.

The poignancy of the Indians' inevitable defeat comes through with moving force in some of the speeches and the questions the "blanket men" and the "long hairs" put to the triumphant whites. Thus Chief Seattle: "The very dust under your feet responds more lovingly to our footsteps than to yours, because it is the ashes of our ancestors." Seattle told his white friends that long after the last red man had perished and his memory had become only a white man's myth, the shores and woods and even the streets would still throng with the invisible dead Indians who had so "loved this beautiful land. . . . The white man will never be alone. Let him be just and deal kindly with my people for the dead are not altogether powerless." And then there is that mildly puzzled profound question of Young Chief at the council of whites and Indians called by Governor Stevens in 1855: "I wonder if the ground has anything to say? I wonder if the ground is listening to what is said?" The Northwest Indian story contains humor and dark tragedy and poetry; fierce action and passive resignation; fanaticisms of loyalty and revenge; farce, wisdom, folly, and every type of mysticism including even voodoo.

Northwest native cookery would make a fascinating book also, with its mingling of many elements: Indian, Chinese, Japanese, New England, Old South, and more than a flavor of Scandinavian and Russian. There are famous dishes in the Northwest indigenous to this part of the country: Geoduck steaks cut from a gigantic clam; Captain Doane's famous oyster pan roast, made from the little native Olympia oysters—a dish, accompanied by whiskey, which played its part in many an informal political caucus of the early days; barbecued hard-shelled crab, served with curry sauce; pies of wild blackberry and salal; Oregon grape jelly; smoked brook trout prepared over a willow fire; goat's milk cheese from Pistol River or the rich creamy American cheddar from Tillamook.

For genuine campfire and fireside yarning it is doubtful if any other part of America can surpass the Northwest. There are all the elements necessary for folk tales and apocrypha: Indians, prospectors, miners, loggers, woodsmen, and fishermen; cowboys, outlaws, and cattle country sheriffs; sea captains and river captains, hermits and mystics, pioneers and old-timers. Yarners like Hathaway Jones of the Rogue River appear, give their prodigious imaginations a good stretch, die, and leave behind a body of humorous legends. Loggers in the land of the big trees add their picturesque quota to the still-growing saga of Paul Bunyan, the mighty giant. The Oregon seacoast which saw Drake fresh from Spanish plunder has many an ancient tale of white men and buried treasure; the most famous concerns the cache of beeswax with its mysterious inscriptions found in the sands of Nehalem. And there are classic yarns expanded into rich fictional proportions from a kernel of interesting truth which no amount of factual denial will ever succeed in killing. Among these is the famous tale of the Rawhide Railroad from Walla Walla to Wallula which was eaten by coyotes in a severe winter; and the Spokane yarn of the lawsuit over the ownership of the errant donkey who discovered the famous Bunker Hill and Sullivan mine of the Coeur d'Alenes.

There is the story of the people of the Northwest themselves, as seen through their own legislation; Oregon's combination of conservatism and innovation; Washington's extravagance and the horseplay and corruption of many of its political figures, along with some genuine liberal fervor. There is the story of Northwest Labor; the marching of Coxey's local army under the leadership of General Jumbo Cantwell, a "bouncer" in a famous Tacoma gambling resort; the rise of the revolutionary I.W.W.; the "massacres" at Centralia and Everett; the early Socialist and Anarchist colonies of Aurora, Freeland, Burley, Home; the far-reaching activities today of Seattle's Dave Beck and his notorious Teamsters' Union.

Finally there is this very moment's drama of hydroelectricity, the Northwest's great new challenging potential; and along with it, an inseparable part of it—tied up with the promise of reclaimed lands and cheap electricity—the new migrations toward the Pacific; the jalopy caravans of defeated people moving out of exhausted country, moving westward filled with hope and fear.

The geologic history cannot be surpassed for mystery and marvel in all this continent. Where else could one find so varied a record of the action of ancient convulsive forces on the surface of the earth? Snowcapped mountain ranges like the Cascades and the Olympics; mighty rivers like the Snake and the Columbia; mountain passes six thousand feet high connecting Canoe and Horse country; gentle rich western valleys like the Skagit, the Puyallup, the Willamette; vast dryland acreage like the Oregon cattle counties of Malheur and Harney; wheat lands like the Palouse; apple country like the Wenatchee and Yakima, Hood River and the Valley of the Rogue—and all the riddles of lost rivers, dry falls, cones and craters and lava blankets that tease the scientific mind.

Is it to be wondered at that in a country of such scope and richness and dimension the people fell victim to the American weakness of the worship of the Big Thing—dimension admired just for dimension's sake? Not long ago I saw the first copy of a *Junior Historical Quarterly* issued by the University of Oregon extension service. In it there appeared an article which showed, by the aid of old maps, that Gulliver's Land of Giants, the fabled Brobdingnag, was actually the Olympic Peninsula. Swift created this mythical kingdom after reading Hakluyt and Purchas and their tales of the legendary kingdoms of Quivira and Anian which lay along the great unknown western ocean. This same magazine quoted from *Harper's* of 1883, "They have discovered footprints three feet long in the sands of Oregon, supposed to belong to a lost race."

Small wonder the Northwestern myth hero is Paul Bunyan, the logger giant. And in truth the far western country was not built up by weaklings. It took strong men to dare the trip westward in the first place, to accept for themselves and their wives and children seemingly endless hardships and solitude; to hew the great trees and make little clearings in the green gloom of formidable forest; to believe wholeheartedly in the future of dry desert lands; to resist the lure of goldfields south, north, and east; to keep exhausted and homesick women on the track; to exert pressure for wagon roads and later for railroads, adequate defense measures against Indians, representation in the states "back home" and all the rest of it. A Northwesterner who knows his history is always anxious to point out to the inquiring stranger that this country was won for America—in the face of marked indifference at the national capital—by the men who settled it, set up their own government, and prepared if need be to fight to keep it. This way of acquiring territory is unique in the history of America.

There's a good deal that the descendants of pioneers might well be proud of in this Northwest country, and there are some things of which they should be heartily ashamed: curious prejudices, tendencies to exclusion and bigotry for which today we have created the word Fascist without at all altering the quality of the thing described. The descendant of pioneers is apt to look with a wary and suspicious eye on the somewhat less glamorous pioneers of the present: those migrants from the Middle West who have been pushing westward since 1935 at an estimated one hundred and ninety a day, searching for green land, rainfall, and a future for their children.

Minority groups in the Pacific Northwest—notably Chinese and Japanese—have not had a very happy history. When the Chinaman ceased to be useful as a railroad builder he was no longer welcome, and the shameful way in which he was ousted from coast and inland cities does not make very pleasant reading, although then, as so often today, there was the curious anomaly of the big interest and the liberal pleading together for racial tolerance, while on the other side of the fence stood the little man who was feeling the Chinese wage scale right in his stomach. Today liberal-minded people are already organizing to prevent the occurrence of similar treatment of a minority in the Northwest with the rising tide of anti-Japanese sentiment that now dominates the coast.

In the Pacific Northwest are clearly set forth those powers of destruction and construction by which man affects the land in which he lives. The Northwest country is still too new to hide its scars and shames. Ugly and meaningless waste has followed in the wake of the mining and lumber industries; towns which just "grew" are usually eyesores in a spectacular landscape. In a ghost town along the Eastern seaboard, when the essential industry has closed its doors and departed, the sight is not always immediately shocking or deeply depressive, for there is some rather gentle air of the past lingering about the place; the houses not infrequently possess the graciousness of line and simple dignity that belonged to a slower-paced era, and there are old trees to hide the illness that has fallen upon the community. Most of the dead towns of the Pacific Northwest, on the contrary, are apt to be grotesquely naked and ugly; for they grew up in a period when architecture, along with all the other arts, had died a shameful death. Here is post–Civil War America set forth with little softening detail from a less "commercial" earlier period. There are exceptions of course—towns that grew and died, or faded, with an air: Jacksonville, Oregon, and Port Gamble, Washington.

Yet not all the picture of the Pacific Northwest's use of resources is a dark or negative one. The great new projects for irrigating land and for generating cheap electricity challenge the imagination with the scope of their promise. But the Northwest country did not have to wait for government help to get its drylands into productivity. Although certain irrigated valleys no longer seem so amazing in the light of the vast program of the Columbia Basin Irrigation Project they do stand as concrete examples of an aphorism from the drylands, "There's no waste country, only waiting country." And these same valleys, irrigated for so many years and caught now into far-reaching economic problems of distribution, present two basic American anomalies: the economic insecurity of the man who grows our foodstuffs; the presence of hunger in the midst of plenty.

The Pacific Northwestener—true American that he is—finds it a heady experience to boast of the statistics which the government issues on the Grand Coulee Dam. He feels himself Paul Bunyan indeed when he tells you that man has built a dam on top of which four ocean liners the size of the *Queen Mary* could be carried with space to spare. But he is beginning to realize that the true story of this enterprise will be told in the uses to which such a gigantic piece of engineering are eventually turned.

The question of what will happen to the states of the Last Frontier is tied close to the heart of the American dream—and when one reads the history of this country there seems little reason to doubt that there was a dream. In the Pacific Northwest one might truly say the dreamer and the awakened one face each other.

What has drawn and still draws people to this country, and so often holds them there, is not alone the economic and social advantages offered by land that is still "open." It is something with a deeper and less tangible pull. The landscape itself beckons. The eye is always being stretched to the tops of high peaks and tall trees, across golden deserts to purple hill slopes, around bends in great rivers and turns of the magnificent coast highways where great waves break far out on the solitary rocks of an old shoreline. Nature is inescapable in this part of the world. The Pacific Northwesterner carries snapshots of his "view" around with him along with pictures of his wife and children. Real estate agents have long recognized the selling force of "view lots" which make up in distant glimpse of mountain, lake, river, or sea for any possible inconveniences in transportation facilities. Nowhere do cities lie so close to scenes of breathtaking beauty, ringed round with shining water and snowcapped peaks. Even in the eastern drylands nature forces the sense of her power and mystery into the human consciousness with the beautiful tortured forms of ancient convulsions. One can go to many places in the Pacific Northwest and forget for a while what is happening in "the world." And perhaps we need these moments of freer and quieter breathing, for certainly something comes back to the average man in the sight of high mountains and within the sound of lapping tides, or in the breathless brooding silence of desert stretches and vast deep canyons thrust into the earth's surface. Here an American can recapture a sense of the legendary beauty and poetry of his native land. Here it is possible again to catch a glimpse of a forgotten vision. "The Last Frontier" people say wistfully, even fearfully, looking out across the great blue stretch of the Pacific. Nostalgia and sadness are in the phrase, but there is certainly also promise.

"Well, we've come to the Jumping-Off Place at last," pioneer women used to say, sitting down wearily at the trail's end, sometimes to weep with their faces turned away, hidden in apron or sunbonnet. . . . The farthest reach, the shore of the other ocean, no more land for track of foot or wheel. So here we pause and stand and take our final root.

CHAPTER II

Historical Background

LOOKING BACK

The Pacific Northwest has recently become very conscious of its history. Everywhere historic roads and trails and the campsites of famous exploring or pioneering parties are being re-marked; old blockhouses, forts of the Indian War days, early cabins, and fur trading posts are now carefully preserved or restored; and the gracious houses of the first days of wealth and leisure are re-furnished by the women of pioneer societies.

From early summer to mid-autumn, one can see in almost any town embarrassed young men going about their normal business wearing an imposing growth of whiskers, and young women swishing self-consciously down the streets in the long full-skirted dresses of another period. These are unmistakable signs of a Pageant, a Fair, a Round-up, a Jubilee, a Stampede, a Potlatch, or just a simple Celebration.

The university town of Eugene, Oregon, gives a performance every three years which might serve as a model of what a good pageant can be when a community of above-average people whole-souledly devote themselves to a spectacle intended not alone to please boosters but to give enjoyment to poets, musicians, and artists. Goodwin Thacher, the University of Oregon professor who writes the scripts, does not do just a "continuity," he does a "poem," a "song." Some three thousand people and five hundred animals take part in these great outdoor performances. All the university resources are tapped, including the departments of Drama, Music, and English, and the School of Physical Education, which helps train the dancers. The Eugene Gleemen and the Women's Choral Union take part. All the rural families from the pioneer county of Lane contribute costumes, equipment, and participants. There is no speaking, only singing, music, and pantomime; and the parade is so complete that the one criticism ever leveled at it (and old-timers can be very critical) was made by a woman from arid eastern Oregon who said that it had "everything except water-witches"—an oversight which the Eugene *Register Guard* was pretty sure would be corrected next time.

At these anniversary celebrations the local papers find delight in reprinting the singularly inept prophecies of certain men who fought the annexation of Oregon Territory when it was a matter of debate in the United States Senate. The eminent Mr. Daniel Webster often commands a lead paragraph with his long-remembered words of the 1840s: "What can we do with the western coast, a coast of 3,000 miles, rockbound, cheerless, uninviting and not a harbor on it? What use have we for such a country? I will never vote one cent from the public treasury to place the Pacific Ocean one inch nearer Boston than it is now."

Senator McDuffie of South Carolina was pleased to state that he would not "give a pinch of snuff for the whole territory." He went so far as to wish that "the Rocky mountains were an impassable barrier"; while even Senator Thomas H. Benton, Oregon's staunch friend, considered that perhaps these rocky peaks had indeed been "placed by Providence" to mark the western limits of the States and set thus a boundary to man's ambitions.

Many of the best minds of the period were solidly against the settling of these distant lands; but there were, fortunately, a number of simple people willing to set out on one of those almost mystical American drives in search of the promised land.

When the local papers publish short résumés of Northwest coast history, many accounts begin with Balboa wading into the Pacific far to the south in 1513, flag in hand, to claim all the shoreline of this unexplored ocean in the name of his country. This included the lands of the Northwest, which Balboa did not see, and it was Spain's first claim to the territory which at one time, from her Mexican seat, she wished to annex to herself.

In the sixteenth century most of the famous European mariners were busy searching for something which did not exist except in wishful thinking, the legendary Strait of Anian, or Northwest Passage to the Orient.

About the time that Henry VIII was scandalizing Christendom with his goings-on a Spanish galleon under Bartolome Ferrelo moved cautiously up the west coast, perhaps as far as the forty-third parallel, which means that Ferrelo was the first white man to reach the latitude of Oregon. In 1579, Francis Drake, busy making life uncomfortable for the Spaniards in the name of Henry's daughter the Virgin Queen of England—a perverse jade who wouldn't say yes or no to the king of Spain on the subject of matrimony—sailed his famous *Golden Hind* along the same wild coast. Some authorities say he reached the forty-eighth parallel, which would be about on a line with the town of Everett, Washington. Others say he certainly sailed no farther than the forty-third parallel. But however far Drake got he gave as his reason for turning back a report of weather conditions which well-read native sons have been resenting ever since. Although it was June the "chaplain" to his roistering buccaneers claimed that they traveled in intense cold and snow. Residents of the Pacific Northwest, who boast of roses in January—although the land lies in the latitude of Newfoundland—quite frankly don't believe Parson Fletcher's story.

After Drake, Sebastian Vizcaino came in 1602 from Spain to Monterey in California and from there pushed on north the following year as far as the forty-third parallel, leaving a record of his passing in the names of such Oregon coast promontories as Cape Blanco and San Sebastian.

In the years that followed, until 1774, so far as records go—though

Oregon Indian myths say otherwise—no alien eye was laid upon that roaring coastline, no outsider caught a glimpse of naked red men with deformed heads, faces painted with mica and ochre; holding their annual food gathering expeditions for fish, roots, berries; fasting and communicating with spirits; performing their mystic rites. While European nations contended for the eastern part of the New World, the western part slept in wild beauty, its snowcapped peaks unassailed, its records of geologic convulsions—exploding mountains, seas of lava, prehistoric oceans—unread by knowing eye. The hundreds of miles of waterways were disturbed only by Indians paddling their dugout canoes, chanting their minor songs on the waters of Whulge, their name for the inland sea; looking respectfully at the Mountain that was God—which no red man dared approach—or at Kulshan, the White Watcher—the Mt. Ararat of their flood legend, now known prosaically as Baker.

In 1774 Spain roused herself for another effort on the Pacific to consolidate her claims there. She sensed a threat in Russian activity far up the Northwest coast and in the gradual pushing overland of the fur companies from Hudson's Bay. Up the west coast then sailed Juan Perez, bringing back little of value except word that the northern Indians would seem to have had white communication since they had iron trinkets in their possession. Perez was followed in 1775 by Bruno Heceta who formally claimed the Northwest lands for Spain and who brought back a report of turbulent discolored water off the shore to the north which was probably the Columbia resisting the Pacific with a fierceness so pronounced that it took years for mariners to fight their way into her waters. Neither of these two Spanish mariners got as far north as Alaska, where the Danish captain Vitus Bering, in service to the fabulous Tsar Peter, had already discovered the sea otters, destined to play such a significant part in Northwestern development.

It was left to Englishmen to publicize the big trade discovery on the west coast. As a result of the travels of Captain James Cook, who came out in 1776 from London, word got back of fortunes in furs to be had in this part of the world. On the return journey Cook's ship stopped at Canton and the sailors discovered that the Chinese would pay fabulous sums for the shabby sea otter furs they had bought from the Nootka Sound natives for sundry metal oddments like old coat buttons and drawer handles.

In spite of Cook's discovery it took some years for trade to get brisk on this distant coast. No names need concern us in this period except that of John Meares, since it is through him, as Philip Parrish has said in *Before The Covered Wagon*, "that the current of history runs." Meares is famed for a number of things, including the launching on this bleak northern shore of the first boat to be built on the Pacific coast; built moreover by fifty Cantonese—the first Chinese laborers to be brought to this country. Word of Meares's activities up north got about among the Mexican and California Spaniards, and they sent a company north to seize ships, build forts, and in general make it plain to the British that these waters belonged to Spain. Meares heard of it in China and took home a full and angry report to London. It almost caused a European war. Meares insisted that he had purchased Nootka Sound—so named by Captain Cook who spelled it as he thought the Indians pronounced it—and there was no one to prove that he hadn't, so in the end after some hot words and musket brandishing Spain relinquished her claims. The Nootka Sound Controversy brought Captain George Vancouver up the coast, as representative for England, and Vancouver can never be forgotten here because he managed to give geographic names that have stuck all these years: the mountains Rainier and Baker, Hood Canal, the islands of Whidby and Vashon, Port Townsend and Port Orchard, Admiralty Inlet, Bellingham Bay, and Howe Sound. Vancouver's lieutenant, William Broughton, named a point on the Columbia River for his master and gave the snowcap he saw in the distance the name of Mt. Hood.

While Spain and England were arguing over their rights, these western waters had begun to give anchorage to Yankee ships whose crews also bartered for furs in summer and wintered in Hawaii. The stage was slowly being set for that markedly bloodless quarrel by which mighty expanding England and the still insignificant but ambitious United States were to determine whose country this Pacific Northwest really was.

THE RIVER OF FABLE THAT REALLY EXISTED

For many years it seemed likely that the tale of a mighty westward-flowing river, rising in a mountain of shining stones and emptying into the great sunset ocean, was but another compound of Indian myth and white man's dreamings. Perhaps no river in history has enjoyed so much enshrouding of mystery as the Columbia, long called the Oregan or Oregon—a name whose genesis is lost.

There was a Yazoo chief named Moncacht-apé who—sometime during the middle of the eighteenth century—got bored with his restricted life in the valley of the Mississippi and set out to verify tales he'd heard of great oceans to the east and west. He went first to see the Atlantic and reported to a French explorer, who has told his tale for posterity, that his "eyes were too small for his soul's ease." He then set off promptly to find the great western body of salt water. He said he got to the Pacific by way of a great westward-flowing river, and if one believes the tale at all it seems likely that this was the Columbia.

Even while the British were still looking for that long-sought Northwest Passage by way of Hudson's Bay, a Connecticut captain named Jonathan Carver had returned from extensive travels in the interior of America with tales of a great river which he called the Oregan—a name he claimed to have got from Indians. Carver had maps, too, somewhat fanciful ones, and he took his maps and his tales and his mysterious river name with him to London, where perhaps he imagined he would have a better audience. Carver averred that the British planned to send an expedition down this river and establish forts at its mouth. But Captain Cook's unwitting discovery of fortunes in furs had already begun to turn a tide of mariners toward the Northwest coast. Unhappily for England's plans the American colonies decided to break their bonds with the mother country and it remained for a Boston fur trader, Robert Gray, to immortalize himself in 1792 by discovering the fabled river—and naming it for his hardy little craft, the *Columbia*.

Gray, undaunted by the names Cape Disappointment and Deception Bay, with which the explorer Meares left record of his failure to find the

River of the West, succeeded in putting his little ship over the bar that hid with such wild fury of foam and wave the spot where the Columbia met the Pacific. Gray sailed twenty-five miles upriver, hoisted the American flag, and planted some Pine Tree shillings in the soil. Vancouver sent an expedition under Broughton up the stream much farther than Gray had gone, to lend weight to England's possible claims. But the fact that Gray—though only a fur trader without government authority—had been there first was to prove helpful later in establishing America's colonization rights by virtue of "discovery" rights.

EXPLORERS ON FOOT

No expedition by foot across uncharted terrain can compare in human interest with an American expedition of 1804 and 1805 made by two Virginia gentlemen (one with chronic melancholia), a party of twenty-nine ill-assorted men, and Sacajawea, an Indian woman won for small change in a gambling game. This was the Lewis and Clark expedition which the far-sighted president, Jefferson, organized to explore the western part of the American continent, to which he thought the United States had as good a right as any other country. Shrewd Mr. Jefferson concealed his real intentions under a display of interest—quite sincere but secondary—in mastodon bones, botanical specimens, and commercial treaties with the Indians, but he apparently had it in his mind to get Americans into the valley of the Columbia in order to add some "rights by exploration" to that "right by discovery" which Gray's river trip was believed to be.

Jefferson's interest in this remote land was probably given impetus by the enthusiasms of an unusual character named John Ledyard whom he met in Paris while serving as ambassador. Ledyard was a well-born adventurer who, though American, had served under English flags and had made the trip with Captain Cook when the possibilities of the fur trade were first perceived. When Jefferson knew Ledyard, he was full of a plan to cross Europe and Siberia to Kamchatka, enlist there on a Russian trader, desert ship somewhere on the west coast, and come back on foot to the American colonies. Poor Ledyard died before he accomplished any of his plans, but he is believed to have sowed in Jefferson's mind the first seed of the idea of an overland expedition.

The Lewis and Clark trip cost twenty-five thousand dollars and took two years. The leaders left a journal which, oddly enough, had to wait one hundred years for publication. This journal remains one of the great chronicles of human endurance and sound psychological practices under trying conditions. Clark had his negro, York, with him and York was a famous dancer. His solo numbers never failed to please the Indians they encountered en route. In fact York's black skin, Lewis's red hair, the company's possession of such miraculous objects as a compass, a magnet, and a spyglass, played no small part in aweing the Indians into hospitality whenever Sacajawea's helpful family connections weren't enough to smooth the way. The company also had a violinist and the violin survived the trip out and back and was often pressed into use to raise the spirits of the men when they flagged from weariness. There were certain medicine show aspects to this important early expedition; the dancing, the freaks, and the distribution by Lewis to the Indians of ointments, eye wash, and Rush's pills. Lewis and Clark observed Christmas as best they could. Even at Fort Clatsop in sodden weather when they were ridden with fleas, and the only food was moldy elk's meat, bad fish, and a few roots, they exchanged gifts. Sacajawea, or "Janey" as the Journals sometimes refer to her, gave Clark two dozen white weasel tails, while Lewis offered fleece underwear, and all the men received either tobacco or handkerchiefs.

When Meriwether Lewis got back to the States and made his report to the president, a good part of it was taken up with an analysis of the conditions for fur trading in the far west, and to suggestions as to where and how to establish centers for carrying on a business which was bound to grow increasingly profitable as the use of furs ceased to be a luxury—possible only for the very rich in Europe—and began, instead, to be a fashion.

In the early years of the fur trade on the west coast the deck of the vessel was the place of business. Bold seamen and traders wove a strange and colorful embroidery of old and new, East and West; London, Canton, Boston, St. Petersburg, Nootka Sound, and the Sandwich Islands. There were chiefs from Owyhee, as Hawaii was then known (a name still to be found in Oregon geography), and Indian chiefs with the wanderlust who exchanged visits. One Nootka Sound dignitary returned to his people from a visit to China wearing a queue into which had been braided so many copper handles from saucepans and frying pans that he could scarcely stand upright. He also had bits of metal sewed to all possible parts of his garments and he set foot on his native soil carrying a large skillet, snatched from the indignant cook in the galley at the last moment. He disembarked a millionaire, for in those days the northern Indians prized metal above all things.

What to trade with the Indians for their furs was a matter of great import to the early men in the Far West, and it remained so, long after the trade had been organized into a land business with posts established in the Northwestern wilderness. Yankee traders, who were a little more on the freelance side, used whiskey to their subsequent discredit and in marked contrast to the Hudson's Bay Company, which, under the canny John McLoughlin ruling at Fort Vancouver from the 1820s to the 1840s, absolutely forbade it as an article of trade. It is said that when the first Indians on the coast tasted firewater—presumably given to them by Vancouver's man Broughton—they were so astonished and ashamed of the way they felt that they ran into the bushes and hid until they recovered. But aversion did not last long. To this day it is against the law to sell an Indian liquor, and whether it is true that he is congenitally unable to handle it or has just never been allowed to learn how to take care of it, one would hesitate to say. Newspapers frequently print stories of the death of Indians from some fancy concoctions they make for themselves with which to while away the rainy evenings of winter. The Muckleshoot Indian Reservation near Auburn, Washington, had a number of deaths recently from some cocktails of "Antifreeze" shaken up with huckleberry and blackberry juices from the summer harvest.

The Yankee "mountain man," after a successful day of exchanging drinks for furs, sometimes found it necessary at night to establish a sober guard over his own person. This guard was required from time to time to fire off his gun to prove that he was still in possession of his faculties. Waking up to find himself in a circle of dead Indians was apparently not too novel an experience for this early commercial traveler.

Tobacco was always a good medium of exchange with the red men. Little mirrors and boxes of paint were in great favor also, for even the fiercest braves thought nothing of sitting in the sunlight making up their faces. Although the shrewd and redoubtable "Father of Old Oregon," John McLoughlin, managed by a combination of good works and fox-like cunning to keep the Yankee traders pretty well out of the Hudson's Bay domain, he was not always completely successful. In *The White Headed Eagle* Richard Montgomery tells of the visit at Vancouver of Captain William McNeill, of the Boston Brig *Llama*, who brought in a cargo of gimcracks which McLoughlin knew at once, with sinking heart, would have an irresistible appeal to the Indians: brightly painted jumping jacks, whistles, and wooden soldiers. The Indians seem to have learned extremely slowly how to trade with the whites. Long after the fur business had dwindled and disappeared, an Indian would do almost anything from committing murder to cutting a cord of wood for a brightly painted tin pail.

The Indians learned slowly but they had their own shrewdness. Tales survive of feasts given to traders of the American Fur Company in which dog, attractively "cooked to a jelly," was the *pièce de résistance*. Fortunately the trader could hire a proxy to eat his meal without giving offense to his hosts, and along with the passing of the dish of dog flesh to this proxy there always went a gift, or bribe, of tobacco. One writer hints that the Indians might have figured out something for themselves: "They knew that but few traders would eat dog meat and anticipated the gift of tobacco."

One comes to enjoy stories of the Northwest Indian with his tongue in his cheek. An Indian who respectfully offered twenty horses for his pick of a family of beautiful white girls crossing the plains in 1842 was amazed to find the father affronted. The interpreter was righteously unctuous in his explanation that white men did not sell their women. The logical red man came back with the remark that he had observed that white men frequently bought Indian girls for their wives and he didn't see why the custom wasn't reciprocal.

In the early years of the fur trade, and for some time after, the wives and women companions of white men were inevitably Indian women. McLoughlin, who played host at Vancouver in frontier splendor to all international travelers of the period, was married to an Indian woman, the widow of Alexander McKay, an Astor partner who died in the massacre on the Tonquin. Although from all accounts a most remarkable woman, Mrs. McLoughlin played no role of chatelaine in her husband's feudal stronghold. This was a wholly masculine world.

The days of McLoughlin were the great ones of the fur trade. The Hudson's Bay Company was an organization so ancient, so haughty, and so powerful that early pioneers suggested that its initials might well have stood for "Here Before Christ." The Brigade of Boats came down the Columbia every June with the French Canadian voyageurs singing as they paddled in all their brilliant finery, donned near the end to effect a musical comedy finish to long weeks of grilling travel, beginning far to the north, working slowly south and west by canoe and horse.

Although the Hudson's Bay Company was the oldest fur company in the New World (its charter for "gentlemanly" exploitation going back to 1670) it was third in the rich Pacific Northwest field, arriving there in the 1820s. The North-West Fur Company of Canada had already planted posts in Old Oregon as early as 1807 and explored the western territory; and there was also John Jacob Astor's ill-starred, romantic attempt in 1811 to found a great fur company at the mouth of the Columbia.

The Astor ship *Tonquin* under a choleric captain named Jonathan Thorn had a dark history. Many of the crew were lost when the stubborn officer tried to launch boats on the treacherous Columbia bar. Later, farther to the north, the ship's decks were the scene of the bloody massacre of all the crew by angry Indians who did not care for the captain's high-handed manners. In the end the ship itself was blown to bits, whether by accident, by the Indians, or by a wounded member of the crew who perished at the scene of his revenge, no one can say for sure.

The Astor land expedition was no better favored by fortune. Members of this group under Wilson Price Hunt endured hardships which become fearsomely credible when one looks into the yawning vast maw of the Snake River, down which they attempted to come by canoe, or when one rides through that beautiful and formidable landscape through which they afterwards passed without food or guides. Particularly when one journeys among the strange formations of the John Day country—still bearing the name of a member of the expedition—does one understand how poor John Day himself went mad from his experiences.

The Astor enterprise which gave Washington Irving material for his book *Astoria* had three articulate clerks who have left us some important sources of Northwest history: Alexander Ross, *Fur Hunters of the Far West*; Gabriel Franchère, *Narrative of a Voyage to the Northwest Coast of America*; and Ross Cox, *Adventures on the Columbia River*. Ross Cox immortalized himself by taking a noonday nap from which he awoke to find his companions gone. He was lost thirteen days in the Spokane country, and survived to tell the tale, which pretty well established a record for that country at that time. The Dorion Woman, sometimes represented in Pendleton Round-up pageantry, was an Indian woman who as a member of the Astor Overland party deserves to rank near Sacajawea for her bravery and endurance. When all the men of the group with whom she was traveling were killed—including her husband, the interpreter—she led her two children on horseback nine days through deep snow, found a lonely spot in the Blue Mountains, and made a camp where she spent two winter months. She killed the horse and the three of them lived on that in a hut of branches and moss packed with snow. She got out in the spring after a fifteen day walk, carrying the children most of the way, with little to eat for a week and nothing for the last two days.

All the ambitious plans of Astor and the hardships and endurance of the men who undertook to bring his plans to materialization came to an end in 1812 when America and England went to war, and the Astor partners sold out to the North-West Company. In turn the North-West Company amalgamated with the Hudson's Bay Company, and thus this latter name is inseparably connected with early Oregon history.

FAITHS

In reading any Northwest history it is impossible to escape the story of the delegation of Flatheads and Nez Percés who heard of Christianity through the words of a wandering missionary group of Iroquois and set out in 1831 to St. Louis in search of "Black Robes" to teach them the elements of a new religion, or as the Protestants asserted, seeking the "Book of Heaven." Although these Indians were said to be looking for Catholic fathers, the first specific answer to their call came from the Methodists who sent Jason Lee to Oregon in 1834 with the expedition of an ill-fated Boston merchant named Nathaniel Wyeth.

Everyone went to Vancouver in those days, since the Hudson's Bay Post was the one great supply center, and Lee was no exception. McLoughlin, looking favorably on missionary enterprise, persuaded Lee to remain on the western side of the Cascades. It was not long before Lee envisioned the future of this fertile untouched land, and saw the need for American settlers. Indeed, the early missionary nucleus has been accused of emphasizing the earthly promise of the new territory rather than the celestial promise which they were supposed to hold out to the Indians.

McLoughlin encouraged the American missionaries presumably because they were allies, standing also firmly for law and order, discipline, and obedience among the Indians. England sent out a Reverend Herbert Beaver ("very appropriate name for the fur trade," as Peter Skene Ogden remarked) to the Vancouver settlement, but he and McLoughlin never got on well. The Reverend Beaver could not bring himself to accept the marriage of white men and Indian women; wrote tattletale letters to the Aborigines Protection Society of London; and in general made himself such a nuisance to McLoughlin that the chief factor gave him a spontaneous caning in the courtyard one day. The caning was the impulsive result of the Reverend Beaver's reply to the doctor's question as to why he was sending such unflattering reports to London: "Sir, if you wish to know why a cow's tail grows downward I cannot tell you; I can only cite the fact."

While the Methodist mission was beginning to flourish in the Willamette Valley, the Presbyterians sent one Dr. Samuel Parker to study the spiritual needs of the American Indian. With him came a religious-minded young physician, Dr. Marcus Whitman, a name destined to dominate in human interest all other names in the field of pioneer missionaries due to the tragedy which overtook this young man and his beautiful wife. They were killed by the Indians, along with a number of children, invalids, workers, and settlers near the mission they had established at Waiilatpu.

The dramatic episode of their death is not wholly accountable for the exalted status of the Whitmans in the Northwest pioneer pantheon. Many disputants have argued about the aims and importance of Whitman's famous "ride" to the East coast in the winter of 1842 and '43. Some say the trip was made only because he wished to save his mission from the threat of discontinuance. Others argue that he "saved Oregon" by going to Washington to see President Tyler and Secretary of State Daniel Webster and persuading them of this outpost's eventual importance to the union. It is certain that he did outline a plan for establishing supply stations along the emigrant trail and submit it to the War Department where it was discovered in the files some forty years later.

In spite of the overwriting and the bitter arguments of which they have been the subject, the Whitmans still have a heart-touching appeal: the delicately nurtured Narcissa, dying so terribly in the wilderness; the impulsive and perhaps even foolhardy but certainly conscientious Marcus, bringing on himself and his wife and companions an ill-merited dark fate. Everything conspired against these good people. An epidemic of measles killed off many of the Indians, who laid the blame at the doctor's door. The effects of a simple purgative inserted in watermelons to prevent stealing were of no help either. Moreover the Indians did not care for the untheatric ritual of the Presbyterians and longed to have the more colorful rites of the Catholic

Church. Even after the massacre such a homely incident as an Indian's over-eating of dried peach pie in the mission kitchen among the survivors, almost occasioned fresh tragedy; the acute nature of the stomachache leading the greedy red man to conclude that he had been poisoned.

A moving account has survived of those last dark days at the mission at Waiilatpu, told by Catherine Sager who was thirteen at the time, a cripple who had fallen under a wagon wheel while crossing the plains. After months of physical agony and tragedy—both her parents died on the journey—she had been adopted into the Whitman home along with her six brothers and sisters. This eyewitness has told how Whitman was tomahawked from behind as he sat in the kitchen; how Mrs. Whitman, already wounded, was carried out of the house on a settee, only to be shot to death in the yard.

Mrs. Whitman, warned by her husband of the seriousness of the situation, leaving her supper untouched the night before the massacre, and going away by herself to weep where no one could see her, becomes to the reader a prototype of all pioneer women in hostile country accepting their fate with resignation. One thinks of the words she wrote as a bride on the way out to Oregon, when they came to the beautiful Grande Ronde country: "This morning lingered with Husband on the top of the hill that overlooks Grand Round for berries—always enjoy riding alone with him especially when we talk about home friends. It is then the tedious hours are sweetly decoyed away." And again when they are debating the possibility of taking the seven orphaned Sagers, including the five months, ill, undernourished youngest, she thinks perhaps of her own child drowned when very small: "Husband thought we could get along with all but the baby—he did not see how we could take that, but I felt that if I must take any I wanted her as a chain to bind the rest to me." . . . And now it is night and she and her husband are both dead. The little thirteen-year-old adopted Sager is left to tell the rest of the story:

"I had always been very much afraid of the dark, but now I felt that the darkness was a protection to us, and I prayed that it might always remain so. I dreaded the coming of the daylight; . . . I heard the cats racing about and squalling. . . . I remember yet how terrible the striking of the clock sounded. Occasionally Mr. Kimball [a wounded man] would ask if I were asleep. . . ."

In the morning: "The children . . . renewed their calls for water. Day began to break, and Mr. K. told me to take a sheet off the bed and bind up his arm, and he would try and get them some. I arose stiff with cold, and with a dazed uncertain feeling . . . I said, 'Mother [Mrs. Whitman] would not like to have the sheets torn up.' Looking at me he said, 'Child, don't you know your mother is dead, and will never have any use for the sheets?' I seemed to be dreaming . . . I took a sheet from the bed and tore off some strips, which, by his directions, I wound around his arm. He then told me to put a blanket around him, as he might faint on the way and not be able to get up, and would suffer from the cold. Taking a pair of blankets from the bed, I put them around him, tying them around the waist with a strip off the sheets. I then placed his hat on his head and he went downstairs. We waited long for him, but . . . we never saw him again alive."

Later in the day, the Indians arrived and went off again and when the house seemed empty the children ventured downstairs. "The Indians had spread quilts over the corpses. Mary Ann, my sister, lifted the quilt from Dr. Whitman's face, and said, 'Oh girls, come and see father.' We did so and saw a sight we will never forget."

The final episodes of the Whitman story cover the captivity of the women and children, the killing of invalids in their beds. Girls of likely age were appropriated by the chiefs; one in particular, Lorinda Bewley, going down in history for her spirited resistance to her fate; a resistance, which, in the end, availed her little, except that two chiefs contended for the honor of having her; and while the Cayuse went off to get a wagon and rope to transport the fiery girl, a Umatilla came and took her away.

Down the years it is hard to realize the terrifying effect of the murder of the Whitmans at Waiilatpu on the Oregon settlers at that time. They were only a handful of people in an unfamiliar country; and they realized that if the miscreants went unpunished no isolated community would be safe in the future. Organizing an army, equipping it and outfitting it, was a very difficult task in 1847 in a country which was still loosely organized, without adequate supplies—where indeed "wheat and promises" were legal tender. Furthermore there was good reason to believe that their own government—

the United States—was coolly indifferent to their fate. Nevertheless they dispatched Joe Meek, the hardy mountain man, overland from Oregon to the capital three thousand miles away to bear the news of the tragedy; an embassy under Jesse Applegate set out for California to ask help but had to turn back because of the impassable snows in the Siskiyous; there was no vessel going out to San Francisco all that winter; the only boat out of the Columbia was one bound for Hawaii which carried the news there and explained the emergency.

After a winter campaign of great hardship and many months of dickering, some Cayuses were hanged in Oregon City for the murder of the Whitmans. There seems doubt—as there was always doubt at Indian executions—whether these were really the guilty ones. Ironically enough it was the Catholic fathers who attended them to the scaffold.

The success of the Catholic missionaries among the Indians would seem to have been a matter of psychological understanding of the Indian nature. Priests were credited with such utterances as "Noise is essential to the Indian's enjoyment" and "Without singing the best instruction is of little value." A Catholic priest invented the Catholic ladder, a diagram of the mysteries of the church presented in simple chronological order by which the competitive red man could measure his advance in piety. On special occasions like Easter the Indian was allowed to express his pleasure in his adopted white deity after his own fashion, and did so with green boughs, plumes, drums, bells, and occasional counterpoint of piercing yells.

The Catholic insistence on the objectifying of the mysteries undoubtedly made a deep appeal to the Indian with his worship not only of the Great Power but of lesser powers—any object which carried a quality of the supernatural. A Catholic missionary in the early days reported finding in one Indian tribe, in the high arid lands to the east, a spotted calico shirt and a white robe. These sacred objects had been obtained from a white man whom the Indians had seen wearing the garments, which they took to be respectively the *manitou* of the spotted disease (smallpox) which had killed such alarming numbers of them, and the *manitou* of the snow. Possession of these rare objects was obtained by the barter of a number of their best horses, and for many years the sacred articles were carried to the place of ritual and there worshipped with the smoking of the great medicine pipe— an offering to earth, sun, and water—and with appropriate dancing and singing. By this worship the Indians hoped to prevent the return of the disease and to bring a snow heavy enough to push the buffalo down from the mountains.

The Indians liked instances of the intervention of the white man's Higher Spirit in matters of daily life; and the successful crossing of the Columbia bar in a great storm in the forties gave the priest and six nuns aboard the vessel a special distinction as bearers of magic power.

The early Catholic fathers were often men of cultivation and remarkable strength of character. Among them the names of Blanchet and de Smet stand first. Both men endured untold hardships with great courage and vigor. Both made trips to Europe to arouse interest in this remote part of the world and brought back bands of nuns and priests for the new field. Of de Smet it is said that his travels, at a time in history when travel entailed nothing but endurance, totaled from seven to nine times round the earth. He crossed the Atlantic nineteen times, made one trip round the Horn and two by way of Panama. He once fasted thirty days before taking a sixty-mile snowshoe trip for which he needed to reduce his weight, and when threatened by a hostile Indian was able to knock the weapon from his hand, throw him, and give him a sound beating with a riding whip, which summary treatment brought the Indian as a convert to the church.

De Smet was also a man of delicate sensibilities, particularly susceptible to the charms of nature and able to express his feeling for it in such phrases as "the rock-hung flower" and, with reference to his own desert home in the drylands of this territory, "a little Arabia shut in by stern Heaven-built walls of rock." Although he mourned the Indians' inability to discard their superstitions he is himself reported to have considered a severe illness the punishment for his "too carnal admiration of nature."

Although the old missions have sunk into ruins, the few descriptions that remain of these oases of garden and brook in the midst of a wild uncultivated country convey a slumbrous charm. In the correspondence of the wife of General Stevens, the first governor of the Territory of Washington, there is such a description of the mission St. Joseph d'Olympia:

"I also had a boat built in which I made excursions down the Sound. About two miles down there was a Catholic mission, a large dark house or monastery, surrounded by cultivated land, a fine garden in front filled with flowers, bordered on one side, next the water, with immense bushes of wall flowers in bloom; the fragrance resembling the sweet English violet, filling the air with its delicious odor. Father Ricard, the venerable head of this house, was from Paris. He had lived in this place more than twenty years. He had with him Father Blanchet, a short thickset man, who managed everything pertaining to the temporal comfort of the mission. Under him were servants who were employed in various ways, baking, cooking, digging and planting. Their fruit was excellent and a great rarity, as there was but one more orchard in the whole country. There was a large number of Flatheads settled about them, who had been taught to count their beads, say prayers, and were good Catholics in all outward observances; chanted the morning and evening prayers, which they sang in their own language in a low, sweet strain, which, the first time I heard it, sitting in my boat at sunset, was impressive and solemn. We went often to visit Father Ricard, who was a highly educated man, who seemed to enjoy having some one to converse with in his own language. He said the Canadians used such bad French."

There is something haunting about the thought of the governor's lady, a homesick New England gentlewoman, floating with her Indian paddler on the waters of Puget Sound at sunset, in the sight of the eternal snowcaps and the high densely wooded hills, listening to the Flatheads chanting the hymns of the Catholic church under the leadership of a cultivated French priest.

This mission was last used by a family of Olympia pioneers who spent a winter in the seventies within its moldering walls. The family remembered it chiefly for its gloom, the fact that the walls had few windows and those built high because of the priests' wish not to have the Indians distracted by the outside world when at their prayers; and also to make it difficult for arrows or stray missiles to find their way inside.

In the 1840s emigrant wagon trains began to unfurl their white sails on the prairies of the Middle West and start their laborious creaking way westward. Occasionally descendants of these hardy folk insist that Grandma said it was all just one long picnic; but this seems a little hard to believe. A Pendleton newspaperwoman who rode in a prairie schooner from La Grande to Pendleton with a group of "pioneers" in the year 1938 assured me that the torture of the movement even on a paved road was almost more than she could bear for two days.

Getting wagons into the last reaches of this new country was an achievement, first attempted by Marcus Whitman who persisted in taking on a wagon from Fort Hall against the expert advice of fur traders. He actually succeeded in getting it as far west as Fort Boise, but he could hardly have imagined what a tide of emigration was to follow in its wake. By the time the tide was at its full Marcus Whitman was dead of an Indian tomahawk.

Through three decades and well into the fourth people crossed the plains into Oregon. The story of their travels makes an oft-repeated but still compelling saga of heroism in the face of Indian massacres, cholera epidemics, dried-up water holes, one day stopovers for women to give birth. It is not easy to determine what brought these beglamored people into the vast western unknown. Certainly there were plenty of stay-at-homes to call them insane when they did it.

But there were other men whose enthusiasm more than made up for the skepticism of their fellows. As far back as 1822 attention had been drawn to the Oregon country by John Floyd of Virginia who, in the House of Representatives, made a report on American rights in the distant lands west of the Rockies and hinted that colonization there was bound to take place. Mr. Bailies of Massachusetts envisioned a canal from the Atlantic to the Pacific which would prevent the eventual colonies in this territory from breaking away into an independent unit and setting up a government of their own. Mr. Bailies, who enjoyed a good rich phrase with the best of his contemporaries, said that he would "delight to know that in this desolate spot, where the prowling cannibal now lurks in the forest, hung round with human bones and with human scalps, the temples of justice and the temples of God were reared, and man made sensible of the beneficent intentions of his creator."

Oregon bills kept coming up in Congress throughout the twenties while the first diplomatic dickerings over British versus American rights to the North Pacific coast began to take place in London. In 1829 Hall J. Kelley, a Harvard graduate and a writer of school books, organized the "American Society for Encouraging the Settlement of the Oregon Territory" and in 1832 set out for the western lands himself by way of New Orleans and Mexico. In California he had the misfortune to fall in with Ewing Young who in turn had the misfortune to be considered, by the mighty McLoughlin at Vancouver, a horse thief, and poor Kelley was not received as well as he had hoped to be. It was, however, Kelley who helped to influence Wyeth to outfit his remarkable, if ill-fated, expeditions, and Wyeth in turn stirred many people to interest, including the impressionable young James Russell Lowell who remembered all his life the sensations he felt when his fellow townsman set off westward on the great adventure.

In the thirties the missionaries began their slow process of colonization. Their reports helped to keep the Oregon Question alive in the minds of those "back home." President Jackson sent Lieutenant W. A. Slacum on the first official visit to Oregon. Slacum made a thoroughgoing and favorable report to Congress in 1837, recommending that we firmly hold out against Britain and demand the land as far as the forty-ninth parallel at least, lest the States should lose the fine waterways of Puget Sound. Slacum's report brought the matter of Oregon's admission to the States before Congress once more, and it remained there through the next ten years.

All the Congressional agitations, the speeches and reports, the stories in newspapers, the letters home from missionaries, began their slow and powerful infiltration through the people who were to pioneer this remote section. Around middle-western fireplaces, at corn huskings and quilting bees, Oregon began to be the most exciting topic of conversation. People discussed the fertility of the Willamette Valley, the advantages of the Columbia River for commerce, the great forests and the salmon-filled streams. Times had been hard in the frontier country and people were restless. Slavery was beginning to cause agitation. Above all there was that characteristic American wish to move out into the unknown. People in the sheltered midwestern valleys caught fire from the pictures of a great poetic landscape to the west; a landscape of vast plains, high mountains, swift turbulent rivers, and, at the farthest reach, a great ocean. Some few were also undoubtedly influenced by a patriotic wish to keep Great Britain from acquiring the land and the waterways explored for the United States by Lewis and Clark and Robert Gray.

The settlers were for the most part men interested in establishing homes, clearing land, raising cattle. The emigration of 1843 is particularly memorable because from this group—along with the settlers who had come in prior to that year—was composed the membership of the famous "wolf meeting" in the Willamette Valley. This was a gathering of settlers to discuss ways of protecting their herds from predatory animals; and during the meeting a resolution was adopted "that a committee be appointed to take into consideration the propriety of taking steps for the civil and military protection of the colony." This was followed by the Champoeg meeting of May 2, 1843, at which picturesque Joe Meek forced into the open the opposing wishes of the French-Canadian settlers—still bound by sentiment to the Hudson's Bay Company—and the newcomers from the States. With his height, his great voice, and his commanding gestures with his coonskin cap he succeeded in getting the two extra votes needed to organize a provisional government the American way, and became a figure for murals and town park statues down the years.

Thus once again the American method of forming a "government by compact" took place: "We the people of Oregon Territory for purposes of mutual protection and to secure peace and prosperity among ourselves agree to adopt the following laws and regulations until such time as the United States of America extend their jurisdiction over us." One cannot read the concluding words of the message of the executive committee elected in this wilderness in 1844 without being moved: . . . "and in conclusion, we desire to impress your minds that although the colony is small and its resources feeble, yet the life, rights and liberties of an individual here are of equal value to him as to one in the city of Washington or London. And it is a duty which devolves on you and on us to use as much discretion, vigilance and caution in maturing and adopting measures for promoting the interests of the little colony, as if we expected our names and acts would be enrolled in the pages of history, or inscribed on pillars of stone when our day and generation shall have passed away."

Jesse Applegate, the "sage of Yoncalla," drew up in 1845 a revised draft of the first governmental laws, and under this for four years the "sturdy, sober, order-loving pioneers" conducted their lives.

No American colonists went north into the state which is now called Washington until after the Oregon emigration of 1844. This emigration numbered among its members an intelligent and well-to-do Quaker, named George Bush—considered a mulatto by early settlers, but according to family records of East Indian descent—and a tough-fibred Kentuckian, Michael Simmons. These men and their families wintered north of the Columbia and eventually explored around Puget Sound and took up claims not far from the present town of Olympia.

The Hudson's Bay Company had had a flourishing farm on Nisqually flats for some years but there were no other settlements and the general opinion was that England intended to claim the lands north of the Columbia. The prolonged and rather dubious negotiations between Daniel Webster, as secretary of state, and Lord Ashburton, a special British commissioner, have led many people to claim that Webster was quite willing to relinquish northern "Oregon" to Great Britain, if Great Britain would force Mexico to sell us California.

A good deal of bitter feeling about the Oregon Question seemed to focus itself in communities in the Mississippi Valley. In 1843 one hundred delegates met in Cincinnati for an "Oregon convention" and there adopted a resolution to the effect that the United States had a right to the western country "between the parallel of forty-two degrees on the south and fifty-four on the north." This was the origin of the famous "Fifty-four Forty or Fight" slogan which elected the Democrat, James K. Polk, to the presidency in 1844 and which was finally settled in 1846 after an outbreak of hostilities with Britain was narrowly averted by making the forty-ninth parallel the northern boundary.

Immediately after the settlement of the quarrel with England the Oregon colonists expected to be welcomed into the Union with open arms, but they had inserted into their provisional constitution a clause which read that "neither slavery nor involuntary servitude, except as a punishment for crime" should ever be permitted in their territory. This roused the opposition of such Southern leaders as Calhoun, and the Congressional session of 1846–47 closed without providing in any way for this new colony.

The Whitman massacre had stirred the Oregon settlers and forced them to a sharpened realization of their need for help from the home government. During that famous winter of 1848 Joe Meek had been dispatched to Washington with news of the colonists' plight. His great virility, masculine good looks, frontier clothes, tall tales, and way with the ladies—aided slightly no doubt by kinship with President Polk—had all of Washington at his feet from the moment he entered the genteel Willard Hotel in his rough costume and announced to the timid clerk that he was "Minister Plenipotentiary and Envoy Extraordinary from all Oregon to the United States of America." The Whitman massacre was thus in no small measure responsible for the passing of the bill to make Oregon a Territory in 1848.

After this period three major events built up the Pacific Northwest and gave it its present character: the gold discoveries in California, Idaho, Montana, and British Columbia; the settlement of the Indian wars; the coming of the railroads.

Discovery of gold in California changed that state's history almost overnight, bringing it from a feeble position of rivalry with the Territory of Oregon to one of easy dominance. The adventurous Forty-Niners have assumed a place in American history which many historians consider they ill deserve in comparison with the more sober missionaries, explorers, traders, and settlers who opened up the Oregon country. Even the Oregon Trail became for many the California Trail, but in recent years the northern states have begun to realize how easy it is for them to compete in glamour of history and beauty of landscape with their highly publicized southern neighbor.

Many of the men who did not go south from Oregon to make a fortune in the goldfields made it by staying home and supplying roaring San Francisco with timber for buildings and all kinds of farm produce, as well as oysters and fish. The Puget Sound region, having also prospered indirectly by the California gold discoveries, grew strong enough to seek independence from the Oregon settlers—claiming that their interests were quite separate—and in 1853 became the Territory of Washington and a state in 1889. Their first governor was General Isaac I. Stevens who had been sent out to survey for a western railroad. Railroads were to play the next great role in the settlement of these lands.

The great days of the Columbia River boat traffic, with the boom period in the mining areas of the Inland Empire, opened up the eastern drylands to settlers other than missionaries who found this country far more beautiful and promising than they had been led to believe. They discovered that animals eating the apparently dead dry grass grew sleek and fat, that there were possibilities in dry farming, that irrigation from adjacent streams created magical fertility. Encroachment on the lands of the proud Indians of this section led to wars and treaties and the forming of reservations.

The railroads were—and still are—a storm center to western people. Their building had been at one time a "sectional issue between the North and the Cotton South" so that southern leaders successfully blocked the establishment of roads to the west until after the outbreak of the Civil War. After the war California, with its spectacular prosperity, was served first, but through the late sixties, the seventies, eighties, and nineties, the railroads began to reach their iron fingers into the Arcadian northern lands. There then appeared on the western scene such great organizers and wily schemers as Henry Villard and Jay Cooke, and a little later James J. Hill and E. H. Harriman. Fortunes were made and lost, towns destroyed or created by the stroke of a pen. Bitter court contests and public name-callings followed in the wake of the westward push of the iron rails.

In the twentieth century the history of the Pacific Northwest has been very largely the history of all of the United States, with certain natural differences growing out of geographical position, lateness in development (making both for advantages and disadvantages), and the discovery and utilization of local resources. Such aspects of the Northwest have been considered in this book through such individual communities as most clearly set them forth.

CHAPTER III

The Seasons

···

The months from April to October in the Pacific Northwest give so rich a variety of experience in scent, form, and color that even the native is often bemused with the weather and nature's generosity.

Spring in the Pacific Northwest might be said to begin officially when people set out on rhododendron viewing expeditions along the miles of the Olympic Peninsula or the Oregon coast. The rhododendron is the state flower of Washington. Oregon chose a more useful plant, the Oregon grape, which bears yellow bells of blossom in spring and purple globes of berry in autumn, besides offering a year-round spot of glistening green in the dankest landscape. Like the Japanese, however, who worship the pink cherry which yields no fruit—since this teaches, they say, "the subtle use of the useless"—the Northwesterner worships the rhododendron which graciously lends its rosy beauty to ugly wastes of logged-off land as well as to untouched forest fringes.

About the time that rhododendrons appear, Scotch broom also comes along to herald the season, and meadows and canyons assail the eye with glitter of brilliant yellow. Pussywillow doesn't count as a messenger of a new season in the Northwest, for it is apt to appear at Christmas if the season is mild, and be gathered for a New Year green along with the dark red berries of the *kinnikinik* or Indian tobacco.

Timed to coincide with rhododendron and Scotch broom, the groves turn white with dogwood and wild cherry, and erratic winds carry the spice of blossoming red currant. Downy plumes of spiraea signal the passing airs; fields display purple and white iris and the sky-blue cornflower. Then west coast forests hide the three-petaled trillium, pale bleeding hearts with lacy leaves, the gentle, secretive brown ginger, and the small precious orchid known as Lady Slipper. Fragrant pink twin-vine riots delicately over logs and mossy earth. Fungus of a thousand varieties, in every tone from white to deepest purple, re-create in the damp woods curiously marine memories, the frills and convolutions of conchs, or coral, or even sea anemones.

When the flat-petaled pink rose opens along every country road, spotted foxgloves are defining the marshy lines of languid streams; and in the seasonal swamp lands, vibrant with frog-song, the beautiful and dignified skunk cabbage defies its lowly name. The air along the coast carries the mingled scent of salt spray, sun-warmed conifers, and the first fruit blooms. Inland it's the scent of sage, pungent with the spring showers, and sprays of flowering thorn. The winds are languorous with wild syringa, the mock orange of which Lewis and Clark took note in their Journal, and from whose straight shoots Indians sometimes made arrows. Up the river valleys travels the breath of mountain balm or cinnamon bush, azalea, pine sap, and last year's needles which carpet the stirring earth. Prairies mark the sun's climb with carpets of purple violet and yellow buttercup, blue lupine, camas, and leopard lily. Mountain meadows display the curious markings of mission bells and arrogant tufts of Indian paintbrush. Shooting stars point the wind with their black-tipped pink arrows.

With early summer, hill slopes yield the tiny wild strawberry of unsurpassed flavor, and then the trout are leaping in the swollen streams. Later the salmon berries ripen in every cool ravine, and so one knows the salmon are running. When summer deepens it brings the wild blackberry, growing on logged-off land, where fireweed also raises its slender magenta wand. Soon follow the great bush blackberries; head high sprawls of burdened branches, yielding lavish harvest to any passerby with a tin pail.

As the earth begins to cool, huckleberry, elderberry, and blueberry darken on bushes in the mountains and along the prairie trails. This is the season when, not long ago, all the Indian women went out to gather camas root for the winter's food supply. They still pick berries, the Indians, and on the roads near White Salmon one may see them picking up one side and the whites up the other. Vine maple sends thrusts of brilliant red and yellow up the rocky slopes of mountain passes and along the boiling rivers. Then the restless madrona—forever peeling its green and brown bark—yields its orange berries to greedy birds, south-bound. Wild geese cry in the night, traveling high above the fog. Ducks rise whirring from freshwater lake and salty cove. Gulls are long since back from the north to cry mournfully on the shore.

After the dry summer, with forest fire warnings posted on every roadside, the good smell of burning brush rises into the air. The mountains take on fresh coats of snow. Against the first gray skies they stand out with startling clarity; they seem to move nearer with a new and formidable intimacy, an almost menacing beauty.

On the coast the rains begin. People withdraw to their fireplaces. The run on the local libraries sets in. It is winter. In eastern valleys alchemy of fog and frost creates enchanted landscapes; bare trees in thrall to crystal, shrubs of spun glass and weeds of spun sugar along the hill slopes where the brief sun has no power. The gray light plays a range of cool and icy blues over these frosted forms, and in the distance they seem to exhale a white breath.

Over the weekends, east and west, hundreds of cars, ski-laden, make the brief trips that take their owners out of tideland and valley rain or frosty fog and bring them to clear mountain air, to ski and toboggan runs and miles of powder snow.

The skiers are still practicing christianias and slaloms on the snowy slopes when the alpine meadows set forth their annual pointillists' display of riotous color along the melting snow line. . . . The Season has turned again.

CHAPTER IV

Where to Play

Y ou cannot drive many miles along any highway in the Pacific Northwest without seeing one of those well-designed wooden road markers which indicate that here is a place where the traveler can find a stove, an open fireplace, a shelter, perhaps a swimming place, certainly trees, ferns, flowers, and flowing streams—in short a public park or a camping ground.

Quite apart from the big national recreational areas such as the parks at Crater Lake or Mount Rainier, the national forests and the primitive areas, Washington has fifty-six state parks and Oregon sixty-two. In addition every town has set aside some local beauty spot as a city park.

The Northwest is park conscious. When the city of Seattle set out to harness the Skagit River for use as power it also created a park high in the Cascades and organized inexpensive tours to this primitive land. These trips have remained popular year after year; literally thousands of people view the dam and reservoirs, wander in the twilight along the roaring green Skagit, eat the power company's generous helpings of good camp fare, and loiter in the adjacent gardens where colored lights play on the waterfalls by night, hidden voices sing *Jerusalem the Golden*, and synthetic birds warble from the subtropical underbrush.

To keep the land as beautiful as it was originally is an ambition belatedly but powerfully rising in the Northwest; and the people of this part of America would definitely like to handle it in their own way. They do not care much for the high prices and the restrictions of the national parks, where "concessions" pretty well determine the kind of holiday the traveler is going to have. They prefer their land left under the jurisdiction of the National Forest Service.

One of the finest pieces of untouched coastline in all the world is that along the Oregon shore. With real envy Washingtonians view the long miles, as untouched in many places as they were when the first brigs sailed warily off the rocky shore. Washington let much of its own coast be ruined with billboards, logging butcheries, and a clutter of cheap buildings. Now it will have its chance to make and preserve a billboardless highway along the Olympic Peninsula from Queets to Long Beach.

No matter what your taste in recreation the Northwest can supply your needs. Parks range from a "splendid stand of virgin timber" with or without camping or picnicking facilities to restricted acreage around an old blockhouse from the Indian wars; from hot, sandy geological and educational areas to damp, green, ferny recreational regions; from sea level and below to thousands of feet in the air.

If you are a collector of rocks, fossil remains, or Indian arrowheads the Northwest is your country. The richest fossil finds are those in the John Day region, the famous Condon fossil beds where, naturally, much that is seen may not be carried away as mementoes; although I once met a Texan who had cut a dinosaur's footprint out of a New Mexican desert—when Carnegie Tech's back was turned—and carried it home to his ranch parlor, and I wouldn't put it past him to try to carry off relics of Oregon's diminutive three-toed "dawn horse" if he came on them.

If something a little rarer than arrowheads appeals to you, you can go into the country of the pictographs and petroglyphs. Here along the desert waterways Indians, antedating any present tribal memories, left strange symbols, painted with ochre and time-resisting native pigments, cut in hard basaltic rock with "pecking stones" of harder quartz. These pictographs represent, with simple emphasis on the essentials of form, hunters and their prey; priests with wands of power; the ceremony of the first born with attendant convocation of animal powers, and so on.

Once you start to search for orbicular jasper, opals from the Hart Mountains, the agates that lie on so many of the beaches of the Northern Pacific stretch, or for the rare type of "iridescent" obsidian found in the Glass Buttes country of Oregon you'll be more than ever bound to a land so rich in treasures for the knowing eye.

If you are a student of wildlife, particularly of birds, then the 160,000 acres of Bird Refuge in Malheur County in Oregon will offer you an unusual field of observation where literally millions of birds gather at seasons' turns to feed and rest. And if you want some days of hearty and exclusively male companionship and some consistent drinking in the name of Conservation and Preservation, try to get to the land of the great antelope preserves in Lake County, Oregon, when the Order of the Antelope holds its annual hunt without firearms.

All year long the fabulous marine flower beds at the Depoe Bay Aquarium on the Oregon coast display their marvelous colors and forms for those who can be torn away from the fearsome spectacle of the octopuses or the beguiling antics of the baby seal.

If you're drawn to geologic mysteries you can visit Washington's Ginko State Park where gems of petrified wood are to be seen, along with relics of the sacred Oriental Apricot, the Ginko, which once flourished here. Or you can view that tantalizing geologic riddle, "the great mystery falls" on the way into Grand Coulee. Big descriptive words wither on the tongue when one tries to convey the magnitude of this ancient waterfall, where a river three miles wide took a four-hundred-foot drop. You can go some four hundred miles south into Oregon and view another "mystery," Crater Lake, that silent and awesome relic of "unfathomable volcanic power" lying in the rim of a mountain which once stood 14,000 feet high.

The best time to see Crater Lake is in the very early morning, just before the sun comes up, and you can have this experience from your bed if you don't mind paying the Lodge's charges for rooms on the lake side. (People in the camp have to get up and dress and take a good brisk walk for their sunrise view. One old Oregonian who remembers tenting on the lake's rim said to me with a growl: "We used to have a pretty good lake until the government got to fooling around so much with it.") Crater Lake never loses the power to inspire a sense of dark mystery, of the presence of forces that might well intimidate man. There is, under certain conditions of light, something almost evilly beautiful about the strange dark cone that rises from the unplumbed depths of blue water; and one comes to understand Indian legends of the lake, and their reason for sending their young men to bathe in it as a part of initiation into manhood. When, in very early morning, the light is beginning to grow, the lake is blue-black and utterly, terrifyingly, still and quiet. Around its rim the peaks and walls of the ancient crater form a black silhouette. Above this sinister wall the sky rests in cold purple. Then the true spirit of the lake seems to breathe from it—a mysterious, deeply lonely, and saddening spirit. As the light grows into blues and pinks and golden fragments of cloud and peak, the lake seems to become less itself, as though it were now putting on the face it wears for the tourists who roar in for a quick look and roar out again.

If you came west to "rough it" almost any mountain trip will give you what you want: the Olympics, the Cascades, the Blues, the Wallowas, the Okanogans, or the primitive area at the head of Lake Chelan.

You have a chance to walk or ride some four hundred miles along the Oregon Skyline Trail, a trip of quite unparalleled scenic variety beginning at the Columbia River, traversing the mountain country of Hood and Jefferson, with their vast stretches of alpine gardens; past the "unconquerable spires" of Three Fingered Jack and Mount Washington; through the great lava "blankets"—viewing in passing those famous cold white beauties, the Three Sisters, South, Middle, and North; and so finally down into the region of lakes, large and small, dominated by Crater. Here with pack on back you can cross the trails of old frontiersmen and skirt the battlegrounds of Indian wars; and even, it is said, camp where young Indians from the northern tribes, newly mated, used to spend their honeymoon days, hidden safely from the warring redskins to east and west.

The visitor can hardly miss the great single mountains: Rainier, Hood, Baker, St. Helens, Adams. They offer everything in the way of accommodation from well over a million dollars' worth of carefully designed rusticity at Timberline Lodge on Mt. Hood, to little overnight cabins with wood-burning stoves at Camp Sunrise on Mt. Rainier. You may force your way to their cloud-capped summits or worship them afar from some gentle meadow; seek their reflections in lonely lakes, circle them on horseback trails; or, on skis, squint up at their brilliant glitter from a field of powder snow. At Christmastime shops burgeon with hundreds of views of these snowy giants, particularly of Mt. Rainier, a mountain so grand, so remote, and so ever-changing that no Indian was ever foolhardy enough to force his way up its steep flanks and thus risk coming permanently under its powerful spell.

You can visit the only mainland seal rookery in all the world, not far from Florence on the Oregon coast. Here in a cavern fit for Beowulf, lit with eerie light from the cave's mouths, some three hundred sea lions roar and splash in the green swells, or slide on and off the big central rock, ruled over by Brigham, chief of the bulls.

The cave was discovered on a calm day in 1880 by a roving sea captain in a little skiff who was once marooned in the cave by a raging storm outside, and was forced to kill a small lion for the juicy meat of its flippers. I can understand the many trips the captain made to this cave of his discovering. I am never able to pass the place without making the mile-long trip down the cliffside to stand in the darkness and watch these creatures, quite unconscious of observing eyes, disport themselves in the restless green tides; the females quarreling, young bucks fighting for precedence, new babies demanding attention. Once I missed, by just an hour, a great battle between killer whales and the lions just offshore.

If it is spring there are strange birds to be seen. Here is the rookery of the guillemot, whose arrival in March signals the new season on the ocean. This bird, living most of the year on the open sea, has curious feet with red scarlet webbings which he uses like a rudder in his long flights. Here also, at the cave entrance, the tufted puffins or sea parrots make their nests.

If you fancy another kind of cave, Oregon has that for you also. Down in Josephine County there are caves underground in a "mountain of marble"; stalactites and stalagmites theatrically lit, earnest young guides to point out to you the Ghost Chamber, Dante's Inferno, Bacon Rind, the Onyx Butterfly, Kate and Duplicate and all the other tedious comparisons with which lecturers seek to beguile the public to gaze on nature's handiwork. Even if you don't like caves you can be extremely comfortable at the Caves Chateau in that rustic, overstuffed, and pleasant style—all chintz and stone and dark wood—which big resort hotels in the West manage to achieve with such apparent ease.

Surely no country anywhere in America is richer in resources for the weary human who wants to rest and restore himself than are these two states of the North Pacific slope. By boat, by foot, by horseback, by bicycle, and even by car, he can come, within a short distance of any city, to utter solitude and peace. There is such an extravagance of natural beauties that no visitor could possibly cover them all: lakes and rivers and ocean beaches; miles of inland sea; snowcaps and glaciers and alpine meadows; rocky canyons, pine forests, green valleys stream-threaded—it would be hard to choose one favorite kind of landscape from among the wealth that is offered.

SECTION II

Some Places and People

CHAPTER I

Cow Country

astern Oregon and Eastern Washington are far more like one another than they are like their respective sister halves, the lush green stretch of seacoast country which the Cascade Mountains separate from the inland. Sometimes when traveling north to south, or south to north, in Oregon and Washington, the sense of homogeneity is so strong that one is apt to think, how sensible it would have been to make these two wet sections one state, and let the dry sections form another. Yet this feeling changes when moving east or west along the mountain passes that separate these two dramatically contrasted landscapes. Then it seems that no matter how sensible it might appear on the maps there must surely be something very valuable in the experience afforded the citizens of these two states, for nature has offered them the chance to understand diverse ways of life produced by sharply contrasted environments.

And in the end one is more than content to leave them as they are.

Eastern Oregon and Washington played their brief but significant part in the colorful drama of the cowboy. Flavorsome Spanish words from the days when California ranchmen penetrated the Oregon country still linger in speech and writing: *vaqueros, riatas, rosideros.* A description of a real round-up in eastern Oregon in the old days sounds very much like the Southwest:

"They were all well-dressed, showy men, wearing bright colors—all roamers of space in light countries love color, for color is the product of light: the best equipped men for vaquero life of any that ever rode the plains, and they all had the fine, well-trained saddle horses, with silver-mounted bridles, hackamoors, mecates, and riatas. They mostly wore rosideros for the protection of their clothes—a buckskin apron that fits like a tailored pair of pants, tied around the legs with buckskin thongs. . . . Altogether with their wide sombreros and gay colors and good form and fine horses, with the sun shining over it all, it made a picture."

This is the picturesque side, the theater side, of the days of the big ranches of eastern Oregon. The other side of the picture is not quite so pretty, for it shows some of the methods by which the rich inland grazing country, with its rare combinations of good soil and water supply, fell into the hands of a few greedy men. Land office and court records from Oregon's Harney County have revealed some of the devices employed—apparently without any marked twinges of conscience—by the cattle barons and absentee landlords to acquire more property than they had any right to: "dummy" entrymen; land falsely described as "swamp" and procured at a dollar an acre; state school lands intended for the use of actual homesteading settlers stolen outright; terrorization of "little" homesteaders by hired thugs, and similar unsavory practices.

Henry Miller, the voracious rancher from California who managed with Charles Lux to acquire some million acres of land and a million head of cattle, owned large holdings in Oregon. One of his most famous acquisitions was the so-called Agency Ranch. At the time of the opening of the country to homesteaders a Miller partner, T. M. Overfelt, made a famous ride of two hundred miles in twenty-four hours—relaying to fresh mounts from ranch to ranch of Miller's vast private domain—in order to be present at the bidding for this choice stretch of cattle country.

The cattle barons came to be cordially disliked. They were held responsible for retarding settlement in order to keep their holdings intact, and lesser men spoke freely against them. It was all part of a general picture of rugged individualism about which present day pioneer reunion speakers find, however, something favorable to say. A paper read at a Harney County reunion in 1937 sympathetically cited these men as products of their time. "Do not blame them!" adjured the writer. "They believed in:

> 'The good old rule, the simple plan
> That they should take who have the power,
> And they should keep who can.'"

Although according to Bill Hanley, "the idea of the vaquero never got north of the Blue Mountains or across the Snake River," Washington too had its big cattle day—if without quite such a Hollywood setting as Oregon's. Many Washingtonians learn with surprise that the setting for Owen Wister's *The Virginian* was not Montana or Wyoming but the Methow Valley in the Okanogan country of the north central section of their state. Wister knew the country through a Harvard classmate, Guy Waring, who went from Newport to the wilds of the Okanogan in the eighties and was known quite simply in all the lonely countryside as "the man at the forks." Wister's introduction to Waring's story *My Pioneer Past* gives a clear picture of the hardships of travel near the century's turn in this beautiful region, still little known and not extensively traveled.

Washington also had its full quota of tough hombres who rode the plains. It had, like Oregon, the day of cattle rustling, followed by the day of the vigilantes. There were long treks of cattle, east, north, even west and south. The famous Cariboo trail trip with beef on the hoof into the mining country of British Columbia is the source of many good yarns. Even that standard "thriller" of all western round-ups and rodeos, the feat of throwing a steer which is known as bulldogging, is claimed to have its origin in the state of Washington. In *The History of Toppenish* (Toppenish is a town in the Yakima Valley), the author has this to say:

"On the day they drove the cattle across the Columbia at Egbert French's ferry, one of the steers refused to enter the water, whereupon young

McCoy threw himself from his horse onto the steer and, grappling his horns, threw him to the ground. This was in about 1866. Alec McCoy believes this was the first instance of bulldogging in the world's history. He had never heard of its being done before. Several men saw the feat and in later years it was occasionally performed on the reservation range by cowboys of daring inclination."

There was in the Northwest a certain development of the native Indian horse. Selected "cayuse" brood mares were crossed with American sires to produce the staying qualities needed for western life. The word *cayuse* came from an Indian tribe called the Cayuses who used to ride along the emigrant trails trading their fresh horses for women's dresses, household utensils, tools, or cattle. The name is now applied colloquially to any western horse.

In both Oregon and Washington the sheepmen came in on the heels of the cattlemen, and then there were the sheep and cattle feuds—not yet completely settled. There are still killings over range rights in Oregon. When the big ranges began to break up, the cattleman would settle on a creek and turn his cattle up into the mountains. Along would come a sheepman, the sheep would eat the outside grass and move on to another good range. This made the cattlemen very angry indeed. But perhaps there was more to it than just the problem of the grass. Bill Hanley, the "sage of Harney County," wrote something about it once that would seem to indicate a psychological tension underlying these feuds: "It wasn't any trouble for me to understand how to run sheep. What strikes at the dignity of the cattleman is the lowness of the service he has to give. They are always a-bleating, working their noise for sympathy, which is a kind of asking for protection. To a cattleman it is a dreary noise. Then they have to be kept in flocks, and given continual human association.". . . and as his final indictment, "He [the sheep] has been herded since before the Good Book was written, and he don't know any more now than he did then."

Whatever your feeling about sheep you'll see plenty of them along the highways in the early spring and autumn in the eastern part of Oregon and Washington. The presence of so many sheep is not the only change that an old-timer would notice coming back to this land which was for so many years a "resting place for Space." Water has been brought to the desert, and the traveler's eye falls pleasantly on stretches of new green, round which communities are springing up as the irrigation projects from the gigantic dams get under way. In certain shallow valleys among the barren hills, trees offer rich yield of fruits. Maps are dotted with town names slowly increasing the size of their type as their population increases.

I find it restful to look at a map and see big stretches of land with only an aimless thread of road winding in a vast empty space. Washington does not have such peaceful big stretches anymore. Almost fearfully each year I look at those white spaces where the Washington map says only Sand Dunes, The Pot Holes, Strawberry Butte, Bald Knob, the Colville Indian Reservation, and I wonder when the little "-villes" and "-tons," the Junctions and Corners, are going to creep in with their ominous small blue lettering. Eastern Oregon is more reassuring. Malheur and Harney Counties remain relatively uncluttered. There are only a few names to conjure with around the Malheur Bird Refuge or the Hart Mountain Antelope Refuge. The names all make a picture to one who has traveled this country, joyously accepting the bumps and ruts, on the way to Blitzen or Frenchglen, or down into the Basque country farther toward the east. Horsehead Mountain, says the map, Alkali Lake; springs named for Mules, Skulls, and Buzzards; Coyote Wells; the mountains, Juniper, Little Juniper, Stinking-water, and Sheepshead. The name Wagontire recalls days when the presence of one in the vast indifference of the desert was a landmark spelling tragedy. The word *Malheur* cropping up in river and lake and county is a reminder of the French *voyageur*. The many Owyhees keep alive the memory of the days over a century ago when Hawaii was spelled Owyhee, and was a regular port of call for ships bound to the Northwest coast. Your directions in this part of the country are from ranch to ranch: Whitehorse, Alvord, Folly Farm. This is truly the Old West.

One of the most enjoyable ways to enter eastern Oregon is over the McKenzie Pass from Eugene into Bend and so along Route Fifty-four. This drive offers all the contrasts possible to this Northwest land—excepting only the sea coast. One sets out from Eugene, lying in the gentle valley of the Willamette, a university town, ringed round with blue hills and blue rivers, and goes climbing up along the roaring cool McKenzie, through a beautiful stand of virgin timber, to the summit where the lava beds stretch their bleak length incongruously through the green country, best seen in early evening when the light plays fanciful tricks with the forms and tones of this ancient cataclysm. Down then from the peak slowly through the wide-spaced pink-boled pines, onto the eastern plain where the mountains rise in solitary splinters from the desert floor.

Given a few days in and around Bend, including the beautiful Metolius country where even word-weary advertising men find themselves writing poetry; out and down as far as the Basque country of Jordan Valley, or to the section of the old big ranches like the famous P Ranch of Pete French; then to Klamath Falls, Medford, Ashland, Crater Lake; north and east to the Snake River Canyon, to Enterprise and La Grande, Baker and Pendleton, up to the John Day country; back finally to the Columbia River and along its barren rocky palisades until they begin to turn green with trees, and you'll have some sense of the enchantment of inland Oregon.

CHAPTER II

Farewell Bend

B end isn't a typical Oregon town—if there is such a thing as a typical Oregon town—and yet it is a town which only the Pacific Northwest—perhaps even only Oregon—could produce. Its citizens range from the distinguished and handsome Mr. Sawyer, with his Harvard accent, who publishes the Bend *Bulletin*, to Klondike Kate, a "convent-bred" lady now well on in years who was once the diamond-bedecked toast of Dawson. Klondike Kate is married now to an Alaskan sourdough named Matson who admired her from a distance for thirty years. She came to reside in Bend because she saw some pictures of it in a movie travelogue and liked the look of it.

Bend does have a nice look. Although it is a mill town, living off lumber, its streets are clean, charming, well laid out along a little park where water fêtes are given annually on an artificial lake. All around Bend lies a famous recreation area of lakes, rivers, and mountains, ski slopes, trout streams, geologic riddles to confound scientists. Regional planning councils give Bend just about ten more years before its adjacent lumber supply is exhausted—unless it adopts some "sustained yield" program to save the timber resources. Will it turn to pulp for salvation, as many similar Northwestern communities have done; or to something newer like rayon? Will it discover mineral resources? Will it die slowly and become a ghost community? . . . When such questions confront a town as lively as Bend one comes suddenly and sharply to an understanding of the dark problems that this whole Northwest region poses.

Many Easterners have been identified with Bend; notably, however, not many of those who trekked through here on their way to the fertile Willamette in the fifties and sixties of the last century. These travelers looked back with recorded reluctance at the green stretch beside the river and named the place somewhat whimsically, Farewell Bend, because of the curve the river made there. But these weary folk were tired of barren hills. They wanted green slopes and verdant valleys, damp underfoot; so they pushed on, and it was not until the late nineteenth century that Bend became a town.

In the early 1900s irrigation came, and shortly afterward the lumber interests found the place. Tom Shevlin, the football hero from Yale, came in 1915 to build the Shevlin-Hixon sawmill. George Palmer Putnam came to edit the paper. People in Bend are fond of telling how Mrs. Putnam tried to break her husband of the habit of dropping his clothes on the floor wherever he stepped out of them. (I'm sure Bend didn't have in those days, and hasn't now, any human creature you could conceivably call a servant.) Mrs. Putnam, it is related, would take hammer and nail and pound George's clothes into the boards wherever she happened to find them lying.

Out of experience in the pine forests around the town, Paul Hosmer got the material for his book *Now We're Loggin*, which paints, with the exaggeration and gusty humor proper to logging vocabularies, a picture of the various types of jobs and human beings which keep the lumber industry going. I can't resist Mr. Hosmer's theory on the decline of the old-time lumberjack:

"A few years ago one could always tell a real lumberjack at a glance. There never was much room for doubt about him. If, through error, you should mistake him for an actor, a farmer or what have you, it was his playful habit to correct you at once by pulling your hat down over your eyes with his left hand and rapping you smartly on the chin with his right, after which he would carelessly toss you into the log pond before proceeding on his more important business of depleting the available liquor supply, which always seemed to pile up on him during his enforced stay in the woods through the winter. He was garbed in raiment peculiar to his calling—stagged pants, a little round hat from which the bloom of youth had long since departed, and a noisy, passionate shirt of many checks and colors. The shirt was always worn outside the trousers, like a Chinese laundryman. It was a half an inch thick and so scratchy that the ordinary human began to itch all over the minute he got into the same room with it. Lastly, he had on a pair of logger's shoes with half-inch caulks in the soles—'corks' in the woods—the most devastating thing in the line of footwear ever devised by man. Corked shoes were to the lumberjack what a tail is to a monkey; in other words, without them he wouldn't be much of anything and couldn't go any place. They served two or three purposes. For one thing they enabled our hero to earn an honest livelihood by spending fourteen or sixteen hours a day on the quarter deck of a short log while said log was resting uneasily on the bosom of a river. If you have ever tried to balance yourself on a log while wearing a pair of store shoes you will understand at once why a cat has claws. The old-time lumberjack was wont to spend several weeks each spring in bringing down the drive. During this time he practically lived on a log, although now and then he found time in which to dash ashore and curl up in a wet blanket for an hour or so of much needed sleep.

"The real purpose of the lumberjack's corks . . . only came to light when the drive was 'in' and the veteran had retired to the nearest saloon to celebrate his return. Here it was you could see the deadly skill with which the lumberjack, as he entered the door, was wont to set his heel down firmly on the pine floor, twist his foot dexterously, and rip out an entire board without batting an eye. After a couple of hearty jolts of bottled sunshine, one snort of which has been known to blow a man's collar buttons a distance of forty feet, it was his custom to kick a two-foot splinter out of the wooden bar rail just to hear it crack. Every kind of hardwood obtainable has been tried out in backwoods saloons for bar rails and floors, but nothing grows that can withstand the joyful ravages of a lumberjack on vacation. Some years ago an American genius retired to the seclusion of his laboratory, and when he came up for air he had the plans and specifications of an entirely new thing in that line. He had invented the modern brass bar rail which cannot be splintered, and it is my personal opinion that the decline and fall of the old-time lumberjack dates from this event. The brass bar has done more to tame the lumberjack and cramp his style than any other one thing, including prohibition. It practically ruined him. If you're a logger there's no use in getting drunk if you can't break something.

"... If a man had gone into the woods early in the fall and worked right through on the job he sometimes had as much as $150 in the spring, $149 of which he immediately spent for rum. The remaining dollar was sometimes used in the purchase of a new hat.

"If he was a good, careful buyer and a conservative drinker his winter wages sometimes lasted three or four days, but most of the boys were not conservative. They were, on the other hand, astonishingly willing, not to say eager, carousers, and it was not unusual for the old-timer to wake up without a dime the day after he was paid off, to find himself in a very poorly equipped jail, where he usually spent the summer.

"When our hero started on a spree he did it in a wholehearted manner that left no room for doubt in the minds of the citizenry as to where he was going. The police force never had any doubts about the matter, either, although it was the custom of the local gendarmes to leave the city when the drive struck town so as not to get involved in anything. Experienced lumberjacks usually confined themselves to misdemeanors and the lighter crimes—not counting manslaughter, as this wasn't considered much of a crime—in the hope that they could get out of jail in time to go to work in the fall, but now and then even an old-timer was apt to overestimate his capacity and get a little too rough with the mayor or some other personage of power, with the result that he got nicked for six months. This was usually disastrous, as by the time he got out all the good jobs were gone and he would be forced to ship out as a bullcook for the winter and make the last ten miles into camp on snowshoes."

People in Bend are glad to tell the inquiring visitor that Clark Gable once worked in a mill here, and that Don Blanding was a cashier in one of the banks. The third time I heard this last item I ventured to remark (it was in the library, a charming building of native woods, suited admirably to the land out of which it rises) that Mr. Blanding might better have remained behind the bars of a cashier's cage instead of fluttering middle-aged ladies with his romantic banalities. This sentiment seemed to endear me to the member of the library staff to whom I spoke. We fell at once into intimate conversation and she offered to telephone Klondike Kate and ask if I might come to call. Unfortunately "Aunt" Kate was not in town, but I learned some further details about her. Aunt Kate, it seems, is the firemen's friend. Whenever a fire siren sounds in Bend she puts on the coffeepot, knowing that her pals will come past when the blaze is out. The firemen's brass band, in return for this service, meets her at the station whenever she returns from any junkets to the world outside. She loves stories about herself and frequently visits the library to inquire if anything new has appeared about her.

Bend's outstanding landmark is the isolated bit of mountain called Pilot Butte, from which the local hotel has taken its name. The Pilot Butte Inn is one of the most comfortable and pleasant hotels in all this eastern Oregon land. The food is good, really good, and there is a genial air of comfort and even of a sort of bourgeois, bad-taste, expansive luxury which soothes the spirit at the end of a long day of naked open spaces. The building itself rambles pleasantly across a green lawn. It is built fittingly of local stone and wood. Inside are rooms full of comfortable soft furniture and some really fearful and wonderful "art." There is a very handsome large piece in one of the foyers, setting forth, as the clerk told me—not without a certain embarrassment—*The Temptation of Hercules*. Hercules—foreshortened in a manner that might well breed envy in Picasso—gazes at his own face in a mirror held by a buxom blonde. What there might have been tempting to Hercules in his own face is a subject I did not take up with the clerk; but his club and the aggressive draping of his tiger skin indicate that he is not going to linger in spite of lures. In the dining room there is also A Large Picture. This is of a lady, in flowing white garments, with her head resting on the base of an organ and a broken flute at her feet. This is St. Cecilia, symbolically represented as forsaking worldly music (the flute) for celestial music (the organ). I hope with all my heart that neither of these fanciful conceits is ever removed from the walls.

Bend has some very conservative inhabitants who live along the river and if you meet them and no others, visit the library, and stay at the Pilot Butte Inn, you may never see the other face of Bend's coin. But it does have another face. I sat for several hours beside GILBRIDES PASTIME—MIXERS, HOT DOGS, COFFEE and saw this other side. Old drunks held rambling conversations bristling with non sequiturs; making shrewd lewd comments about a recent drowning in a nearby lake. A young woman in a fetching get-up of pink cotton slacks and black cowboy hat with a cord under the chin went by on mysterious errands. At the end of one of her brief journeys she entered Gilbrides and took a great many heavy clinking silver dollars out of a cigar box. A synthetic cowboy, with incomparable languorous grief, sang (Drop in a nickel for this one!) "You left me in sorrow, you drifted away." All Gilbrides' habitués found this a most moving sentiment presumably. I heard nothing else in the time I sat at the curb.

CHAPTER III

Among the Basques
with a Scotchman

When we went to visit the Basques in Jordan Valley we stopped in Vale to pick up the judge of Malheur County to take with us as guide and raconteur. Judge David Graham from "Auld Glesca on the Clyde" over forty years ago, and proud of it, is a tall man with a slight stoop and the burriest of Scotch accents. He obligingly changed into riding trousers and boots, took his overcoat and a safety razor and set out with us.

All the way down and back he never stopped talking and we were glad he didn't. Although Vale, Oregon, lies in the midst of one of those open white patches on the map that I so enjoy looking at, the judge of this remote county had read, apparently, every book of any worth published in English. He began young and has kept at it ever since. As we rode he said, looking off to the right: "When I first came out here from Scotland, just a young laddie tending my uncle's sheep, I lost *Nicholas Nickleby* on the ridge between Juntura and Drewsey." I looked. The "ridge" appeared to be a stretch of some seven rolling hills. "Carrying everything I had in a flour sack," he said, "those were the days when . . ."

He was off. "When" so many things: Sheep coming in to take the place of cattle; life getting tough in towns like Lakeview; memories of "cat houses" in Ontario run by a cross-eyed blonde named Trixie Bennett, alias Rose Hanley, and her villainous French boy friend. Yarns and more yarns, and swift telling comment on the things we were seeing.

"Old woman lives here. Great rock collector. No children and every day's the same to her." Of a man, disappearing with swift slinking motion into a shack beside the road: "Murderer, but we can't pin it on him. . . . Murdered his partner in a mine fight." "No, Bob wasn't immoral, just non-moral; been among livestock all his life and thought nothing of it." "She's as holy as Coca-Cola." "Van Gogh was quite a fellow. He could have painted this country."

Judge Graham had once been the marrying judge of the county and had many a tale of "indigents and nit-wits" who had come to him for "splicing." After one particularly stupid pair had left his presence he turned to the witnesses and remarked: "Two hearts that beat as one, two heads that think as none."

He stopped talking only when we got out to look at the views. He let the wind from vast spaces blow over us and quiet us, and he was always the last one to get into the car—looking back reluctantly over his shoulder—although he has known this country intimately for half a century.

"There's nothing pretty about eastern Oregon. It just fascinates you, that's all," was his opinion; and certainly there is some curiously compelling quality in this land. There are places where it seems to break and flow like vast turbulent waters. In fact this land was once all ocean and it is as though the ocean has left its rhythm here, with tides of hills and mesas, breaking surf of buttes and rocks. In one place there was a beautiful wide view where we stood for many minutes, looking at the long—the singularly long—flat mesas that seemed to move out into space like the prows of ships. Over and over one thinks here of the sea; the same abstract rhythmic sense, the same soothing, yet never dull, monotony.

There was a single farm in a valley I cannot forget, lonely and lovely, with a square of poplars defining the yard and, peering over the buttes that surrounded it, red spears and thrusts and juts of dark solitary rocks. What the moon must do to such a setting comes at once into the mind, and one does not wonder that in such a land people must hold themselves to the earth by collecting its relics in stone and petrified wood. Almost every lonely house along these lonely roads has a yard bristling with weird gardens of onyx, quartz, chromium, jasper, and copper.

Down in Jordan Valley for all their years of solitude the transplanted "Bascos" seem to have little need of devices to keep themselves gay and sane. We put up for the night in a sprawling farmhouse. We found Mama Madariaga, the mother of eleven children—"seven grandchildren; ten by Christmas" (with a hearty poke in the ribs and a big laugh)—putting up some sixty bushels of peaches in a canning shed in the backyard of the old farm. We were late and we were very hungry and there were six of us, but Mama Madariaga was quite unaffected by this sudden incursion of outsiders. Before we had more than time to walk out in the cool evening light as far as the one drugstore for some medicinal whiskey, she had our supper ready for us: food with foreign flavor, old recipes out of the Pyrenees handed down these many years, a tomato soup with clabber in it; little fish, split, boned, dipped in egg and crumbs and then fried; Spanish meatballs with a hot red sauce; fried chicken; shoestring potatoes; lemon and coconut cream pie, and great mugs of dark brown coffee, served *au lait* as it is in Basque country.

After supper we went out and wandered about the streets of this little town, cut off from the outside world by deplorable roads for so many years. Some of the Basque faces are quite handsome, dark, passionate, merry, and yet with a curious reticence in them. It has been suggested that the American Basque is reticent because he does not like to be laughed at; he speaks a most extraordinary native tongue; must, in learning a new language, make speech mistakes, and to avoid being an object of derision he takes refuge in silence with strangers. We stopped to talk with some men in front of a filling station, men in blue denims and old faded hats—high crowned, not cowboy hats. The judge talked to them. They replied monosyllabically; there was a good deal of soft laughter, and the whole feeling became momentarily very un-American. We looked for the one dress characteristic we were told could still be found in everyday garments among the Americanized Basque who was born in the Pyrenees—the collar button kept closed no matter what the temperature. Finding it pleased us, for we knew we would have no opportunity to see any other details of native dress—the beret, the scarf, the full skirt, or the rope-soled shoes.

The Basques came into the high range country of Eastern Oregon and Idaho during the eighties and nineties of the last century. They are still for the most part sheepherders and farmers, an industrious hardworking lot who never appear on relief rolls, collect old age pensions, or send their boys to C.C.C. camps.

The Basques still speak their native tongue in Jordan Valley—although it is slowly being allowed to die among the young people. In the *Commonwealth Review*, Cressman and Yturri tell a charming tale of the difficulties which lead the Basques to encourage their children to learn to speak English well and quickly. A Basque who lived in cattle country went to a neighboring ranch to buy some chickens with which to start a flock of his own. He asked for some hens. When the owner was putting the chickens in the crate the observant Basque protested in some agitation: "Some bull hens! Some bull hens."

We watched the card games in pool halls, some curiously quiet, some very noisy. The judge, who was no stranger, unbent the villagers a little. We spoke of Spain and it brought head-shakings. The Basques were passionate Loyalists. They know that times are bad at home. It has been suggested that the new critical attitude of many of these pious people toward the Church has its root in their low opinion of the role the Catholic powers played in the tragedy of Spain.

We ended at a charivari dance where we saw some really beautiful Basque girls, delicately made, with blue-black hair, sparkling eyes, and smiles which lighted their faces in a most bewitching fashion. Some of the younger ones go out now to the state university and arrive home looking very *Mademoiselle* and properly stereotyped. The young ones are friendly and gay and utterly without self-consciousness.

We left the dance about midnight, went home and were hardly abed before most of the dancers arrived at Madariaga's for midnight supper. We remained in our rooms but the judge got up and reported on it to us the next morning at breakfast. Papa and Mama both prepared the meal: ham, and their favorite hot sausages called chorizos. Papa was garbed only in his long woolen underclothes, having had no time to dress. When we saw Mama at breakfast she confessed to us her chagrin and humiliation—not at our having been kept awake—but at the fact that she had not been forewarned about the festivities and so had had no time to prepare the freezer of ice cream which the Madariaga household always provides for these impromptu post-dance gatherings.

In the morning we went to call on Marie Marquiña, whom we had met in the general store the night before, and again at the dance, and who had promised to show us the church. Marie's home adjoins the old pelota court, some one hundred and twenty feet in length, with stone walls fifty feet high. The court is slowly moldering away since there seem to be few men left with the stamina or the time to play this fast tough game brought over from the Pyrenees.

Marie took off her apron and went with us to open the church. Although it was Sunday, of late years there are only infrequent services by itinerant priests from Boise or Ontario. The girls of the community painted the interior, a complicated quite hideous and very touching piece of work, all squares, in a number of sickly colors. Marie's attitude toward the whole matter seemed markedly impersonal and practical. She apparently felt little awe, indicating the Host in casual fashion, showing us the different robes of purple, white, green, and black for Easters, funerals, Christmas, and festivals. She said that many of the robes had disappeared. Probably some of the priests had taken them. She seemed to bear little rancor toward them for what appeared to us arrant thievery.

Just before we left, the Madariagas took us out to the cobbled backyard and showed us a large board of faded and weathered red with Chinese script on it which they said came from an old "joss house" in the wild frontier town of Silver City, Idaho, just over the line. They wondered if it had any historic value. If it had they would gladly part with it. A Madariaga girl told us that the old silk curtains from this same temple had kicked around the local school for some years also. As we rode away I couldn't but think of the curious fact that these people were so interested in preserving—even if belatedly—the relics of the Oriental in the Far West, and have apparently so little wish to keep their children aware of some of the richly individualistic and picturesque qualities of speech, dress, and ways of life that they brought with them into the American mass. It seems sad that these enriching elements are allowed to die out and the monotony of "Americanism" completely dominate all such cultural fragments.

We left Jordan Valley by Sucker Creek Road, a beautiful trip through those Aztec and Inca forms that lava upheavals and erosion often create. It was wild daisy time and they were growing head-high along the road. The sage itself was unusually bright in tone and very large—a sign of fertile soil. The yellow blossoms lent sudden heightened life to the dreamy flat wash of hill and desert. Here and there were poplars, turning and beating their leaves in the infrequent wind. Fences had horses tied to them, dreaming in the hot light. Toward evening the shadows began to slant down from the rosy hills, running a range of all the possible blues and violets. The land laid its unforgettable hand upon us. We shall have to go back.

We saw the new green stretches of alfalfa watered by the Owyhee dam which sends its long siphon over the landscape like a great white snake—the longest siphon in the world—carrying water to Dead Ox Flat from the rockribbed Owyhee reservoir. Here in the valleys stretches the great Vale-Owyhee project for which the government is spending twenty-two million dollars to put waste land into production. The contrast is still viewable; utterly gray and dead-looking land abuts sharply on fields of almost electric green. The sweet scent of alfalfa lies on the air and bees are busy making alfalfa honey in neat houses along the roadside. The judge pointed with pride to the new sugar beet factory at Nyssa, the "newest and most modern" in the United States. Not far away was a brown-tented government camp for migratory workers.

Everywhere one sees signs, "Government Grazing Service," reminding one that this is still sheep and cattle country. This is big land. Harney County alone exceeds in size the combined areas of Massachusetts and Rhode Island. Eastern Oregonians are glad to see the land come into use, because it justifies their faith of many years' standing; but they hate parting with the sense of leisure and space that uncluttered country gives a human being. Very special qualities seem to be produced here by comparative isolation; by the necessity for developing patience and an almost Oriental time-sense in the years when roads were so impassable that a few miles might be a matter, not of hours, but of days. People in this country can always take time off, without any guilt, to go excursioning. And the country itself produces a big-dimensioned type of human: eccentric, difficult to live with in all probability, but with that quality, so hard to define yet so easily recognizable, which we refer to as "character."

CHAPTER IV

Burns

B ill Hanley's famous Bell A ranch of ten thousand acres lay just three and a half miles from Burns and the Double O of sixteen thousand acres lay some thirty-five miles to the southwest. Riding his cattle through this eastern Oregon landscape helped Hanley to create his homely, sometimes profound, and very American philosophy. His ways of thought and expression were in the same vein as those of Will Rogers, who was one of his many friends. His often trenchant, but always kindly, aphorisms and his quiet wisdom, Anne Shannon Monroe set down before his death in a book called *Feelin' Fine*, a phrase which was his own invariable description of his condition. Some of these close-packed phrases reveal the man's nature:

"Everything is in understanding. Even with a flea; when you know he always hops up and never down that helps you to get rid of him."

"Brains is an awful responsibility. Man's been wobbling around with 'em ever since it happened."

Of young men of rich families who got into difficulties: "Just taken off milk and put on money, what can you expect?"

"Everything passes. . . . Man's only job is to deliver what is in him to the age he lives in."

He loved all animals and even kept coyotes as pets. "Once when I'd bought so many cattle, and wasn't selling any, and had more coming, with no money or credit to take care of the load, right in the midst of my worry, a fellow comes along with a yearling coyote he'd raised a pet. I bought it; paid $10 for him. After that when I was overworried I'd just set down with him and begin to scratch him under the chin a little, and commence to howl, and he'd set up and howl, too. You could howl with a coyote when you couldn't howl out loud by yourself. We'd just set and tell the heavens how cruel the earth was to us."

Bill Hanley died fittingly enough after Hanley Day at the Pendleton Round-up, thus giving western newspapers a chance to use the headline, "Last Round-up!" The end of another Oregon cattleman, also associated with the town of Burns, was less glamorous. Bill Brown, who once controlled 136,000 acres of rangeland and owned more than ten thousand horses and twenty-two thousand sheep, died in the early winter of 1941 in the Methodist Old People's Home at Salem. At his death the newspapers recalled some of the more picturesque details of his life. He always rode in his socks and rode like a centaur. He would write checks—and they were big ones in Bill Brown's palmiest days—on anything handy, a piece of wrapping paper, a tomato can label. Thirty-mile hikes after supper were nothing to him. He never married, never drank, never swore, never lied. He kept no books and his wealth was a matter of conjecture, but he was counted a rich man until the depression following the first World War. Then, "flat busted," he ended his days in an Old Folks' Home.

Burns did not get a railroad until 1924, although it was for years the capital of the old cattle country, and is today the administrative headquarters for the Taylor Grazing Act, making it still the center for livestock business in this part of the world. Pete Stinger, on whose ranch the village first sprang up, got cheated out of the honor of having the community named for him. I can't but think that Stinger would be a fine name for such a town, with the particular quality of color that cowboys and Indians give these high, dry, dusty, and zestful communities.

Burns has a town crier who fills in the weekly gap between newspapers by announcing major calamities or events of local interest. We heard of a woman who went to Burns to give a lecture. Alone in her hotel room she was amazed to hear her name being cried through the streets. She rushed to the window and thrust out her head to hear the announcement of her presence in the town and the purpose of her visit.

In Burns one remembers that smart Indian princess and "chief" Sara Winnemucca who, in the late seventies, persuaded the government to allow the defeated Paiutes to leave the unfamiliar Yakima land, where they were banished after their ill-timed war, and return to the part of Oregon they had fought so hard to keep. Sara guided her people through almost Israelitish hardships, the worst of which was hunger. None of the other Indians would share food with the Paiutes. They were even kept away from the Wishram salmon fishing and had finally to subsist on grasshopper meal, provided them by a life-saving plague.

One sees Indians all through this country; Indians who, unlike coast Indians, still retain some of the more picturesque and suitable details of their native dress; men with braids and big high-crowned black hats; women with bright scarves and moccasins of bead work and deer hide. These Indians are not infrequently camped along the highway, sometimes with a shiny car and—we hate to tell it—a pup tent, not a tepee.

CHAPTER V

John Day Country

John Day, the unfortunate Virginian who endured such hardships when crossing America in the winter of 1811–12 with the
Astor overland party that he eventually went mad, has left his
name to a spectacular and little known section of Oregon.

It seems fitting that this fantastic, tortured, and highly colored landscape
should bear the name of a man who died insane. And yet it has a beauty which
is at times almost tender—particularly in those places where the colored
strata of the gorges show a wonderful pale green, a lunar green like moonlight
on dusty sagebrush. To bring these unfamiliar shapes into more intimate
meaning one is compelled to turn to the language of medievalism. Crenella-
tions, bastions, turrets, castellations, towers are the only terms by which to
describe these tokens of the fierce terrestrial struggles of another aeon.

Between Canyon City and Dayville lies the Painted Canyon; peaks and
cones, fierce red crests and gentle flowing slopes of palest beige, sudden
angry scarlet, or smooth vermilion, outcropping along the banks of a languid blue stream. Yet in this fantastic countryside, wherever possible, lie
green fields, river-fed, hay stacks enclosed in little fences. And there are
white-faced cattle and a scattering of sheep feeding in the lush strips beside
the water.

The back roads yield spectacular scenery. A trip between Dayville and Prineville by way of Mitchell gives vast views from the tops of winding mountain grades. You see twin peaks, very high and marvelously, smoothly conical—as they are through all this crater country—guarding a valley of half-sculptured forms. A gigantic cock's comb of dark red stone defines the line of a sloping hill. Here and there rocks sliced through as neatly as though done by a great knife stand like a part of a very old wall. Spirals of red lava mount the great hills, as evenly, row on row, as though laid out by man for planned effect.

Whenever you see a human beside the road, you are startled; human life does not seem to belong here. Returning a rancher's dignified greeting we speculate whether, living in the midst of such abstract rhythms, natives must not become in time very remote and impersonal like island-dwellers.

The people we met in the towns were comfortingly hospitable, human, and natural. When we were visiting the charming old white courthouse among the trees beside the stream in Canyon City we were spied by Mr. Clinton Haight, the editor of the *Blue Mountain Eagle*, who sent his son Bill to invite us to lunch. We ate in the backyard, among the inevitable collection of curious local stones, an excellent meal, stretched by Mrs. Haight with easy grace to include three extras. There was good talk. Mr. Haight proved to be another of those Northwestern characters who give a sense of homely stability in a shifting world. There is nothing in the least stereotyped about these men. You are free in their presence of the well-dusted clichés of the city dweller. They think independently and act eccentrically if they choose to, and yet when they speak it is with authority, as though their words have grown out of long silences and much experience in living.

The banner head of Mr. Haight's newspaper reads, "Freedom is the Right to be Wrong." Mr. Haight's personal column The Cock-Eyed World puts into print his observations and philosophy. Not long ago he wrote:

"Fie Fie on the Cock-eyed World for shooting its taxpayers. . . . Never let a taxpayer die. If he gets sick the government should send four or five doctors to his bedside and give him a free blood transfusion, or anything, to keep his breath going. If taxpayers die, or we shoot them in wars we can never hope to Bal. the Budg."

From Mr. Haight I heard what I was to hear many times in the North-west. There is total agreement that Hitler is a madman who must be stopped. Mr. Haight is not quite as humorous about him now as he was when he wrote: "They tell us that Hitler was a paper-hanger in Austria. And then he went mad. We don't doubt it. The last time that we papered the ceiling on the kitchen we went crazy. Get up on a ladder with about 15 feet of ceiling paper wrapped around your neck and it will drive anybody mad."

Mr. Haight thinks Hitler may be mad but he isn't responsible for every-thing that's wrong with the world. He doubts whether it matters essentially who wins this war, we're in for a general upheaval. And let's not go on laying it to the Germans or the Japanese. The fight for religious freedom was won; the fight for political freedom was won; the big fight now is for economic freedom. Men don't want to work so hard for so little. . . . England has com-pleted her cycle. All life goes in cycles. Whether she wins or loses her day of dominance is over. America too has completed a cycle. Mr. Haight said: "There has come an end to the kind of democracy I knew."

When he said this everyone in the garden was silent and a sadness seemed to creep out of the very air around us. This is a ghost town, Canyon City. Joaquin Miller's cabin clings to the hill above it: "Sail on, sail on and on." But "whither now?" one asks despairingly.

But Mr. Haight did not allow us to be dispirited long. He took up yarns of the "old days." He regretted that I had come some months too late to know an old character who had just died. On his ninety-first birthday he had gone into a local soft-drinks place and shot it up just for old time's sake. (There are no bars in Oregon.)

Then he had a story about the man who used to bring in the great wag-ons of whiskey in the early days when this was big-time mining country. (A sign on Canyon City's entrance gate says in fading letters, "Canyon City pro-duced $20,000,000 in Gold Dust.") This teamster, coming along with his load one day late and hungry, passed a neat little cabin and a garden of pota-toes. He said to himself, "I wonder if this fellow knows the law of the road that the first three rows of taters belong to the passing stranger." So he got out to help himself and just then the owner, an old man with a long white beard and a much longer and very black musket, appeared. He proceeded to chase the teamster, who, as he shot around the house, said to himself, "Man, if you ever thought, think now!" The third time round the house he gasped, "By God! I got it!" As he flashed past the wagon body for the fourth time he reached in and brought out a bottle of whiskey. Facing his pursuer, he cried, "How about a drink?" "Now you're talking sense," said the old man. "Why didn't you mention it sooner?"

After lunch Bill Haight took us for a tour. First up the steep-pitched hillside to Joaquin Miller's cabin, perched on the red hill. There were some of his poems tacked on the walls, and mementoes of his life, including, presumably, "Papa's last whiskey jug" which his daughter contributed on the occasion of the opening of the cabin as a local museum. In one corner was a branding iron. Young Haight implied casually that it might have come in handy for a poet who—what with love and literature—hadn't much time to care for cattle of his own. There was a photograph of Joaquin, the perfect showman, with well-cared-for flowing beard and hair, dashing hat, and embroidered shirt and boots. Small wonder his impact on the London of the early seventies was so forceful. Miller the poet and stud, pony express rider, world traveler and student of sorts, the county judge who changed his name from Cincinnatus Heine to Joaquin in honor of a Mexican bandit—here was a combination of qualities and talents unlikely to occur again in these degenerate times.

All this put us in the mood for the "museum" of Mr. Brown down in the town and for talk of the famous Whisky Gulch celebration which takes place in Canyon City every June when the Grant County pioneers get together to honor their oldest members and to recall the dramatic bad days after the prospectors, looking for the fabled Blue Bucket mines, came on gold in Whisky Flat. The Pony Express went thrice weekly from this roaring center to the metropolis of The Dalles. There were a good many outlaws whom the decent citizens buried in a separate cemetery which has now become one of the local sights. Whenever there was gold there was also bound to be many a beautiful woman, and Mr. Brown has souvenirs of this legendary period in the back of his garage. Little music boxes, sliver-thin high buttoned boots, embroidered silk slippers, handsome hand-tooled side saddles, battered bits of old china. In the window is a little model of Canyon City in the old days. Above the saloon there is a sign which reads, "HURDY GURDY DANCING AND GAMBLING—NO BET TO BIG TO CALL. BRING YOUR POKE AND ANTE."

Mr. Brown also has a corner given over to a collection of pictures, many of them of young women in various states of deshabille, ranging from a Kentucky Whiskey miss (Moonlight Brand) stripped to the waist, with hyperthyroid bosom and flowing brown hair, awaiting her fate with marked apathy, to a recent photograph of the seemingly unreluctant Miss Mae West. With admirable catholicity, Godey period scenes of mothers with tots clustered at the knee have also been included in this collection; and, scattered here and there, are some snapshots of well-developed gentlemen, presumably wrestlers. Whether this was all just a riot of Freudian free-association or whether Mr. Brown had some definite end in view, I lacked the courage to inquire. On the whole it seemed to present a rather happy eugenic picture.

I felt sad parting with Canyon City. The houses along the street had a sweet ancient air—more gracious of line than most houses in pioneer country, a dreamy feeling of prosperity once there, perhaps to come again. People still strike it rich in these parts. The Haights had just sold a chromium mine. I heard the figures of the sale and found them astounding. Not that the Haights will change their way of life. I'm sure I could drop in from the courthouse next summer on a Monday at lunchtime and find Mrs. Haight hanging out the wash with the old German "help" named Carl, and the editor of the *Blue Mountain Eagle* letting his meat loaf and potatoes with spicy brown country gravy grow cold on his plate while he discusses European politics, religion, or the fantastic rocks that border his garden paths.

All through this part of Oregon the land is wild, the history wild. The town of Mitchell might stand as an example. Desperadoes, Indians, and cloudbursts have wreaked their will on the place. A nine-foot wave of water rushed over the bluff above the town in 1884, and again in July 1904 a thirty-foot wall of water roared down the canyon onto it.

Prineville is having a lumber boom now, and so farewell to some more of the beautiful rosy-boled pines through which we climbed; seeing deer feeding quietly; looking back from open notches to the bare bright stretches of the weird landscape we were leaving. Prineville's history is definitely on the lurid side. It was started in 1868 by one Barney Prine who, with almost Old Testament speed and directness, established the place by building the town in one day, dwelling house, store, blacksmith shop, hotel and saloon— all under one roof, all of willow logs ten by fourteen, one story high. Subsequently it was "Bloody Prineville" with sheep- and cattlemen having it out with spirited gunplay in the streets, so that local associations of cattlemen were ironically dubbed "The Crook County Sheep-Shooter's Association."

One feels new movement all through this section of the country, a sense of shifting populations and fresh migrations, new seekers, dreamers, malcontents, jobless. One feels it in new roads, new industries, reclaimed acreage. It comes sharply when, stopping the car in the twilight to ask where we are, we learn that it is a C.C.C. camp high in the mountains. A boy comes up close to the car. His young sensitive face shows in the headlights; he has a soft Southern voice. "What part of the South are you from?" A pleased small laugh. "Alabama, ma'am—we're all from Alabama," and one feels the stir and turn of the population of this country—Alabama boys high on a mountain road in the Ochocos of Oregon.

CHAPTER VI

Gold, Uncivic Potatoes, and a Centenarian

Although the town of Baker looks calm enough today, lying peacefully in the shade of its locusts and cottonwoods, it had a wild history. The visitor is reminded here, as in Canyon City, of the search for the Blue Bucket gold mine, prompted by an emigrant's tale of finding enough nuggets "to fill a blue bucket" which sent frenzied men digging up every eastern Oregon canyon. Griffin's Gulch yielded gold in 1861 and since that time nearby mines have produced some $150,000,000 worth of gold. The memory of the great stampede is kept alive by a display in the staid First National Bank of the many forms that gold can take; and among the quartz, the nuggets, the wirelike strands, and the dust, is a single lump weighing eighty-six ounces and valued at $2,500.

Baker was built up as a merchandising center for the mining communities encircling it. Its past is lurid with tales of robberies, hold-ups, sporting houses, dance halls, murders, and all the rest of the frontier picture. Yet, with typical American incongruity, "The city commissioners in 1881 passed an ordinance prohibiting small boys from shooting marbles or riding velocipedes on the sidewalks, and required one citizen to remove his potato patch from a lot on a principle street." Houses of ill repute were one thing, presumably, and marble games and potato patches another. A growing city has to develop civic pride.

I find the assertive vertical of the ten-story Baker hotel, "one of the largest buildings in the state," a similar piece of incongruity in a country where horizontal space would seem distinctly not to be at a premium—but that's the only possible criticism I could make against this comfortable stopping place.

If, while in Baker or any adjacent community, you ask any questions about the old days you are at once driven out to Medical Springs to see Baker County's oldest resident, a fabled character named Dunham Wright, aged ninety-nine in 1940. A sprier centenarian I never expect to meet.

We drove up to the old Wright house, long and sprawling and tree-shaded, with the Medical Springs spa just across the road. We entered upon a most 1890 scene of Patriarch in Midst of Family; the old man, now paralyzed—legs only—with his little spotless white beard and his bright blue eye, white shirt and broad-brimmed white hat, in the midst of a group of laughing and talking people, all seated under a long arbor through which the wind was blowing from the bare brown hills. His daughter, a white-haired, plump, gay woman, announced in loud clear tones, "Papa, here's Nancy Ross come to see you from New York. Not Betsy, but her niece." After the laughter at this witticism had subsided the old man fixed me for a moment with his bright blue glance, dropped his eyes to my nail polish and drawled with finely placed ironic emphasis and a mounting appreciation of his powers of observation and humor: "Laws sake! Look at all that blood! Terrible wounded in every finger. Think you could still sew a flag single-handed?"

When the roars at the old man's wit had died down there was a chorus of eager voices urging me just to ask him anything I wanted to know. "The trouble isn't getting papa started, it's getting him stopped. He has such a wonderful memory." A slight hesitation on my part was fatal, for a well-meaning man—no longer young except by comparison—stepped up and said in the old man's ear, "Tell her about the Black Hawk War." Mr. Wright responded like a race horse to the gun; and after that I had some difficulty getting him down to comparatively recent times like 1860. He sat there remembering with vivid detail the stories his own father had told him. Some of them were about Lincoln. Mr. Wright is a descendant of the Hanks family and he told, with a nice sense of timing and good dramatic feeling, how his grandmother, a Hanks and a midwife, was up early getting breakfast before going over to the Lincoln cabin to deliver the expected child, "when Thomas Lincoln thrust his head through the cabin opening and drawled, 'We got a new baby over t' our house this morning, and we think we'll call him Abe.'"

At one point Mr. Wright dwelt with loving detail on a contrasted picture of the lives of the women in pioneer times and at present. After painting an unappealing picture of the past he again announced, with heightened sparkle of his bright blue eye, that he hoped to have his audience in the aisles for the second time, and launched into a descriptive passage about the twentieth century woman: "Now today a woman goes into her Queen Anne House or Bungalow" (you felt he meant them to be capitalized); "she unlaces those close-fitting stays" (slight fixing and abrupt removal of the glance at this point); "she takes off her toothpick shoes, she puts on something loose and comfortable, she draws down all the blinds and she goes out and says to whoever is running that house, Don't disturb me for a week. I'm just plumb wore out."

I managed to get in a question then about Joe Meek. "Yes," he said, "I knew Joe Meek—saw him often—had an Indian woman." This seemed an odd thing to emphasize in a country where such alliances were fairly commonplace. He went on then to tell the story of Joe Meek waving his coonskin cap in the air at the Champoeg Wolf Meeting and shouting "Divide! Divide!"—so whether apocryphal or not one might as well accept the story as these old people tell it. Indeed, interviewing the old settlers is one way to appreciate the manifest inability of the historian to arrive at "truth." What really happened is pleasantly confused with wish and dream and yarn and promise; so that one carries away few facts but something perhaps more valuable: an enlivening sense of the quality of life in these old people. No dwindling and fading, becoming parasitic and looking toward the next generation for the answers; but a sort of intensification of the life forces, a real expression of the "personality."

The Northwest is proud of its old people, and they are a tough-fibred lot. "Seven-months babies" born on the plains are to be found at ninety, exceptionally hale old women. On a country road on the Olympic Peninsula an old farm woman in her seventies had an almost mythological encounter with a maddened ram which broke her bones and pinned her to earth, but she lived to describe it to her grandchildren. In central Washington a man of seventy-four was riding a bad horse which fell with him. He climbed back on with a broken leg and rode the twelve miles home. Five months later he was up and about as well as ever.

Mrs. Mary Ramsey Lemons Woods, who lived in the eighteenth, nineteenth, and twentieth centuries, died in Hillsboro in 1908 at the age of one hundred and twenty years, seven months, and eleven days. At one hundred and sixteen she testified in court with what was said to be remarkable clarity. She had lived under the administration of every president from Washington down to Theodore Roosevelt, and among the lot of them favored "Teddy" and "Old Hickory." The Oregon Pioneer Association crowned her "Mother Queen of Oregon" when she was one hundred and twenty years and five weeks old, and she sat up and wore the crown and had her picture taken.

To children in the Northwest some years ago Ezra Meeker, coming annually into town with his famous ox team, his long white beard, his oft-repeated tales, and his zeal for getting the Oregon Trail marked, was a figure as ancient as God. Actually this spry old man was in his late seventies and eighties when he traveled with his oxen from the Pacific to the Atlantic, establishing monuments along 1,800 of the 3,000 miles.

CHAPTER VII

Enterprise—A Lost Hat— The Canyon of Hell

We went to the town of Enterprise because it is the way in to Hat Point, the Imnaha, and Hell's Canyon of the Snake. It lies in the land of the Blue and Wallowa Mountains and is a gate to some of Oregon's greatest scenic wonders. Enterprise goes its own easy way, regardless of visitors and possible publicity. The town has always been noted for simple good will, democracy, and hospitality, and it will probably never change. I came away hoping that Hat Point (named for a creek which was named for a hat which a tough pony bucked off the head of one Alex Warnock many years ago) would never get a big dark National Park hotel perched on the rim of the Snake; that the nearby countryside would not ever discover the profits to be made in dudes. I even hoped that the hotel would stay just the same, with the starched lace curtains, the poison-blue walls, the keys that wouldn't fit the locks, and the absolutely kindly and unselfconscious managers who made no more of visitors from afar than of the rancher's wife in from the hills to see the dentist.

Mr. Charles Zurcher, the state senator from Enterprise, took care of us. Mr. Zurcher is a modest man but an original thinker. He has ideas about important questions like Money and he is glad to tell you what they are, but he doesn't push them at you. His carefully thought-out theories on that teasing abstraction, the Gold Standard, have been gathered together in a short article called *Money and its Functions as Understood by a Small Town Merchant*, and part of this article has been published in a survey along with the theories of such well-known financiers as Henry Ford and Frank A. Vanderlip. Mr. Zurcher isn't awed by this honor—although it pleases him—but his constituents think it a fine thing that Charlie Zurcher who sells insurance and denim overalls, cowboy boots and "store" clothes, has received some national recognition for his ideas.

Mr. Zurcher says he started to think on the subject of Money "away back in 1920 when the Federal Reserve Bank took it upon itself to restrict credits in the whole country and practically ruined the livestock business of the Northwest." Although Mr. Zurcher's stock ranch and dairy farm were making money he had to sell out to protect his creditors, and it took him some sixteen years to pay off his debts. He says: "Although when I looked over my ranch in 1920 I discovered that I had more real wealth than I had in 1919, when I undertook to turn it into gold it took more of it than it did in 1919, and I began to wonder who it was that determined in *what* debts should be paid. I could easily see that a pound of butter at 16 cents would spread as many slices of bread as it would have done at 50 cents, and that a beef steer at $40 would feed as many people as it would at $100. I began to wonder what real wealth was, and from there on I evolved my theory."

Briefly Mr. Zurcher's complaint against America's money standard is that when the dollar is fixed at so many grains of gold, regardless of the market price of gold, it is no longer an "honest" dollar. In the operation of the present money standard, hardships are worked on the man whose possessions are in things like stock and wheat, while the man with "intangible" possessions is benefited.

Mr. Zurcher writes: "Suppose that Kansas City, Missouri, had bonded itself in the year 1865 in the sum of $100,000, and that the bonds called for payment in buffalo tongues, in the year 1933, at the rate of one tongue for each dollar of the bonds. Do you think this city would be able to redeem its bonds in accordance with the specific terms of the contract?"

In Enterprise the local Lions entertained us and we saw, after dinner, a movie made by the Pacific Power and Light Company called *The River of the West*; all about how electricity serves these vast relatively unpopulated stretches of country. Could this have been a bit of propaganda brought into being by the threat of the cheap power from the Bonneville and the Grand Coulee projects?

On the day that we took the famous trip to the Snake River canyon we left Mrs. Campbell's with a well-filled picnic hamper and the memory of good black breakfast coffee "perked" right at the table in individual percolators. Mrs. Campbell is a handsome dark-haired lady who serves Enterprise with a restaurant, gift shop, lending library, magazine stand, and place of rendezvous—a feat which entitles her to classification with Barney Prine.

It is difficult to describe the landscape on the Hat Point trip. You go up 7,000 feet and then move along at the top of the world. It is so big—this landscape—that one can hardly grasp its dimensions. It has none of the solemnity, or the forbidding depressing grandeur, of many steep rocky outlooks. The rolling slopes are all so golden, so russet, so strokable to look at, that the effect is gentle rather than grim. And there are no silences to compare with those that come up out of vast openings in the earth's surface. This Snake Canyon is another of the Far West's biggest items. It seems amazing that anything as large could have remained unmeasured by geographers for so long a time; "lost" one might even say. It gives one a fresh idea of how much of this Far Western country is still unexplored and unknown. Not until Richard Neuberger wrote an article in the April 1939 *Harper's* had many Americans so much as heard of the canyon. Even the *Encyclopædia Britannica* gives it only passing reference; and yet the comparisons to the Grand Canyon of the Colorado are staggering:

"Hell's Canyon averages 5,510 feet in depth for 40 spectacular miles. Here 6,000 foot expanses are not uncommon. At one point the canyon is 7,900 feet deep; a mile and a half from rim to river. This considerably exceeds the 6,100 maximum depth of the Grand Canyon."

Neuberger also says: "The Snake River is the least known major waterway of the continent. Millions of Americans have never heard of it, yet it is more than three times as long as the Hudson and its drainage area is eight times as great—including nearly all of Idaho, and parts of Washington, Oregon, Wyoming, Utah and Nevada. Only three rivers in the United States—the Columbia, the Colorado, and the Tennessee—excel it in hydroelectric power potentialities."

Looking down these incredible perpendiculars one must think of the men of the Bonneville and Astor Overland Expeditions who tried this Snake trip with great loss of life and terrible suffering. Very little has changed hereabouts since then. The local people emphatically don't want it made too easy to get into this part of their country. They like it left inaccessible and remote, so that it takes at least some will and endurance to get up to that final ridge where there was no one the day we were there but an exceptionally handsome forest ranger with his horse and his dog, his soft pale hat and twangy friendly drawl, "One of the Marks' boys" from down some valley far below us. The land is sheep and cattle country and the people don't see any possible advantage in making it a national park or monument with high prices and regimented recreational activities.

Eating Mrs. Campbell's sandwiches, hard-boiled eggs, and cake with an inch of frosting, we looked down, thousands of feet, to the pale green river winding and churning below. From our picnic table we could see the approximate spot to which Grace Edgington and Len Jordan took their degrees in philosophy from the University of Oregon and a lot of courage, and went to raise sheep and a family some fifteen years ago. The only way out from their ranch is by airplane or boat—at certain seasons. At Christmas, Len's mother, a charming and dignified white-haired lady from Enterprise, goes in to see them—if they don't come out. The captain of the craft which bucks the treacherous Snake has provided her with a rocking chair in which to take the trip. It is necessary to spend a night in the canyon, sleeping on the boat, for there is no possible landing place in a canyon with sheer vertical walls. The Jordans have raised three remarkable children in their self-imposed isolation. The seven-year-old, on being told that he didn't know "straight up," replied solemnly, "I do too, it's perpendicular."

It was pleasant to sit in the high, sunny, pine-fresh air and look far across to the Jordan ranch and think about people living this way in these times.

That night in Enterprise we rode in the moonlight around Wallowa Lake. The C.C.C. boys have made a monument and a quiet enclosed place at the end of it for old Chief Joseph's grave marker; and the local residents hope in time to get Young Chief Joseph's dust transferred back to this land for which he and his people were willing to give their lives. Looking at the blue magic of the hills in the moonlight, it is easy to understand how cruelly painful it must have been for the Indians to relinquish this lovely rolling country of hill and lake and gentle valley.

CHAPTER VIII

Pendleton Round-up

In 1940 the Pendleton grandstand burned to ashes just three weeks before the famous Round-up was to begin. The fire—believed to have been deliberately set by a pyromaniac—started at 9:15 while the stand was full of spectators watching a softball game. Fortunately everyone escaped, although the grandstand was completely gone by ten o'clock. By eleven the leading citizens had met at the brewery to talk it over. They were in bed by two with the new contracts let; and sixty hours later, the work was under way.

This indicates the attitude of Pendleton citizens toward their annual show. The speed with which the grandstand was rebuilt—in concrete this time—was made possible by the instantaneous pledging by Pendleton people of the money needed.

The social life of Pendleton revolves around the yearly Round-up, and it is a whole-town job. Nobody makes money on it—except indirectly through a four-day boost to local business. Men who have worked like demons for the Round-up year after year always tell you that they are content to break even. Money goes only to the professional cowboys who compete for prizes, and to the Indians, who get paid for every tepee, every papoose, and every costume they bring to the Indian grounds.

Once the professional cowboys—the "turtles"—got tough with Pendleton and tried to make their own rules. Pendleton let them go and put on a strictly amateur show until the professional boys came round to the citizens' way of seeing things. Inquiry about this row brings out such picturesque explanations as: "Well, for instance, in bull-dogging, the turtles wanted to come out lap and tap with the steers." One lets it go at that! Everything is amiable enough now, seemingly. The turtles deem it a real honor to win the Jackson trophy given yearly to the best all-round cowboy. This trophy is a silver statue of a bronco being ridden in spectacular fashion. Mr. Phil Jackson, who owns the Portland *Journal*, comes over every year to present the award—thus pleasantly linking the coast and the inland. (The Jacksons were formerly an inland family.) The *Journal* Special lies out on the tracks beyond town and there's never any extra room on it. The whole state of Oregon lends at least its spiritual support to the Pendleton show.

In the Pendleton papers a similarity has sometimes been pointed out between their show and the Oberammergau pageant. The devotion to an idea and the hospitality are certainly comparable, but the quality of the entertainment is rather more robust in Pendleton.

At Round-up time all Pendletonians keep open house. Breakfasts of two hundred, lunches of seventy-five, dinners of one hundred and fifty are commonplace among the leading citizens. There is something especially appealing about the sight of cowboy shirts, boots, scarves, and suntans in the midst of the restrained Victorian setting of a Pendleton home. Cowboy crooners teeter dangerously on the backs of chairs to sing their drawling ditties, scratching matches on their elegant, incredibly tight, dress-up pants of thin striped wool, bucking the chair precariously as they recite the whimsical character of the *Strawberry Roan*. A cocktail party in Pendleton at Round-up time is quite simply Scotch or Bourbon—and plenty of it. One sees an ancient Oriental in a white coat, carrying hors d'oeuvres, walking among the guests and speaking to them with the easy grace of an old and privileged servant.

The Indian director—who also runs the Pendleton Woolen Mills—puts up a tepee on his lawn and there at lunchtime sit famous chiefs in imposing splendor of avoirdupois, black braids, eagle feathers, and brilliant shirts; among them a two-hundred-and-fifty-pound Indian known to his white friends simply as Clarence Burke but to his Indian pals for many years as Yetet-amout-sette, which is to say Man-Sitting-on-a-Mountain, until on a recent Fourth of July he changed his name to Whet-yat-mūs-te-yaika-pee, or Sun-Setting-on-the-Mountain. This name-changing required quite a ceremony with the distribution of six or eight blankets, beaded belts, and other valuables.

"These are pick-up men," the hostess says, introducing elegant gentlemen in gay silk shirts who are subsequently to be seen sitting their saddles with that hard flat stockman's seat, doing their brilliant stuff in the arena. Lunching with one of them we speak, before long, of politics. He's all for change, summing it up with a brisk western aphorism: "If you've got a balky horse and trade him for another, you aren't any worse off than you were."

Everyone goes to Hamley's leather shop to see the prize saddles inlaid with silver and of a very beautiful fine workmanship; to buy the soft squaw shoes of buckskin and bead-work, shapeless beautiful buckskin gloves, or Hamley's famous "lifetime" leather kits, into which men love to put their shaving oddments. The Hamley store throngs with Indians and cowboys, trick ropers, visiting Easterners, movie stars, dudes and ranchers—and most of this same motley and colorful crowd will in all likelihood be seen later under the green trees of the Hamley residence having a buffet supper.

Everywhere you see Moorhouse's fine photographs of the Indian as he was before greatness and strength had vanished from his face. You see also the portraits of some of these great old men and women done by the Episcopal rector of the town, Fred Wissenbach, a rebellious and cultivated Bavarian who fled Munich and came to the New World a number of years ago to become a minister with parishes at Sheridan, Wyoming, and Pendleton, Oregon. You'll particularly notice on posters the sweet, sad, sardonic, and beautiful face of an old Indian, a face with grace and suffering in it, which belonged to the much-loved Poker Jim. Poker Jim was what people affectionately call a character. He was named White-Geese-Sounding-on-Waters in his youth, but the name was dropped as time wore on and he began to display such unusual talents at a well-known parlor pastime that a newspaper reporter once remarked, "If white geese were in the picture they were the palefaces who got into the game." Poker Jim was a prodigious gambler. Asked once about his biggest poker game he replied, "Maybe play poker all week; no sleep, win hundred twenty-five horses, nine hundred dollars in gold." He gave only one piece of advice to neophytes: "Two pair not much good."

The Round-up is an animated monument to democratic cooperation, good will, and good management. The whole show moves with a briskly professional air. There is never a lag in the speed. The voice from the loudspeaker keeps on and on, "Riding in the east, riding in the west, riding center." At Pendleton they still use the snubbing horse and unmask the bucking broncos in the middle of the arena. This, one is told, is the last place in America where one may still see it done as it was on the plains: everywhere else chutes are now used exclusively. Trick riders and ropers perform their deceptively easy feats in front of the grandstand. There's always a flutter for Monte Montana who is called—with quite shocking understatement—simply a fancy roper, when in reality he's a magician of the first order. I don't believe a single thing I see him do and when I am told—as I always am— about his charming wife (and she is pretty), his little boy, his ardent religious nature, and his refusal to drink, he certainly doesn't become any more real. The woman seated beside me in the box suggested that trick roping should be taught in the schools; kept alive as an American art; raised at least to the dignity of tap dancing, which is available now to most undergraduates. I thought it a sound suggestion.

The Indian beauties in their white beaded buckskin dresses line up for judging. They've been selected before they appear in front of the grandstand—this in the interest of speed which is of prime concern to the men who manage the Round-up activities. Selection takes place actually after a morning parade in the little green town park. One or two visitors usually help to judge, along with a townsman and the Reverend Wissenbach, who points out to strangers that Hollywood standards are not Indian beauty standards; that there are traditions in saddle equipment that count for points, and these traditions should be encouraged; that wristwatches, red nail polish, and beadwork of modern pattern must count against the entrants, no matter how sparkling their teeth and eyes. Anna Wannasie, a little Indian woman, kept the girls in line the time I helped to judge them. She was to be heard admonishing them to sit up straight, throw out their gum and smile whenever looked at. Anna Wannasie looked charming herself in a very beautiful and valuable old red velvet dress, sown lavishly with the prized elks' teeth. She wore braids and the little pointed basket of a quite Schiaparelli chic that some of these old Indian women still wear. I said to her, "You should have a prize. You are beautiful." She tittered shyly, and murmured in a low voice, "Booby prize!"

She had a delicate quality not often seen in Indian women as they grow older. Melissa Parr, a great beauty who was once chosen Queen of the Round-up (there have been only two Indians ever honored in this fashion), is growing middle-aged gracefully; and there was, until quite recently, a famous old matriarch, Molly Minthorne, whose picture is in every Pendleton scrapbook. She always rode horseback in the parade in buckskin ceremonials and her little conical basket-hat. She lived to be over one hundred and six, and she maintained up to the last that Marcus Whitman had been poisoning the Indians and deserved to die by the tomahawk as he did.

Actually the Pendleton Round-up isn't just a four-day hey-hey. It keeps alive a real interest, among Indians and whites, in preserving the fast-disappearing picture of the life that was lived here so relatively short a time ago. The Round-up parade is one of the best places to get an authentic idea of the chronological development of the West. Beginning with the naked Indian hunters (and there is no finer sight in the world than a painted Indian in a breech clout and war bonnet, riding a good horse), the parade comes up through the war parties; the squaws setting out on food-gathering expeditions with their children and their *travois*; the white trappers and their Indian wives, with real animals in cages; Mormon carts, hand-drawn by men and women, because of the belief that such conveyances were less attractive to the Indians; rangers and emigrants sometimes singing those songs so tellingly designed to strengthen flagging spirits, bring the relaxation of homesick tears, or picture of a brighter land just over the next range;

Catholic and Protestant circuit riders; buckaroos; *aparejo* outfits, the Pony Express, stage coaches, twelve-mule freight teams, democrat wagons, pack outfits, and so on.

People who ride in the parade have sometimes been several days on the road, getting into the atmosphere of the thing. In 1938, a group of people started from La Grande, along the Oregon Trail. They wore the clothes of the period of the first emigrants. They came in covered wagons, on horseback and with ox teams, camping at night beside the road, cooking over open fires, sleeping in blanket rolls. Among them was Jim Blakely, an old rancher and former sheriff whose gentle weathered face shows nothing of the experiences he went through in the days when "there was a man for breakfast every morning" and such names as that of the outlaw Hank Vaughan had special and terrible meaning. Well on in his eighties, Jim Blakely still sits his saddle erectly and flatly in the best cowboy style; and sits it all day long, not only at the time of the Round-up, but every day on his home ranch. No one gets a bigger hand than he when he passes the grandstands in the arena parade and raises his hat in courtly fashion.

The Happy Canyon show at night carries the historic pageantry still further. Birds fly up, deer wander, the Indian has this rich and beautiful land for himself. Then the whites come, the wars are re-fought, the mad bad gold days allow a Frankie and Johnny melodrama. As a show it is almost too perfect, and so it does not touch the heart, as mine at least has been touched, by far less perfect performances of similar scenes in other towns. Sometimes the very ineptness of these local pageants moves one with the realization of how gropingly and earnestly western people are trying today to evaluate their recent history.

Probably the most poignant moment in all the Pendleton pageantry comes when, from a seat in the grandstand in the afternoon's clear golden light, you see the covered wagons billow up like great slow sails on the yellow hill across the valley. They begin their tortuous descent of the slope. Indians ride up against the blue sky. Faintly across the distance one hears their cries for blood. The wagons circle and prepare to defend themselves. The Indians set fires. . . . Suddenly tears prick the eyelids at the realization of those qualities of hardihood, endurance, and simple stupid courage which lie so deep in the American character.

Much of the equipment worn in the Round-up Parade is quite priceless, chiefs' robes and chiefs' *coup*-sticks preserved for many years. The Indians put on a further exhibition in the library showing their costumes, food, types of basketry and weaving, with women to demonstrate the old ways of doing things—all this in the hope that the Indian will thus be encouraged, before it is too late, to preserve some of his vanishing traditions.

Sometimes the Indians choose to be buried in their ancient priceless garments, and this is always a matter of great personal anguish to George Strand who manages the parades and is always on the lookout for "museum pieces." Melvin Fell, the Indian Director, likes to tell a story about George's collecting zeal. It involves an old Indian who grew very religious, so much so that he became a deacon in the Presbyterian church at the reservation, gave up all his Indian ways, and even refused to take part in the Round-up parade. Just two years before his death, however, he suddenly reappeared in the parade wearing his famous buckskin suit, worn with a white man's hat to indicate that he was not really crossing back over the line. The next year he appeared completely accoutered with feather headdress and buckskins. The next year he died, and in his will he stipulated that—in spite of Presbyterianism—he wished to be buried in full tribal regalia. George Strand mourned so publicly over the loss of these beautiful garments that when the Portland papers announced that a recent Indian grave near Pendleton had been robbed by vandals, Melvin Fell, reading the item over his breakfast on a trip to the city, said aloud to his wife, "I'll bet that's George!"

On the last night of Round-up festivities the Indians sing and dance for themselves. Charlie Wintermute and Melvin Fell, in big felt hats, cowboy boots, and shirts of extra fancy pattern, sit in the moonlight looking on until far into the night, accepting the rating of Indian judges on the best dancers and singers and handing out awards of shirts and blankets from the Pendleton Woolen Mills. For the last dance the two white men are usually honored by some Indian women with whom they move—not too awkwardly at that—in the curiously hypnotic measures of these old Indian dances.

In spite of the constant activity of the Round-up there is always time for a tale or two of the Old Days. People come up and ask if you've met So-and-So yet. "You should, he's a great character—won't be with us long."

Some of the best yarns come from George Strand who still wears his conventional trousers down around his hips like a cowboy and who looks very much like an Indian—until he puts on Indian clothes, so his wife says. "Then he's just funny." Perhaps George's most famous story is the one about Motanic, the Indian wrestler, and Frank Gotch, the world champion whom he took on for a local bout while the latter was barnstorming America with Jim Jeffries.

Motanic was one of those prodigious Indians who make the Paul Bunyan myth seem at least humanly possible. He could pick up a hundred pound sack of wheat in his teeth and toss it lightly onto a handy pile. The story is a simple one of an Indian who didn't understand white men's wrestling rules. He thought that a throw was a win and when he tossed Frank Gotch onto the floor he took his applause smiling, only to find himself the next minute lying on the floor in a hammer lock. The only thing he knew to do in retaliation was to sink his teeth into the most available portion of his opponent's body and hang on until George, his friend, persuaded him to let go. Then George had to stand guard outside the Indian's dressing room with a gun until white tempers cooled down a bit. When he went in he looked sadly at his champion and said in a tone of rebuke, "Motanic, why for you bite him there?" "Why for he twist my arm?" inquired Motanic, still thoroughly confused about the whole business.

George Strand won his place among the Indians long ago by enduring "when just a punk of a kid" a half hour in an Indian sweat bath to prove that he was man enough to take the first Indian census. The Indian sweat bath is built like a round oven, about three feet high, and the heat is beyond reckoning. George was able to bear it only by sticking his nose as far into the ground as he could get it and holding it there. He didn't dare give up before the old Indian who shared it with him, or he would lose face. Nothing ever sounded sweeter in his ears than the grunt with which the old man indicated that he had had enough, and leaped out of the steam and into the river flowing by.

This was about 1910 and the Indians, understandably enough, didn't trust the white man's motives to any great extent. George had made his way into the reservation on horseback and informed the chief of the Walla Wallas that the president wanted a census taken. No-Shirt, the chief, unconvinced of the truth of this statement, rode twenty-five miles to the nearest station, spent a large sum of money wiring President Taft, waited until he got the reply and then rode back. When he returned George Strand took the figures about his possessions—mostly horses—in front of the assembled Indians, hoping thus to get a good start on the census. But word had already gone out through the reservation and the Indians just quietly got out of sight. Whenever George and the posse rode up to a camp the women took to the bushes and hid, and so finally there was nothing to do "but grab a kid and hang on to him till he started squalling; this'd bring a squaw out of the bushes to claim her young, and she only got him if she told where her old man was." It seemed most of the men were having sweat baths, and that's how George was challenged to take one himself and endure the whole ritual, including having his skin scraped with the edge of a knife "just like hog-scraping."

CHAPTER IX

Grande Ronde Country:
An American Family

W hen the Round-up was over we found rest in the town of Union. We stayed with the Millers in their big white neo-Gothic house, set down in a stretch of vivid green lawn, with flowers in star-shaped beds, an old carriage house, tennis courts, and winding cinder paths—a scene so upstate New York in its quality that it seems a mirage when one comes upon it at the end of a long barren drive among sagebrush and juniper.

The Millers on their father's side descend from one of two Swiss brothers who, aged fifteen and seventeen, came to America and eventually into the Grande Ronde Valley in 1861 when the land was still covered with head-high rye and bunchgrass in which "stock could not be seen at all, but had to be tracked around through the vast ocean of grass." On their mother's side they descend from a Scotch-Irish family which left Indiana for Oregon in 1834 with a missionary group.

Mr. Miller is a sheepman, blue-eyed, steady-keeled, puzzled by the whims of the wool market, with South American wool saved while the American product goes begging. He figures there is nothing else to do but to keep on producing good, essential products which ought to have value, and running his ranches as he always has. Mrs. Miller, who in her middle years still has the figure of her dancer daughter, rises at five o'clock every morning; has a silent hour before the family gets up; studies Unity; does setting-up exercises and then, like as not, puts up fifty quarts of fruit or rides out into the hills to look for lost sheep.

Although the boys, Rodney and Odin, went out to school they both came back to help on the ranches. They use the same lazy drawling careless speech of their father's cowboys. Rodney sings cowboy songs: *Git Along Little Dogie, Night Herding Song*, accompanying himself on the guitar. Odin, who breaks his own wild horses, is not ashamed to paint paintings which are entirely and simply "abstract." Also he would like to be an aeronautical engineer. He is married to a delicate little creature from another ranch who "walks on her toe calks" like a young colt and whose name is Fonda. Odin and Fonda in fancy costumes take part in a horseback quadrille performed every year at the County Fair.

There are two Miller daughters, Bethene and Elida. Bethene went out into the world and became a dancer. She lived in England a number of years and toured the world with the Jooss Ballet. She came home in her late twenties because she didn't know what she represented to herself and thought she might rediscover in Union. She is now beginning to write it out, trying to get a childhood in eastern Oregon and a maturity in the capitals of Europe to make an integrated piece. Elida is a costume designer, a horsewoman, and a teacher in a private school in Portland.

The Miller house is big with many rooms. On the walls are some eastern Oregon "primitives"—paintings of the Grande Ronde valley in the old days, done by early settlers with a hankering to get its shifting magic put down on canvas. Mrs. Miller paints too, and some of her pictures adorn the walls. There's a music room with a large portrait of Bethene in chaps and cowboy hat, done by an exiled Russian, Alexander Koiransky, a great critic of the old days who reputedly ghost-wrote Stanislavsky's *My Life in Art*. Bethene studied with him at the Cornish School in Seattle where "Korey," seeking a receptive ear, recited to her long passages from Baudelaire and the Greeks, read from the Ecclesiastes as the summation of all wisdom, and sought to share with her—as with any others who would care—his vast anachronistic learning.

The Miller library ranges from a Home Medical Book through *Lessons in Truth* to John Donne and Isadora's *Life*; from the *History of Union and Wallowa Counties* to the *Bauhaus* catalog of the Museum of Modern Art.

All America is in the Miller house; its ambitions, its gifts; its native independence and its European borrowings; its blending of soaring wish and humble doubt; the hard worker with the hand, the dreamer, the artist, and the mystic sitting down together at the same table; the going out and the coming back, and the growing question; Who am I? What is this America of which I am a part?

All around Union and La Grande the country has a peerless beauty. There are the Blue Mountains and the superb Wallowas, and the lovely gem-like valley of the Grande

Ronde, a valley thirty-five miles by eighteen, charming and fertile, with abrupt hills rising from it, covered with pine and fir, spruce and tamarack. Along Catherine Creek, where the big fish lurk, one sees the delicate thorn trees on which the early Catholic fathers grafted their first fruit.

Many people in the past looked down into *La Grande Vallée*—so named by the French *voyageurs*—and found it beautiful and enticing; Bonneville, Fremont, Narcissa Whitman riding with her husband. This land produces poets and writers. La Grande has a fairly imposing list of literary names for a community of some eight thousand. Not all the poetry is entirely happy in its choice of descriptive terms. In looking at these softly rounded, gentle, and feminine hills, it is quite impossible to keep the comparison of the bosom out of one's mind, and one poet whom we read with intense pleasure yielded to the metaphor without a struggle, producing thereby a rare—and wholly unconscious—Surrealist bit:

> While on thy peaceful bosom, reared by man's toiling
> hand,
> The homes of thrifty farmers and thriving cities stand.
> The iron steeds undaunted, through mountain barriers
> break,

And dashing o'er thy bosom the sleepy farmers wake.

Ella Higginson, one of the Pacific Northwest's best known poets, wrote a sonnet which manages to convey some of the soft, yet strong, intimate yet aloof, quality of this beautiful country:

Ah me! I know how like a golden flower
The Grande Ronde valley lies this August night,
Locked in by dimpled hills where purple light
Lies wavering. There at the sunset hour
Sink downward, like a rainbow tinted shower,
A million colored rays, soft, changeable, bright.
Later the large moon rises, round and white,
And three Blue Mountain pines against it tower,
Lonely and dark. A coyote's mournful cry
Sinks from the canyon—whence the river leaps,
A blade of silver underneath the moon.
Like restful seas the yellow wheat-fields lie,
Dreamless and still. And while the valley sleeps,
O, hear!—the lullabies that low winds croon.

CHAPTER X

En Route: In Sheep Country

From Union to Walla Walla after the Round-up heat through the Blue Mountains, with the surprise of fresh snow melting in patches. The sheep are coming out early. Beside the road are five dead ones, struck by a passing car.

Far off through a notch the sun is shining in a distant valley; the characteristic yellow and purple checkerboard landscape glimpsed through the fir spires.

Everywhere one sees the beautiful keen faces of sheep dogs and the old grizzled vacant faces of the herders. A man who has had sheep for many years near Grand Coulee told me that the new sheepmen are of a higher grade; but certainly the ones on the roads around Grande Ronde looked anything but intelligent. Such a lonely life seems peculiarly suited to only a few types of men. Yet perhaps in these days of stress and tension there is something appealing about mountain solitude and the company of animals rather than humans.

A rancher's daughter told me of an old herder who came into the farm kitchen from the mountains one day when she was alone. He sat down by the fire to warm himself and after a few minutes he began to call his dog, "Round 'em up Jack! Get 'em boy!" He then became the dog and began to bark and cry at the sheep as the dogs do. After he had kept this up for some time, changing from himself to his dog, the girl went upstairs and locked herself in to wait for her father's return.

In the yard of this same ranch I saw under a tree a piece of carving in wood, painted with lamp black, with bottle caps for eyes, and a tin plate hat. This, the girl said, was called the Nigger's Head. A lonely sheepman had carved it, colored it painstakingly and placed it in a tree near his remote mountain camp. The camp was known for many years, until its final abandonment, as Nigger Head Camp. Was this head the alter ego of the solitary herder?

Out of the mountains the snow becomes rain. There has been a very heavy fall of it and the newly plowed slopes near Weston are washed with curious sinuous patterns. Far off on the skyline the rain is falling in a gray veil like smoke. It is lit behind by the setting sun and the whole effect is highly theatrical.

Why do the towns of Milton and Freewater have such really oversize imposing churches? one wonders—realizing in the wondering that these are the questions that take infinite research to determine. But one remembers, seeing them, that we are coming to the country of the big missionary names, Whitman, Spalding, Eells, Walker.

CHAPTER XI

Walla Walla: Missionaries, Vigilantes, and a Rawhide Railroad

The town of Walla Walla maintains a singular air of charm and detachment. It nestles in a circle of hills truly blue in spring, casting sunset shadows which are indisputably purple even to the grimmest of realists. Walla Walla has an almost smug air of self-satisfaction, like a woman who knows how attractive she has made herself by consistent work and unflagging will. The town is dignified enough to rise easily above the cheap jokes of Easterners who want to know what sense there is in repeating the word twice. You're apt to get a somewhat condescending answer from a local resident: It means the meeting of the waters; it's Indian; it's got a lovely lyric roll, and that's that! Walla Walla citizens even managed to rise above the unfortunate popularity—not so long ago—of a very silly song which went roughly like this, "Talk about this town, talk about that town, talk about Walla Walla," and which rhymed the last syllable with "holler" as I remember it.

Walla Walla has the feel of some old upstate New York town. It's not New England—not quite austere or architecturally pure enough for that—but it has that look of solid comfort and composure, that indefinable but so apparent air of living on the past which old places like Auburn or Cazenovia seem to convey.

Inside the houses one finds heirlooms and "antiques": camphorwood chests, melodeons, and glass that came round the Horn, carefully preserved little fanciful landscapes of moss, shells, and fungus made by territorial ladies when they began to acquire their first leisure, or samples of weaving left from older and less leisurely days when women had to grow their own flax and make their own cloth in the gentle Oregon valleys in which the first emigrants settled. For Walla Walla and early Oregon are intimately connected. There are many blood bonds between this eastern Washington town and the first Oregon settlements in the valleys of the Willamette, the Tualatin, and Umpqua.

Here people really know their history; remember and tell the tales of their grandparents. Local "experts" spend hours re-locating forts, houses, and missions, and with maps and old journals in hand, they retrace various emigrant routes over the Blue Mountains. It is whispered that Mr. W. W. Baker is about to challenge Mr. T. C. Elliott on his routing of the Whitman party. A real community interest will be taken in this if it occurs. I met hardly a person who didn't take exception to the facts of an article on a boy pioneer by Honoré Willsie Morrow recently published in the *Reader's* Digest. Walla Walla citizens do not forget that Mrs. Morrow in her book on the Whitmans had Narcissa standing dreamily gazing at Mount Hood from the mission, and that is physically impossible.

The solemnity with which the Whitman legend is treated in Walla Walla can now at least be spoken of with some detachment but there was a day when no ripple ever stirred the worshipful aura that hung around the name of these martyred missionaries from whom the college and the hotel and other local landmarks take their names.

Walla Walla, with one of the oldest and most "literary" of Far Western Colleges, Whitman, and the first of the private girls' schools, St. Paul's, is naturally dominated by educational and cultural interests. Henrietta Baker Kennedy recalls that her grandfather had to learn his Latin every morning before he got his breakfast, but her young daughter is quick to suggest that the reason might be that at the time tuition at Whitman College was ten dollars without Latin and fifteen with.

The town abounds in clubs of every possible kind. In more earnest days a requirement of the Cosmo-Literature Club was the ability to be at home in a foreign language (requirement now relaxed). The Archaeological Society, an unusual institution for a town of this size, was founded in 1906 and still functions in a lively fashion. There are groups studying current events, reading aloud, nodding or shaking their heads over art Classical and Modern, and for some years the dramatizing of Dickens and the presentation of his plays in costume was a popular activity. The town has had for thirty-five years a quite notable small symphony orchestra. In spite of this the Walla Walla musical audience had only whistles and catcalls for a recital of percussion music given by John Cage and his group a season or so ago—thus distinguishing itself as the only city in the Northwest visited on the Cornish group's tour which displayed no interest in modern experimental music.

The town, like many New England communities of a similar type, and like Portland the "western Boston," has developed some outstanding personalities. There are a good many delightful women with a talent for some one of the arts; and men of the type of Mr. Frank Baker, who happily combines personal charm and a sense of civic responsibility; and more eccentric and colorful characters like Mr. Nesmith Ankeny.

Mr. Ankeny would be flavorsome under any circumstances, but set against the dignity and charm of his home full of family treasures the impact of his conversation makes itself particularly felt. Mr. Ankeny is likely to begin by announcing to the stranger that he is not one of the "more awestruck" members of the community. (This, one takes it, refers indirectly to the fusillade of bromides which accompany the sounding of the names Whitman, Spalding, or Eells on all public occasions.)

Mr. Ankeny's angle on the Whitman myth is original and refreshing. He thinks Joe Lewis, the bad Indian, was at the bottom of the whole business, "sent east to Dartmouth and educated, no good could come of that." (I thought that Tom Hill was the Dartmouth-educated Indian but did not interrupt.) Joe, according to Mr. Ankeny, had a crush on the beautiful blonde Narcissa—a lock of whose famous hair now hangs in the Whitman museum, recovered after the massacre—"and an Indian'd go full length for a blonde any day." Joe tried to kidnap her once, according to Mr. Ankeny, and failed, so he stirred up trouble among the Indians but unfortunately the other boys shot her and Joe didn't get her after all. This is the only place I ever heard this story, but it might as well be added to the Whitman apocrypha now as later.

Mr. Ankeny recalls that in his youth the small boys of the community, fed up with the Whitman legend, used to sing among themselves:

> *Old Doc Whitman he come west*
> *To trade in furs and skins,*
> *He got his danged old skull smashed in,*
> *By the bloody Inji-ins.*

Mr. Ankeny resents "makin' capital" out of what was taken for granted on the part of everyone in the days of opening the west. In his opinion no praise is too high for Jesse Applegate, "the sage of Yoncalla," but he would withhold it from some of the better advertised names. Squirming with irritation in his Victorian chair, Mr. Ankeny disposes of an ignorant west coast pioneer "authority": "Why he's so ignorant he don't know but what Christ was shot by the Cavalry. He knows there's a word like that somewhere in the story."

Mr. Ankeny's own family line, maternal and paternal, saw a lot of history made in the early days. He says he guesses "plenty of ghosts" could walk through the old Nesmith place at Rickreall—Phil Sheridan, Ulysses Grant among them. While Grant was visiting, "the W.C.T.U. gave some kind of a blow-out and the general was missing for three days, hidin' out."

Sure there were some rough times in the past, "but you'd be surprised how a good hangin' purifies the air." There were big men too. You can't beat men like Roubidoux and Sublette, Jim Bridger, Kit Carson, Joe Meek. To the question as to whether these big-dimensioned men are being made in America any more he has a ready answer: "Let an emergency come up and the good men'll show again. You're apt to find a second-grade article until Hell begins to pop and then you'll find the real goods. The thing to ask yourself about any man is, how'd he be in a stampede? . . . Never knew an American to win out back-trackin'."

His attitude toward the Indians is a mixture of sentiment and rough humor. There is an undeniable moisture in his eye when he recalls an Indian like Jackson Sundown winning the Pendleton Round-up saddle "when in his fifties and dyin' of t.b." But lest you've noticed this unseemly weakness he quickly goes into some ironic remarks about "Old Chief No-Cuffs, Old-Man-Afraid-of-Soap."

Mr. Ankeny likes his life, the place where he lives, the banking business. He distinctly does not care for big cities. The pleasantest three weeks of his life were spent with a general in the army who passed the time by systematically working out the destruction of the big cities of the world, one after another. Mr. Ankeny twists with pleasure at the memory. He supposes he doesn't like cities because "who was it said, 'Timid birds fly in flocks, eagles fly high and alone'—that's a city! Bunch of timid birds in flocks!"

Walla Walla is a good town in which to wander. You feel that something quite precious and very restoring in a mad world is being preserved here. Life is slow-paced. Not even the students from the college disturb too greatly its gentle rhythm. You find yourself wanting to loiter beside monuments, like the slab of stone on the campus, near the wooded amphitheater, which marks the spot of the Indian council grounds, and gives credit to the Nez Percé Indian, Lawyer, for saving the day for the whites. Walla Walla streets are lined with magnificent trees and bordered with little running streams, along which the townsfolk plant gardens and make outdoor eating places. Everywhere in Walla Walla the lawns are so well kept, so vitally green and fresh-looking, that one understands what was meant by the old resident who wrote a book of local history and—after some chapters on the wild days of the vigilantes, drunken cowboys, treacherous Indians, and Negro lynchings—ruminates mildly that "the greatest contrast between the Walla Walla of the past and that of the present is to be found in the condition of the yards and lawns."

It is hard to believe that Walla Walla was ever dusty, tawdry, or crime-ridden, and yet in the sixties and the seventies times were rough and tough. Cattle thieving and other crimes became so general that the vigilantes organized to perform justice without benefit of jury, and "it suddenly seemed as though nature had granted trees a new and startling fruit, for it became a very common thing to see dead men's bodies dangling from limbs. In one month during the busy season thirty-two men were reported as having been mysteriously hanged." There are still people who remember the Hangman's Tree on Second Street—said to have been used because of a specially well-placed, long and strong horizontal limb, making the task easy for amateurs.

It is perhaps not wholly without significance that the dignified post of bursar in conservative Whitman College has been held for many years by a man who has written millions of words about the old wild days of the "Real West," for the kind of adventure magazines that are printed on low-grade paper. Mr. Marquis's best market is—or was—in England—and there may be something in that fact too.

Even in those rough days the citizens had a certain regard for scholarship. In an account of the ill treatment of Negroes and the final hanging of an innocent named Slim Jim, the following description of deportment in the face of disaster is found: "He looked about and saw blood upon the floor and upon the archway leading into the forepart of the shop.

> 'The noise of battle hurtled in the air,
> Horses did neigh and dying men did groan,
> And ghosts did shriek and squeal about the streets,'

solemnly recited an old man who prided himself upon a knowledge of Shakespeare."

In Walla Walla one always hears the famous yarn about Dr. Baker's Rawhide Railroad and how the coyotes ate the tracks during a hard winter. This story concerns the enterprising building in the early seventies of a private railroad from Walla Walla to Wallula, to connect the inland empire and the navigable waters of the Columbia.

Dr. Dorsey Syng Baker went to the Ladd bank in Portland (that famous first national bank of the Northwest) and asked that their New York correspondent purchase and send out, by way of Cape Horn, two narrow gauge locomotives, one hundred pair of car wheels, and one thousand plug hats. The plug hats were the bribe by which he intended to get the finery-loving Indians to drag the heavy cargo around the falls at Wishram.

When Dr. Baker got the locomotives and the car wheels to their destination, and the Indians had gone off well satisfied with their plug hat rewards, the young railroad builder proceeded to have wooden rails laid down from Walla Walla to Wallula. When these rails proved to be unsound, since they needed constant renewing, he turned to that ever reliable "metal" of the Northwest pioneer, rawhide. Dr. Baker had the wooden rails "plaited" with the rawhide all the way. The summer sun hardened them and made them almost as good as steel, and although in winter the rains tended to soften the material, preventing the operation of the road, this proved to be no very vital handicap since there wasn't any winter traffic anyway.

All would have gone well if there hadn't come a winter so severe as to be known simply in pioneer annals as The Hard Winter. During the coldest days, wolves and coyotes came down and ate the tread off the rails so that guards with guns had to be established to keep the railroad intact.

This story Dr. Baker's son flatly denies:

"The word rawhide . . . came into use for the reason that in a portion of the road built by Dr. Baker, strap iron was used in the very early construction period, instead of the usual steel rail. The word strap was thought of as a strip of leather, and . . . the word rawhide railroad became attached to this remarkable piece of construction, although such material was never used in connection with the road at any time."

Mrs. Kennedy reminded me that the railroad had some fancy dodges such as charging extra for "Fast freight" which was put on the cowcatcher. (It got there first.)

CHAPTER XII

Yakima Valley: Two Towns, Irrigation, and Indians

T he towns of Ellensburg and Yakima lie in the same valley, the beautiful valley of the Yakima River. You enter through any one of a number of scenic passes which all repeat the familiar pattern of these old western trails, now highways, moving from lush deciduous valley, upland through firs, downgrade through pines to arid desert—or in the reverse order.

In summer these two dryland towns lie cupped in brilliant green among the bare hills growing only sagebrush and greasewood. The fertile gardens of the towns speak tellingly of that Far Western miracle, the blooming of the desert when water is brought to the rich volcanic-ash soil. Yakima—in addition to its great diversified farming area—ranks next to Wenatchee in apple crop statistics and thus faces many of the same problems.

Irrigation made these towns, tamed them too for that matter. The famous Sunnyside Canal of Yakima dates back to 1891 and marks the town's first big stride ahead; a stride greatly accelerated by the coming of the United States Bureau of Reclamation in 1905. In the old days, when this was cattle country, life had a true frontier flavor with ready gunplay and long distance traveling for everything from revenge to groceries—including love. There was some cattle rustling and "slick-earing," but since these were offenses comparable only to murder they never gained much local popularity.

The flavor of this part of the past comes through strongly in Jack Splawn's book of reminiscences which he calls after Kamiakin, the last great chief of the Yakima Indians. He has left a picture of the look of the bottom lands in those days before the century's turn when thousands of cattle were driven in from the lower Yakima for summer grange. Even the sage country had plenty of bunchgrass fit for cattle grazing. Splawn says: "There were no flies of any kind to disturb the stock and there was cool clear water, in numerous small streams that wound through the grassy plain. The cattle became so fat that they had to hunt the shade early in the morning. It was a veritable cattle heaven.

"With no market for agricultural products everybody was in the cattle business. The only labor attached consisted in putting up wild hay and fencing the ranches. Commercial crazes and get-rich-quick schemes had not yet reached this wild and beautiful land. The people were honest and happy. They sold their cattle once a year, but the trader knew that he would get his money."

Cattle were rounded up in this valley and driven from here over the Snoqualmie Pass to the coast, or up north into Canada to the mines. Ellensburg was once a stage-coach stop on the run from The Dalles north to the mining country of the Okanogan and the Cariboo. When the railroad finally got to this part of the state in the eighties it helped open up the country, but it also created the usual amount of bad feeling. The railroads established a new town called North Yakima just a short distance from old Yakima City, and this quite arbitrary act considerably angered the old-timers. The more practical souls decided to move since the railroad offered a building lot free to anyone who brought along his house. So Yakima City picked itself up and moved itself on wheels, stores conducting business as usual en route. Eventually the north was dropped from the new name and the old town became Union Gap.

Smoldering resentment engendered at this time may have been in part responsible for the famous raid that Yakima citizens and neighboring farmer folk made on the railroad coal cars in an icy winter early in this century. The railroads insisted that they had no coal to sell. The people saw it passing through the town and decided to take action. They were already thoroughly disgruntled because of high freight rates and poor equipment for transportation, so one cold day some determined citizens went down to the tracks where coal cars were standing. Farmers bravely drove their rigs across the tracks and everyone began to collect fuel in any available container. One man is remembered for removing his overalls and filling the legs with coal, tying up the ends and running home in his long underwear. To appreciate the acuteness of the fuel problem which led to such seeming lawlessness one need only take a look at the treeless hills of the surrounding countryside.

Between the towns of Ellensburg and Yakima there has existed at times a rather jealous spirit. During the state fight over the location of the capital, both Ellensburg and Yakima contended for the honor, although if they had been willing to work together it is likely that one of the towns might have won over Olympia. Anne Shannon Monroe, that literary descendant of the youngest of Lewis and Clark's scouts, spent her childhood in Yakima and in her memoirs recalls something of the antagonism that existed between the two communities. The old French proprietor of a Yakima hotel, looking out at the dust eddying down the street in one of the famous valley blows, would remark with a shake of the head, "By Goddy, but she blow like hell in de Kittitas," which was to say in Ellensburg.

The note of contention occasionally steals out of the printed page in spite of the golden shimmer which memory tends to lend the past. Even the missionaries could not get along together. The prodigious Methodist, Father Wilbur, who could and did lick, single-handed, spiritual backsliders and any "bad actors" who tried to sell liquor to the Indians, is said to have gone to President Grant in 1870 to get him to say that the spiritual welfare of the Indians should be assigned to Methodists rather than to the Catholics.

The town of Ellensburg, which began as a trading post called Robbers Roost, has had its rough edges nicely trimmed for quite a long time now. The Central Washington College of Education brings into the town the kind of activity which attends an educational center; and the citizens are now detached enough from their early history to make pageantry of their not-so-far-distant past. This they do at the time of the September Rodeo which competes in spirit, if not yet in size, with the Pendleton Round-up.

If you have come from the south into Ellensburg for the Rodeo you've beheld the gentle Klickitat Valley guarded by the snowy top of Mt. Adams and you've wound up the Satus Pass to coast down into the valley of the Yakima with its poplars and haystacks, its grazing horses, peaceful cattle, bands of irrigation ditches, and, far off through a bend in the enfolding hills, you've seen the blue fangs of the Cascades. This is proper Rodeo country.

The Satus highway was once an Indian trail going to and from the salmon fishing at Celilo Falls on the Columbia; and it was over this pass in 1861 that Mr. F. M. Thorp came with his family to establish the first white settlers on the lower Moxee. Pioneers in the valleys of the Yakima and Klickitat made it into a wagon road in the seventies; and for a rip-roaring decade all traffic by stage and freighter came and went that way, and thousands of head of cattle, when this was still Cow Country.

Although Ellensburg people do not measure their days and the weeks of their year with reference to their annual show as Pendletonians do, they take it quite seriously. For one thing they take the Indian seriously. This valley remains perhaps the most Indian-conscious section of the state of Washington. You can't talk long on any local topic without finding Indians creeping into the conversation. And this isn't just true of the old-timers either. Clifford Kaynor, the publisher of the Ellensburg *Evening Record*, has three pet topics: the Rodeo, irrigation in general and the Kittitas unit of the Yakima project in particular, and Indians. In this range of interests he might stand as a prototype of civic-minded valley citizens.

Mr. Kaynor knows Indian myths and he has sat with the old men and women who can still tell them. The Rodeo edition of the paper always includes Indian stories and the townsfolk are regularly reminded that this country was a great Indian council and root-gathering place; that there are still faint traces of the old two-mile straightaway race track of the Indians, pounded four feet into the earth in the neighboring desert; that the natural landmarks in this countryside formed the kernel of Indian myths; that the hissing and rolling sounds of the names of streams and canyons are all from the Indian tongue: Quillamine, Shushuskin, Naneum, Taneum, Manastash.

Without the Indians there would be no Rodeo. They give it color and that faint quality of nostalgia which has so powerful an appeal. Out near the Rodeo grounds they set up their tepee village. At night the tepees with their pine poles and flour-sacking sides catch the shadows of the poplar trees on their white surfaces. Lengths of pink smoked salmon hang from the limbs above the cooking pots. There may be zippers on the door flaps but the chant of the bone game is the same ancient chant and the flat beating of the sticks and the steady "ay-ya-ay-ya-ay-ya-ya," the seamed dark faces in the pale light, can still stir the blood strangely and a little fearfully. There is left to these ancient red-skinned people a certain dignity and beauty; particularly in the faces of the old men below their high-crowned dark hats. They walk softly past with a plaid shawl drawn up over the mouth, and something sinister and romantic breathes from them. One often sees white men with weathered faces and Indians speaking together earnestly and simply like old friends. Eavesdropping, one can overhear discussion of the same old problem; the fate of the Indian, the natural man, in the face of the advancing technical world of the whites. Now it is the fishing rights at the falls of Celilo on the Columbia of which they speak, and one old Indian with a seamed and solemn countenance recites with impressive gravity those often travestied phrases promising the Indian his hunting and fishing rights as long as the grass shall grow and the sun shall turn in the sky.

Although the squaws in the afternoon parade of the Rodeo may have ridden past wearing beadwork which would make a purist wince—the Victor trademark, for instance, the fox terrier and the phonograph of the old advertisement—when in the evening the Indians step out of their ancestral tepees on the dimly lit Rodeo grounds and the wagon trains wind down the dusty hill beside the grandstand, there is a heart-stir in the realization of what these people lost when the whites moved in on them.

The Yakimas were a people rich in lore and in time-honored tradition. Not all of this has been lost. A Yakima newspaper man, Dean Guie, and the press of the Yakima *Republic*, have put out a little book called *Tribal Days of the Yakimas* which sets forth some of the more interesting facts about these neglected Indians. There is also the book of myths recorded by Mourning Dove who was a particularly beautiful and intelligent Indian woman. She was born in a canoe on the Kootenai River in the Moon of Leaves which is April, in 1888, while her family was traveling with a miner's pack train. She grew up to recall and eventually to write down the delightful vanishing legends of her people: *Why Mosquitoes Bite People; Why Garteisnake Wears a Green Blanket;* the tricks and prowess of Coyote the culture hero of the Yakimas.

In the beginning of her book Mourning Dove pays tribute to a "blue-eyed Indian," Lucullus Vergil McWhorter, whom the Yakimas adopted many snows ago into their tribe and to whom they gave the name He-mene-Ka-wan or Old Wolf.

Everyone in Yakima and the surrounding countryside knows about Mr. McWhorter and his ardent, quite unsolicited, and entirely unrewarded fight to help the Yakima Indians resist the Jones Bill. The record of this fight has been published in a little book—now a collector's item—entitled *The Crime Against the Yakimas.* The Jones Bill, according to Mr. McWhorter, showed marked evidence of the CLOVEN HOOF (set out boldly in large letters), in offering the Indian twenty irrigated acres from his allotted eighty, if he would part with the remaining sixty.

It was the purest altruism and love of the Indians which led Mr. McWhorter to champion them against the Bureau of Reclamation, and like most people who are inspired by philanthropy no one on either side trusted him. The Indians felt he must be getting something out of it or he wouldn't care so passionately. Mr. McWhorter is now an old man and says he is not bitter—not against the Indians anyway. He can understand why they would be suspicious of him: "brought up not to believe a thing they see in the forest—for a good Indian hunter begins by distrusting his own eye—why should they believe anything in the world of humans?"

Mr. McWhorter, with his flowing white hair and his pierced ears, sits among his Indian books and his collection of drums, buffalo-horn beakers, baskets, pictures of such long-haired pagan cronies as Many Wounds and Yellow Wolf, talking gently of things he has seen and heard; about Chief

Moses who was really a "good Joe"; about the famous trip he made to establish the site and the circumstances of the killing of the Indian agent Bolon which had helped precipitate the local wars with the Indians. The visitor has to promise not to use any of the best yarns, however. Mr. McWhorter plans to publish them himself. He is really grateful that politics lost him his insignificant post in Yakima because this has freed him to write all day long. The Caxton Press in Idaho recently brought out his book on Yellow Wolf, and he is deep in plans for the next one. Yellow Wolf was the cousin of the famous chief, Young Joseph, and in his book Mr. McWhorter presents the red man's view of this great campaign of the Nez Percés.

I asked Mr. McWhorter how he came to be so interested in the Indians and he turned toward me quickly and said almost beseechingly, "You tell me!" He was born in West Virginia where there were no Indians left, but at the age of fifteen he got his sister to pierce his ears and he grew his hair long, to the not inconsiderable embarrassment of his older brothers who cut it off one day when the family expected some visiting circuit riders. He has dug in his family history for Indian remains but all he ever found was a maternal great- or great-great-grandfather who was supposedly captured by Indians and carried far away to the Northwest; returning home many years later and leaving a legend of aboriginal qualities he had acquired during his years among them, such as the ability to move silently through the forest without rustling a leaf or bending a twig. Mr. McWhorter might have "harked back" to this remote ancestor but he doesn't quite see how. I suggested casually that he might have been an Indian once. His eyes sharpened and brightened. "Reincarnation? I've thought of that. I often dream about country I never saw, dream it in detail. Moses Splawn believed he'd lived before. He told me once that one of the things he remembered best was a great battle in which he took part called the Battle of the Oaks. Doesn't know when or where, but remembered it all vividly."

This kind of talk led to the question as to whether he had ever seen any evidence of special occult powers among the Indians. Mr. McWhorter says he never did, although he was once invited out to look at an Indian who could swallow boiling water and handle hot coals without injury, but he took ill on the trail and never got there. He doesn't doubt Indian prowess of this sort. The other local authority on the Indians, Dean Guie, says that the Yakimas and the related tribes still believe in dreams, witchcraft, and omens; that women still go forth in their ceremonial basket-hats to gather roots for medicine and love charms; that the Indians find no reason to doubt that one medicine man may covet and steal another's "spirit power"; and if the theft is consummated, "the rival bereft of his guardian power may die."

One cannot lump these Indians. There were, and are, good and bad ones, materialists and mystics, killers and peacemakers. Locally there were some bad black crimes to be checked up against them; the kind of crimes of which the "old blanket men" were heartily ashamed. As late as 1908 and 1910 the Yakimas threatened an uprising because they felt they were losing valuable water rights and a great part of their land. The chief who recommended taking to the war path died, however, and plans for the uprising were abandoned.

On the Yakima Indian Reservation, about forty miles from Yakima, the traveler finds the well-preserved remains of one of the most historical and most delightful spots in this part of the country. This is Fort Simcoe erected in the middle fifties during the Indian uprisings. The white-painted office buildings, with their fine construction and well-built fireplaces, and one of the four hewn-log blockhouses guarding the sallyports, still stand in an oak grove in the midst of rolling hills. The place was once an Indian council ground, perhaps because of the presence of a cool spring called by the Indians Mool-Mool, meaning Bubbling Water.

Near Yakima also stands the old Ahtanum Mission founded by the Oblate fathers in 1852. It was burned down once during the Indian wars when Major Rains encamped on the spot and his soldiers, digging potatoes, unearthed gunpowder. The priests had been accused of taking the Indians' side in the controversy and this seemed final proof. Before officers could intervene the enraged men had set fire to the buildings. Later, in the sixties, the Jesuits rebuilt it. It was at this mission that lands were first irrigated by whites in the Yakima Valley.

Camping in our trailer outside Ellensburg on the river, we talk with two little boys coming to pasture three goats. They live in a tar paper shack down the road. They are "transients." Their father is looking for work. School begins tomorrow but they can't go for at least a week, because they are all going to pick hops. We pass the father on the road, a thin man with anxious face, stooped too early. He is looking for the future in the fertile valleys of the Pacific Northwest.

The next morning we turn toward the high mountains, taking the Chinook Pass along one side of Mt. Rainier, leading us back to green Fish Country. We wind away from the bare brown hills, along the cool streams into the country of towering rocks and giant trees; up and up until the American River is lost in the chasms below us, and we are up above the treetops, in among the clouds which, at the summit, break on the rocky pinnacles and scatter down the green sides. There is one place where we stop and look back from the foggy cool world in which we are standing and see the hot sun shining on the barren yellow hills of eastern Washington.

Down again into the sun of the Pacific slope, thinner and less bright. The road winds along the Ohanepecosh and then through deserted meadows and among the sagging barns of a country which once proudly erected a large roadside sign advertising itself: "Big Bottom Country." It still stands, in need of paint. What happened here? Why is the land deserted? The fields are still green; the streams still flow; the mountains still guard the pass, now traffic-thronged. What of that man with his children and goats and his tired stoop and his tar paper shack only four hours away over the Cascades?

CHAPTER XIII

Apple Valleys

I remember being told years ago that the Kaiser of Germany wouldn't eat any apples except Wenatchee Valley apples, and as I wound easily down spectacular Blewett Pass (where women drivers used to give up at the hairpin turns and have hysterics behind their wheels) I wondered idly if—until the invasion of Holland—the Kaiser had, perhaps, still gone on eating apples from this sweet green valley among the yellow hills.

And was it, I wondered, going into second gear behind the great truck loaded with boxes of apples on the tree-lined main street of Cashmere, an Indian potentate who loved *Aplets* so much? The word greeted me on a big sign, "APLETS, THE SWEETEST THING TO GIVE." Have they, then, abandoned "THE CONFECTION OF THE FAIRIES" as a good advertising slogan—with the box cover of Titania sitting up all golden-blonde in bed, receiving the gift—immemorially associated with every childhood Christmas?

My companion thought it must have been in all likelihood the Sultan of Turkey who had loved so much this delicate confection of walnuts, apple juice, and gelatine; and certainly it is a proper Near Eastern delicacy, we decided—buying a box at the corner drugstore—although without the cloying sweet heaviness of Turkish paste.

These are questions I thought—about aplets and potentates, and kaisers and apples—to put to Major Clifford Chase who, as secretary of the Washington Apple Association, must concern himself over markets and menus, slogans and publicity, to keep the Washington apple business—and for that matter all the other American apple business—as healthy as the people who eat one a day.

When I got to Wenatchee Major Chase wasn't available, but there were a great many other people willing, anxious even, to talk about the state of the apple industry in their valley.

One of the best places to see this rich little valley—once a sagebrush waste—is from the hill not far behind the ranch of Marvin Chase, the Major's father. You go up past orchards and sad old barns, through sage tangle and sandy soil, until you stand under the odd rock formation called The Squaw's Saddle—fittingly named, built high front and back the way the old saddles still to be seen in Round-up parades were built.

In spring the whole stretch of land seems fairly to float in misty white and delicate pink. Spring is the season of hope in the Wenatchee Valley, even in these bad times of the San Jose scale and the codlin moth, government regulations, European war, depressions, orange juice for breakfast instead of apple sauce, and all the other factors which are ruining the Wenatchee rancher's once prosperous business. Autumn, at the opposite swing of the year, is the time of reckoning and, of late, autumn, though of a high colored and opulent beauty with its laden trees, has brought little lift to the hearts of the folk in the valley.

Marvin Chase remembers when there wasn't a blade of green in all the sere landscape. His memories go back to the end of the nineteenth century when he and a man named Clarke put through the first irrigation project in this waste land; and he has seen the quite incredible wave of prosperity rise and rise in this valley and then fall with sickening reverberations.

The facts of this dramatic rise and fall are relatively simple, even if the reasons behind it are complex and intangible. This small valley some seven miles square, or a little over thirty thousand acres, produced at one time the highest gross income per acre of any like size piece of land in all the world.

Here in this valley five percent of the country's apple trees still produce twenty-five percent of the country's apples. The Wenatchee Valley apples are the Delicious, Rome Beauty, Winesap, Yellow Newton, and Jonathan. The Wenatchee Valley taught Europe to eat red apples, and the credit for the kind of apples grown here goes in part to Mr. J. J. Hill who interested himself in the dramatic reclamation of this "useless" land, and had his European agents determine what type of apple could be most advantageously sold abroad.

In the great days of the apple crop an acre of apples was easily worth a thousand dollars at harvesttime. Now all over the valley trees are being uprooted or cut down because the profits are no longer to be had.

One of the chief factors in this tragic decline of the apple industry is the codlin moth. We stood beside an acre of trees which had been sprayed at a cost of one hundred dollars to an already bankrupt man, and cut open apple after apple to look at the little white worm at the heart of the fruit which would grow until big enough to cunningly bite the stem in half, drop the apple to the ground and then crawl out and into the bark of the tree to go on reproducing its own kind. Sprays of lead and nicotine have not stopped the spread of this deadly pest. The government experiment station, said Mr. Chase, has over one hundred and five experiments on the codlin moth alone. "Twenty years ago," he added, with characteristic dry wry humor, "I would have said to you that I knew a lot about apples—that we all did. Now I say we don't know anything. . . . It's with us here just the way it was with the farmer I talked to once on the Nisqually flats. 'Yes,' the farmer said, 'I can just about make a living but it's impossible to make any money.'"

It costs money to raise apples. It takes the land and the water rights first, and then the trees, and their cultivation, and lately there has been added the heavy burden of spraying. Some thirty gallons of spray to a tree are used each time, and every tree gets from six to ten treatments. Some estimates say that it runs into fifteen hundred dollars an acre in these times to harvest an apple crop. With good luck there are about twenty packed boxes of apples to a tree. It costs in the neighborhood of a dollar to grow, pick, wash, and pack each box of apples. Then the costs of refrigeration, hauling, and selling must be added, which push it up some fifty to sixty cents more, so that it is necessary to sell apples at $1.65 a box just not to go broke—and a lot of apples don't sell for that amount.

Many of the farm packing plants which made the autumn life of this section so rich in color are gone now and a great share of the work is done in the plants in the valley towns. Here trained workers (many of them local housewives who plan to augment their incomes each autumn at apple time), do the amazingly deft, quick-eyed, and quick-handed work of sorting and packing the apples. The migratory workers—for whom the government has now built a new modern camp in Wenatchee—are, for the most part, only pickers of the fruit; the least important of all the many tasks that are involved in harvesting apples. In the packing plants the apples are bathed in special rinses to remove the sprays; then run through driers, under the eyes of trained sorters; and finally moved along runways where their weight automatically drops them into compartments filled with like-size fruit. From here they go to the packers who with lightning speed mound them into boxes, each wrapped in a special paper and marked Extra Fancy, Fancy, and Choice.

With things the way they are in Wenatchee there are bound to be a lot of people who shake their heads over such a tremendous outlay of money for new farmlands as represented in the neighboring project at Grand Coulee. Mr. Chase, who suffers as much as the next one when he sees the millions of bushels of culls that go to waste in this valley yearly, wonders if we'd better not do a little concentrated work on better distribution of foodstuffs before we get any more farmland reclaimed from sagebrush. What is more, he thinks—and his opinion carries weight, for he made the first Columbia Basin Survey where the Grand Coulee project lies—that in the end, in spite of all the dams and all the plans for lifting the water of the Columbia River some 350 feet, the Columbia Basin acreage will be finally irrigated by gravity from the Pend Oreille watershed—to the north of the Coulee drylands.

On this opinion I didn't get a chance to question Rufus Woods, the hearty editor of the Wenatchee *Daily World*, the only prophet who ever lived long enough to be respected for his prophecies in his own home town. Mr. Woods, genial and expansive, was too full of beaming memories of how people used to refer to his "wild scheme" for irrigating the Grand Coulee in such phrases as "Baron Munchausen, thou were a piker!" Meaning, piker compared to Rufus Woods. Mr. Woods's position today in the whole matter of the Grand Coulee Dam and the irrigation of the Columbia Basin is a little delicate and certainly ironical. He is an ardent black Republican and he lived to see the Democrats make an honest man of him, so to speak. Be that as it may he is certainly Wenatchee's Great Man now, and has been ever since *Life* published his picture tilted back against a porch in Ephrata, Washington. With Billy Clapp and a third crony, Gale Matthews, he is accepted by many as responsible for the first agitation about this gigantic reclamation scheme. However, as with all miracles, a large body of apocrypha has grown up around the attendant circumstances, and there are an increasing number of claimants for the title of Father of the Grand Coulee Project. An engineer named James O'Sullivan has some pretty imposing evidence to offer about his right to the honors, if honors are being distributed in this large fashion; and around Spokane you'll hear that the Ephrata boys are all just upstarts and that E. F. Blaine is the indubitable father of the project.

Without entering into the controversy it is a matter of record that in July 1918 Mr. Rufus Woods gave headlines in his paper to the Coulee idea as follows:

FORMULATE BRAND NEW IDEAS FOR IRRIGATION

GRANT, ADAMS, FRANKLIN COUNTIES

COVERING MILLION ACRES OR MORE

Such headlines and Mr. Woods's consistent plugging for the idea led sober citizens to shake their heads until years later Colonel Goethals and government engineers lifted the onus of insanity from him by finding the idea a feasible one. (Some heads still shake, one should state in all fairness.)

When his newspaper carried the above headline, however, Mr. Woods generously gave William Clapp full credit: "Last and Newest and Most Ambitious Idea Contemplates Turning of Columbia River Back into Its Old Bed in Grand Coulee, the Development of a Power Plant Equal to Niagara and the Construction of the Greatest Irrigation Project in the World—First Conceived by William Clapp of Ephrata, Wash."

I had been told that Mr. Woods was a great authority on the Civil War, a collector of Lincolniana, and a firm believer in the innocence of John Wilkes Booth. I didn't have time to discuss it with him, but I'd hate to take bets on Booth's guilt. If Mr. Woods could live to see the dream of the Grand Coulee become a reality he'll probably live to see the name of Booth cleared for posterity.

CHAPTER XIV

Beautiful Deep Water

The only way to get to the head of Lake Chelan if you don't use a horse is to go in by boat from the foot of the lake. Chelan, which means Beautiful Deep Water, was carved by glaciers from an earthquake fissure, and glaciers still overhang its rocky sides. At the upper end the region is virtually untouched, a "primitive" area of snowcaps and rushing mountain streams—though now a through road from the Skagit project to the lake's headwaters threatens, and sentiment is divided as to its value.

The fifty-four-mile boat trip affords material that is not wholly scenic. The dwellers along the lake's rocky shore who come down for supplies or mail reveal in face and dress every type of recluse. When I went in, in the autumn of 1940, we carried not only hunters and their supplies but many boxes and barrels for the booming mines at Lucerne. We even carried a red-haired beauty operator with an electric dryer and a permanent-wave machine whose friends saw her off in Chelan with hearty cries of "Hope you make your fortune." When we arrived at Lucerne she drew on her dark green suede gloves and stood hatless, poised but nervous, as the boat pulled up to the dock and the people crowded down to look over the passengers. We disembarked a blind man with terrible scars who had drilled into live dynamite in the mine wall some time back. Why he was returning no one knew or could say. At one place a jolly man who had found space enough on the sheer drop of the lake's shore to have a charming garden and a grape arbor brought magazines to the boat crew. "I put *Friday* on top," he said, with a marked German accent. "Read it. It's the only magazine that dares to tell the truth." All the boat crew nodded their acceptance of this verdict. Later I saw them reading it—whenever the passengers let it drop. The lead article was Theodore Dreiser's defense of Harry Bridges.

If you have the right company on the boat trip you can hear some good yarning. You'll hear about Harry Hunt who came out to stay six months and stayed for thirty-five years. It's the climate. Nothing like it. Unique! In summer the warm air rising from the plain of the Columbia sets the air in motion in the Chelan Valley, and this air blows from snowfields and glaciers. Result, ten to fifteen degrees more coolness than in the valley of the Columbia. In the winter the lake as it cools forms a high cloud wall hundreds of feet above its surface which deflects the cold wind, while the canyon's walls slowly yield their stored-up summer heat. Result, the lake is ten to fifteen degrees warmer in winter than the adjacent valleys.

Well, whatever it is, climate, view, or remoteness, those who once fall under the spell of Lake Chelan seem not easily to shake it off. There are plenty of romantic refugees along the lakeshore, including American businessmen fleeing from—or with—notorious love affairs. There was a German nobleman who married a commoner and who had to go back to Germany when Hitler came to power because he could no longer get any money out of the country. Perhaps the best yarn of all concerns a man named Maxwell who built a famous house on the upper lake, wainscoted with marble, the woodwork throughout of "solid mahogany." He also built a boat entirely of teakwood taken from the attic of an old sea captain in Bangor, Maine. Maxwell was enamored of a lady who had been his secretary and they set up housekeeping in the wilderness. This lady remains famous for an encounter with a captain of one of the lake boats, when she dared to criticize the kind of service he was giving. She invited the captain to come ashore and meet her like a man. He did so, and the beating he received caused him to sell his boat and leave the country for good.

CHAPTER XV

Grand Coulee Dam: Man's Biggest Job to Date

Honest catch phrases to capture the public's attention are hard to make under any circumstances. When faced with the task of describing the gigantic dam at Grand Coulee the problem becomes almost insuperable, for Hollywood has succeeded in reducing such gargantuan words as colossal, tremendous, amazing, awe-inspiring, to pygmy stature through overuse. In dealing with Grand Coulee then one is inclined to begin with the most terse and unembroidered terminology: Quite simply, this is the biggest man-made thing on earth, and likely to remain so for a thousand years.

Why some phrasemaker thought of calling it the Eighth Wonder of the World is hard to imagine. It hardly makes sense to put up the Grand Coulee against such forgotten awe-inspirers as the Mausoleum at Halicarnassus, Babylonian hanging gardens, or the lighthouse at Alexandria. With the pyramids, however, there would seem to be some common ground for comparison. This is not in size alone—the dam is three times bigger than the largest Egyptian pyramid—but in the perception of Grand Coulee as an almost mystical symbol of power, the carrier of a message that few can read. This is, at any rate, what it seemed to me when I visited it; once in 1938 when it was in the early stages of construction, and again in 1940 when the great wall of concrete had been flung across the opening in the naked hills through which the Columbia moves its mighty weight of water.

Curiously enough one gets at first no sense of the vastness of this great piece of construction. Partly this is because the tourist approaching from the southwest winds in a car on a hard-surface highway down the long-dry bed of a prehistoric river, and his eye has been stretched to the top of the rocky cliffs and towering red palisades which mark the course of this ancient torrent. Furthermore, in all likelihood, he has been over to Dry Falls Park and gazed into the immense empty basin of what was, in the Pleistocene era, the most mighty waterfall ever to drop its volume over a cliff. The river in whose path the falls lay came from the melting ice of retreating glaciers of the Ice Age, and the great series of waterfalls were more than four hundred feet high and three miles wide. People who have seen Niagara can get some idea of the dimension of this torrent when they learn that these falls were two and a half times as high and five times as wide, and the volume of water pouring over them was as much as one hundred times that of the present Niagara.

Approaching from the southeast the visitor first sees the dam from a point several miles away, and the form seems insignificant. Even on nearer view the setting in a canyon a mile wide and sixteen hundred feet deep dwarfs the actual structure. If the first visit also falls on a day when there are few men working so that there is no chance to see humans reduced to ant size in relation to the great wall and the gigantic machinery, it is hard to grasp the almost astronomical computations which bulletins and government lecturers must use in speaking of the dam's size.

There are views, however, from which the vast construction does come slowly—or suddenly—into meaning. One of these is from behind the dam on the left, where one looks at the long thread of passageway, like a fly walk in comparison to the flat stretch of concrete above and below, and one is informed that four standard-gauge railroads run on that seemingly slender thread, carrying materials to the dam face.

This span of concrete holding back the waters of the Columbia is of a magnitude almost too great to grasp when thought of in terms of man's constructive ingenuity. Pygmy waves of the river fretting at the base are actually thirty feet high. One lets the eye travel up. In relationship to these apparently puny waves the dam's measurements begin to assume their relative significance: height above bedrock, 550 feet; length of dam at crest, 4,300 feet; and on that crest there will be, in time, a 30-foot highway for motor vehicles.

A good deal of brain-cudgeling has gone into the assembling of statistics for this dam so that the average citizen can get some grasp of the size of this job the government is doing with his taxes. Here are a few of the most startling of these facts:

"The finished dam will occupy more space than the entire population of the United States—men, women, and children—and will weigh more than twice as much." (There are more than 130,000,000 people in America!)

The concrete which has gone into this dam, the power plant and appurtenances, could build a monument as high as the Washington Monument and covering six average city blocks. Or to put it another way: the same quantity of concrete could build two twenty-foot highways from coast to coast.

The artificial lake to be formed behind this dam will be 151 miles long and will contain 10,000,000 acre-feet of water, or enough to give every human being in America 25,000 gallons.

"When fully equipped, the power plant at the Grand Coulee Dam will be, by far, the largest in existence. It will consist of two separate but similar power houses, one on each side of the river. Each will contain, when completed, nine generators of 108,000 kilowatt capacity. The initial installation, which will be only *three* generating units, as compared to the final total of *eighteen*, would light New York City and Chicago, or furnish the entire electricity requirements for an industrial city the size of Pittsburgh."

One bright autumn day I drove up the rutty and now disused road to the great mountain of waste left from the gravel taken out of the nearby hills. This mountain of superfluous sand is some nine million yards in volume. What, I speculated, would be the opinion of the origin of this mountain thousands of years hence, when the truth is lost and geologists begin to do their mole-like research? It was only in the fifteenth century that the Shogun Yoshimasa left in his Kyoto garden a cone and a platform of white sand, yet already there is no agreement as to whether he had the sand brought from the Korean shore to make a moon-viewing platform and a cone for the moon to strike on, or whether the sand was to serve some more utilitarian purpose like sprinkling garden paths afresh for imperial visitors. How the experts will disagree among themselves on this artificial mountain near the great concrete dam! And how they will puzzle over the more than twenty-two-million-cubic yards of overburden removed from the riverbed and piled up in adjacent canyons!

I was permitted to enter the dam itself. This is an honor and—when it comes to women—a real distinction. One awed engineer assured me that I shared the experience only with six prostitutes from Coulee City who got by the guards one night disguised in tin hats and dungarees; betraying their presence later by such uncontrollable expressions of awe—drawn from them by the sheer dimension—as "Jesus Christ Almighty! Would you look at that!" As for me, I was reduced to almost complete silence as I walked the length of the great structure, down the long echoing tunnels, up the flights of stairs. (There are some eight miles of galleries in the dam, primarily for inspection purposes.) With a little shiver of foolish apprehension one realizes that the powerful Columbia is, in some places, only four feet away, pressing with all its force against the concrete wall.

Major Hutton, who is director of information, walked beside me, telling me illuminating facts about size and weight and number, dimension and dollars, years and volumes, and although I heard him I knew I wouldn't remember any of it and would have to check later, for the whole thing was becoming a gigantic symbol to me. The major's voice was like a precise factual chorus, a sort of monotone of materialism holding me to the world of statistics and uses, but what I was actually feeling was a sense of almost frightening exhilaration. This was a structure made by man. Pitting himself against one of the world's mightiest rivers and one of the country's most barren wastes, man set himself the task of chaining the torrent and bringing the useless earth to rich yield. If by flukes of circumstance, the shifts of politics, and the greed and chicanery of those in power, no use is ever made of this vast structure, it will still mean something for him with the wit to read the message.

For here is man acting as a constructive rather than a destructive creature, controlling nature instead of yielding to her whims and deprivations. Here is man seizing from time itself its compulsive power so that with invisible electric forces at his command he turns night to day and makes it possible for five thousand men in six years to do a job far greater than the construction of the Pyramid which took—if Herodotus is to be believed—one hundred thousand men and twenty years. Here is man moving mountains about at the rate of seventy tons a minute; placing concrete sometimes at twenty-seven tons in sixty seconds; shifting a great river on its bed to expose its rocky base for construction purposes, and then calmly rolling the river back where it belongs. Here is man truly invincible if he could but see it. Nothing stopped him here! When the walls caved in he devised a freezing system to hold them in place. When the exigencies of construction required a new form, he invented it, and perhaps the most challenging aspect of the building of Grand Coulee Dam is the story of the new mechanical devices which were brought into being. Who can read the almost frightening symbol of remote control by which this vast undertaking was directed; a symbol set forth in a quiet room far from the noise of machinery; a room with electric buttons and dials, tubes and lights and an animated diagram by means of which the progress of the dam might be seen almost as an abstraction and from which impersonal "brain" went forth the orders to the men far away in the bright sun sweating at their tasks.

Major Hutton was good enough to show the colored movies he has been making of the work on the dam, and looking at them I thought again of the importance of the marvelous mechanical forms which were used here; forms developed strictly, often beautifully, and always directly, out of *function*; showing the ingenuity and creative power of man at its highest bent. At a time when billions and billions of dollars are being spent in a mad world for more effective mass murder and the destruction of cities, surely one may well accept with a certain amount of equanimity the expenditure of millions of dollars to indicate the forces for positive expression which lie within the human being. These are the tools of man, one realized, thrilling deeply at the awesome size and the technical perfection of the cranes, or the cofferdams which moved the river from east to west and back again. These great precise and beautiful forms stood up even in contrast to the serenity and majesty of those mountains which the major had included in his movie to indicate the source of the water which the dam will use to irrigate adjacent drylands.

There are, of course, a good many different ways of regarding the Grand Coulee Dam. The dam itself is, after all, only one of the most tangible parts of a mighty whole, known as the Columbia Basin Reclamation Project. Those last four words are the true test—to many people—of the waste or the value of this gigantic undertaking.

And what are those ends which this great venture is to serve? A government booklet states in simple words just what the Grand Coulee project hopes to accomplish:

"A dream of 50 years, the irrigating of a vast tract of rich desert and dry-farming land in central Washington, is about to be realized through the construction of the Grand Coulee Dam, and a system of canals that, in time, will cover an area 60 miles wide, east and west, and 85 miles long, north and south, and bring to it the life-giving waters of the Columbia River.

"When fully developed, the Columbia Basin Reclamation Project will reclaim over 1,200,000 acres of land, regulate the flow of the Columbia River for the benefit of downstream power plants and irrigation, and develop electric energy to be used in pumping for irrigation and for other purposes, on the project and elsewhere."

That's the simple statement of purpose. Now let us see what people think about the eventual happy conclusion of these estimable purposes.

The average citizen may find it hard to grasp the gigantic figures of tonnage, mileage, acreage, kilowatt hours with which the government bulletins fairly bristle. But he has some grasp of the significance to him of the following statistics:

Dam and Power Plant	$181,101,000
Interest	15,000,000
Irrigation Project	208,532,200
TOTAL	**404,633,200**

This is the cost.

As to repayment: After the expenditure of $260,000,000 future development will be financed out of income from the project. The entire cost of the dam and power plant and much of the irrigation is to be recovered with interest, so the government plans, from the sale of power; after which the government will enjoy a good income from a project which will have cost it nothing. This, it is pointed out, is quite a different thing from such other types of government projects as river and harbor improvements, and navy and army programs, in which the beneficiaries do not in the end repay the government.

In general people realize that this project put jobless men to work. They know that the money spent for wages and the purchase of equipment was pretty well distributed over forty-eight states. The citizen who reads knows about the government's plan for control of speculation in the land that will be irrigated; that the acreage will be bought at dryland prices, only forty acres to an individual, eighty to a man and wife. In the end they still have questions to ask, however, and these questions are everybody's questions and it seems likely that no one has the answers ready to hand: Where are men from the exhausted land in the Middle West—the men who need this fertile soil—going to get the money to start a farm out here, even with all the help the government offers them on borrowing? What are we going to do with more farm produce in a country where—unless a war economy temporarily changes it—the farmer cannot dispose of his goods at a living wage anyway? Is this marvelous new boon of hydroelectricity merely going to mean that the last great stretch of beautiful unspoiled country—the Pacific Northwest—will become industrialized, its streams polluted, its quiet mountains humming with transmission lines? Are westerners going to live to see the grime and filth of a Pittsburgh here in the Last Green Playground?

Well, these questions have so far no adequate answers. Yet there is this to think about, in Major Hutton's words:

"The National Resources Committee proposes to take out of cultivation 75,345,000 acres of submarginal and other lands, on which economical farming has proved to be impossible. Nearly half a million farms would be involved.

Droughts and wind erosions have, within recent years, driven 100,000 farm families from their homes on the semiarid lands of the Great Plains.

"Recent reliable statistics of population indicate that there will be in the continental United States 131 million people in 1940, 138 million in 1950, and 141 million in 1960. If an adequate diet is to be available at reasonable cost, the harvested-crop of the country must be increased by about 40,000,000 acres in the next 25 years.

"With a growing population and a shrinking stock of arable land, reclamation by irrigation becomes increasingly important as a national problem."

That much is indisputably true! If Americans in the Pacific Northwest can keep this in mind they may be able to work out the difficult problems of the prevention of the evils of industrialization in this still unruined countryside; and a better distribution of goods and supplies east and west.

Meanwhile, for years, the building of this dam has been the "biggest show on earth" playing to hundreds of thousands of visitors, with as many as eight thousand in a day coming to observe the developments in what has been called "a kibitzer's paradise."

SECTION III

Cities as Symbols

CHAPTER I

Seattle

....

Seattle is a hybrid. You cannot make it into a single piece no matter how you try. It does not seem to have that homogeneity and that centralized core which even the visitor feels in Portland, Oregon. Of the two cities Seattle is certainly more dramatic and even more grandly beautiful with its extravagant display of ranges of snowcaps, the winding waterways of its inland sea, and its scattering of lakes. From any one of Seattle's many hills one can see views so stupendous and breathtaking that the sprawling city sinks into insignificance. Nothing can ever take away from Seattle the dramatic splendor of its natural setting, and it is perhaps the challenge of this setting which makes one wish for Seattle a destiny somehow comparable in greatness to the landscape in which it lies.

Although Portland has had its quota of rowdy and glamorous days, the memory of them does not seem to stick as it has stuck to Seattle. From the beginning Portland maintained threads of connection with the world of the eastern seaboard. Even the naming of the two towns is not without significance. Portland was named as the result of a coin-tossing between two New Englanders, one from Portland, Maine, and one from Boston, and the gentleman from Maine won. Seattle was named for the chief Sealth (which ineptness at Indian gutturals soon altered to Seattle), and this kindly old man, who accepted the whites in a spirit of philosophical resignation, had to be persuaded that his body would not turn in its grave every time his name was uttered before he would give consent to the town's naming.

When in 1909 Seattle held its Alaska-Yukon-Pacific Exposition it announced to the world awareness of the elements which should, by geographic placement, determine its development and give it its quality: Alaskans, Indians, Canadians, Eskimos, and Russians, the Pacific Islanders, and the Chinese and Japanese. These were Seattle's neighbors and her business associates. They might also have been her teachers as well as her pupils. Seattle, near the century's turn, gave promise of becoming a really unusual American city. She gave promise also, of course, of a glittering success commercially—and although the booster drive has run down a little and Seattle moves now at a more dignified pace, she is still as rich in economic resources. What Seattle has lost with the years is something more intangible, and among her losses must surely be counted a failure to affect a cultural rapprochement with other lands and peoples on the shores of the Pacific.

If in Portland you were to ask for the names of the people to whom you should talk if you wanted to get some idea of Portland's core, there would be an almost one hundred percent unanimity on names. In Seattle it would depend entirely on where you asked as to what reply you got. One concludes that there is no fixed nucleus of true Seattleites. When one begins to ask about the old days and the old-timers only one name occurs to everyone: "Of course there was Rolland Denny. He died not long ago. He was the baby, you know, who was weaned on clam juice." From the clam juice the memories range back through the familiar anecdotes of the landing in the autumn rain in the wilderness on Alki Point, the disconsolate women—"The foundation of Seattle," said Washington's historian Edmond Meany, "was laid in a mother's tears"; the indomitable spirit with which the pioneers named their first settlement "New York-Alki" or New York By-and-By; the hard days when the founding fathers drove teams, carried great logs to the waterways, met at the cookhouse for social functions, fought the big fire, fought the railroads—all the same stories of simple heroism and hardship which distinguished Pacific Northwest community life in the early days of pioneering.

In accounts of Seattle's history, however, one comes upon evidences of an intangible but apparently powerful animating force which the newspapers still revive annually around Potlatch time, and which is known simply as The Seattle Spirit. People really believe in the presence of this spirit and when you start digging back into history to determine at what moments it manifested itself most significantly, you come on such incidents as the following:

In 1874 when Seattle had lost its chance of becoming the Northern Pacific Railroad's tidewater terminus, Seattle citizens decided not to let Tacoma, the railroad's choice, leave them behind in the race for Puget Sound supremacy, just another "sawmill town." With admirable directness and vitality the citizens from all walks of life set to work to build their own rail-road, bound for Snoqualmie Pass and a connection between Seattle and Walla Walla. Although the women did not work directly on the job, as the Russian women did in the Moscow subway in this century, they did go along to hearten the men with basket lunches and encouraging words. The May Day Picnic which inaugurated this civic enterprise makes a pleasant and heartening picture of community endeavor when recalled down the years.

Another instance of the appearance of this famous Spirit was during the big panic of the nineties when Seattle had no bank failures because the businessmen all stood together, all banks cooperated, even the newspapers played their part by underemphasizing the panic's proportions. Again, when the Johnstown flood preceded by just a short time the disastrous wiping out of Seattle in the great fire, the citizens refused to accept the suggestion that their fund for Johnstown aid be kept at home instead. Seattle wanted to show the world that it could rebuild itself and help another stricken community at the same time.

This legendary spirit also manifested itself at the beginning of the Klondike Gold Rush when—with every city on the Pacific coast competing for the big business of outfitting the Alaskan gold diggers—Seattle became the trade center. This she did, not so much by virtue of advantages of setting (there were other towns even nearer to Alaska which could have done as well, given the opportunity) but by inaugurating and maintaining a barrage of publicity about herself which magnetically drew all travelers. This was undoubtedly Seattle's most colorful period. The town thronged with every type of human being from seasoned rogues to such timid innocents as clerks from some distant Eastern store with the accumulated hoardings of a group of their fellows, charged with the responsibility of bringing home a fortune for all the subscribers to their Klondike jaunt. There were beautiful women and bad men and plenty of fools, among the latter a number of Englishmen bound for the Northern icefields outfitted with such useful equipment as valets, lawn tennis sets, portable bathtubs, Irish setters, and cases of pipes. There was no more idleness in Seattle. Practically anything could be sold to the men waiting for passage on the overcrowded boats; and they bought condensed food, ice climbing equipment, Skeeter-Skatter mosquito lotion, dog teams, and warm blankets. The Pacific Northwest in general, and Seattle in particular, enjoyed a boom that lasted until the next business depression.

Still another example of the Seattle spirit—a spirit sometimes forthright to the point of brashness—might be found in the exchange of letters and telegrams from the city to Andrew Carnegie when Seattle was ready for help on a library, the 30,000 volumes of the first one having burned in the fire. Seattle assured Mr. Carnegie that the city would give $50,000 annually to maintain the library if he would give the building. Mr. Carnegie wired back that he was not at all clear as to why a town of 80,000 inhabitants needed to tax itself that sum when Atlanta, with much greater population, had assumed no such burden. Seattle flatly put both Mr. Carnegie and Atlanta in their respective places by wiring in reply, "Increase in population from 1890 to 1900, Atlanta 37 percent; Seattle 88 percent. Seattle's population all white and all readers." And when the building was nearly built and they needed $20,000 more, Seattle sent a Reverend Mr. Llywd to Scotland to importune Mr. Carnegie as he paced—in some irritation—the railroad platform near his Scottish retreat. The Reverend Mr. Llywd got the $20,000.

The human embodiment of this spirit was found in Asa Shinn Mercer. Asa Mercer was undaunted by the niggling opinions of more timid folk, unparalyzed by hair-splittings over matters of good taste in publicity; a man to recognize a need and complete any job he took up—no matter how difficult. Mercer, as first president of the territorial university, induced young men to take an education in return for cutting cordwood on the university grounds. He went east in the sixties to persuade decent young women from New England to come out and supply the bachelors of the Northwest with good wives. When he went back for a second cargo of Civil War widows the assassination of Lincoln left him without powerful support and the New York newspapers launched vicious attacks on him, but he was apparently neither broken nor unduly embittered by the experience. He had only been facing a fundamental problem with simple direct action, and if the world found it bizarre and in bad taste Mr. Mercer could not greatly care.

Today the knowing visitor comes to the town famous for its spirit and he comes seeking a romantic mingling of the East and the West, the Indian and the Yankee, the Chinaman, the Norwegian, the Russian and the Jap, the Sandwich Islands and the Yukon, and like as not—if he has Seattle friends who take him around—he will go away disappointed. For he will not take kindly to local pride in the quick assimilation of Neon-culture and old world grandeurs. There are plenty of American cities like this!

Sometimes if the visitor is articulate, or famous enough to be asked his opinion, he speaks out about his disappointment, and Seattle is peculiarly sensitive to such criticisms. Muriel Draper told Seattle that she had come three thousand miles to see some authentic bit of Americanism and she saw only a synthetic culture, a syndicated ghost of New York. Tabu for her! Lewis Mumford, requested to say what he thought of the way the town was laid out, implied that it was too bad it couldn't be torn down and a fresh start made. Seattle citizens, recalling how the topography of Seattle had been altered with almost god-like will—hills leveled, the dirt used to fill the tidelands, grades changed from 35 to 3 percent—found this criticism galling. When Mumford left for Hawaii a local paper bitterly commented that the critic had sailed for Honolulu "which up to this time has been known as the pearl of the Pacific." When Harold Laski came to deliver lectures at the University of Washington in 1938 there was no dinner table topic for months except the monstrousness of paying for the opinions of a left wing liberal with money from the fund of a deceased capitalist. . . . Sometimes this insistence that all visitors give only praise, leads one to wonder if Seattle is not rather like a human being who has failed to fulfill his potential destiny—abnormally afraid of any intimations of the truth.

Prosperous Seattle citizens pride themselves on the astonishment with which the Easterner visiting their "outpost" views the charming club rooms at the Sunset or the Rainier; the amazement with which he sees a flunky with a striped vest and brass buttons lurking behind an ivy-grown brick façade; the surprise that awaits him in dining at the Olympic Hotel where superior French food is served by stereotyped waiters of approved obsequiousness; his polite awe at restricted residential sections with gatekeepers to ask the destination of the visitor before admitting him to fastnesses of beautiful timber, magnificent views, pools, tennis courts, and a famous golf course, as in the Highlands, or to somewhat less private fastnesses, but with almost equally imposing façades, as in Broadmoor.

There is real pride in the University of Washington with its ten thousand students attending classes in expensive and cautious stone copies of the period known as Gothic (singularly incongruous on the slopes of the blue Pacific). Near the campus is the Shell House where the famous racing shells of Washington cedar are made by the Pocock family, who have the kind of monopoly of which one can approve. These are the shells which have carried victorious Washington crews across the finish line at Poughkeepsie so many times, and the years of work that a few Seattle men put in to get western crews accepted among the eastern elect leads one to question deeply the meaning of American democracy. It is perhaps the rarer Seattle citizen who would point with pride to the name of Vernon L. Parrington on a campus building—and apologize at the same time for the truly formidable ugliness of this building named in the great man's honor. The visitor is not apt to be spared a reminder to take a ride on the streamlined ferry, the *Kalakala*. This lovely Indian word means Flying White Bird and many people do not understand why a few other people tear their hair at the idea of a "streamlined ferry" moving at roughly seventeen knots on the Sound between Seattle and Bremerton, with no quality which could be thought of as "flying," since the streamlining was built over the vibrating shell of an old and battered boat. Guides with a sense of flavor will take the visitor up to Harvard Avenue to view the cold stone pile which Samuel Hill built, in the face of one of the most magnificent local views, to entertain the Crown Prince of the Belgians who never came. Now the mansion is the home of a Russian gentleman married to the daughter of Seattle pioneers, and here the Grand Duchess Marie—while in Seattle selling her clothes to a local store— was entertained at a dinner of old world regality. The same guides who tell the visitor these stories may well indulge in a little dramatic contrast and take him down to the Skidroad where sailors are on the prowl, floosies with freshly bleached hair wait at the entrance to shooting galleries, and jobless men with broken shoes and empty eyes look for cigarette butts along the curbs near the totem pole.

Finally, among Seattle sights and matters for impersonal pride (though not for general financial support) is the museum in Volunteer Park, given to the city by Dr. Richard Fuller and his mother, commanding an incomparable outlook over lakes, seas, and snowcaps, guarded by huge stone figures from the Ming Tombs, and marred only by unsuitable doors of metal crochet. The museum contains an exceptional collection of Oriental art and makes an admirable attempt to bring itself into vital connection with Seattle community life.

There are in Seattle little back eddies where scraps of the old influences may still be found: Japanese restaurants where excellent *sukiyaki* and good green tea are served in a peaceful room; or Chinese ones where something more exotic than chop suey can be had if you know how to order. There are even remnants of a once picturesque postwar Russian colony, in little restaurants decorated like a Petrouchka set, where dark bread and *shashlik Caucasian* can be had; and there are a few Scandinavian places—though not as many as one might expect in a city where the Scandinavian element is so large that one is told it accounts for Seattle's famous "cold" audiences. Cold they may be, says a prosperous and civic-minded citizen who gives a great deal of time to the Symphony and the Chamber of Commerce, but Seattle is nevertheless the greatest "sucker town" in America, and takes more "series" of concerts by dancers and singers than any other place.

There are two Seattle restaurants worth mentioning for preserving an authentic flavor which is neither tea room nor merchant's lunch. Blanc's manages to retain a pleasantly non-Rotarian atmosphere of twilight and gilt, assignations and dark red plush. And there is Manca's "since 1871" where the food is designed for men who could still eat with gusto and passion, and the menu's chronological list of this restaurant's movements is a story of the rush toward Big Stakes in a Hurry: St. Louis, Denver, Las Vegas, Pueblo, Salt Lake City, Seattle. Seattle ends the list. There's no place to go from here, you realize, idly reading Manca's menu while waiting for your eggs scrambled with clams, or your cold boiled King Salmon, Manca style.

But of all Seattle sights and institutions there is none to compare with the great public market down on the waterfront where all the lavish yield of the sea and nearby rich agricultural valleys is displayed. Here are all sorts of special little shops where you can get Chinese rice, begonias, old copies of *Scientific American*, phonograph records from Siam, or Mt. Rainier painted on velvet. Here also, among Seattle matrons with their neat paper shopping bags, float aimless tide-borne fragments of humanity, men from flophouses and dumps, thin men in bizarre garments, standing always as Mark Tobey— one of the few painters who uses this material—once said, "as though up against absolute emptiness—a big blue open space, a vacuum."

Waterfront stores deal in sourdough outfits, loggers' clothes with the rain-resisting red plaid mackinaws, sky-blue denims, pea green or bright yellow seamen's slickers, Indian sweaters of oily gray and white wool. At the end of any of the piers—Pier 7, for instance, where Annie Grimison, who is *not* Tugboat Annie, runs the Skagit River Navigation Company—all the life faces toward the sea and one can feel the magnetic pull of ocean winds and salty tides. At sunset an old spell falls over the sky and water and one can forget the Neons spluttering behind one up Seattle hills. Once there were only these waterways leading out to the world. Indians paddled here and buried their dead in canoes along the winding shores. Little yellow men from across the Pacific first set foot in the New World here. Many a strange cargo has sailed in or out of this harbor, guarded by snowcaps and towering banks of firs. Many strange cargos and strange craft still sail. "But it's not the same," the old boys mutter. "Nothing's the same any more." "But there is still the sea," you say, refusing to think of scrap iron shipped from here to Japan in spite of protesting picket lines. . . . Yes, there is still the sea. It laps the barnacled piers, oily and salty, and warm with the color of the sunset blazing behind the Olympic Mountains as they define the western sky in serene and snowy beauty.

There is still joy to be had in the sight of the old four-masters at rest in Lake Union—one of the largest freshwater ports in the world. And on a misty night at the Ballard Locks—with the long clean stretches of concrete and the lamps burning dimly in the fog—one can often capture a good sense of repose and purpose. Here again one feels man's power to affect his environment constructively. By devices which work with such seemingly child-like ease, great ships are lifted from Puget Sound into Lake Washington. Of a summer Sunday one can sit for hours at twilight and watch the pleasure craft, with sun-browned quiet crews, slip through here to the home harbor. And at the locks—which are second in size only to those at Panama—one may go into the old clipper St. Paul, now a museum, and walk about among Indian kayaks, or the binnacle from Byrd's Antarctic ship.

With delight the stranger comes on the row of totems on the ferry dock at the back of the Old Curiosity Shop—their blues, reds, browns, and whites, faded with years of sun and rain, setting forth forgotten genealogical facts about Indian tribes long since vanished. Wandering into the shop itself—in summer full of tourists buying spurious Indian handiwork—the knowing can still find treasures: the rattle of a Kwakiutl medicine man, Haida masks, good basketry from Neah Bay. Indian pieces of quality are usually bought by outsiders and make their way into collections a long distance from Seattle. It is strange how little of the culture of the Indian, his ever more rare old artifacts one finds in private homes in the Pacific Northwest. Perhaps Indian basket collecting was a "fashion" at just the wrong time or with the wrong people. Whatever the reason, it is rare to come on any masks, or carved bone or wooden figures in the proper Norman-English, Modified Monterey, or Colonial houses of the Seattle people who can afford to "collect."

There is a line in Seattle's most popular guidebook which reflects the general attitude toward the Indian in the lay mind. The writer is speaking of the fine examples of Northwest Indian arts inadequately housed and notably unvisited in the Washington State Museum at the University. She says: "The Alaskan exhibits are most engrossing and show the manual dexterity of the Esquimaux to be all that has been claimed for it." With this illuminating remark the subject is catalogued for all time!

The great IS IT ART? row rocked Seattle to its cultural and social foundations in the early autumn of 1940. At the annual Northwest show given in the Seattle museum the judges awarded the prizes to paintings which were indubitably "abstract." You would have thought from the resultant explosion that this was the year of the great armory show in New York when people abused poor Mr. Stieglitz, only later to accept him as a prophet. The Readers' Columns of the Seattle newspapers bristled with every cliché to which pen could be laid: "Little Harry, my seven-year-old, could do it better"—"It's not beautiful," and so on. The only encouraging sign was that people did read about the controversy, and if they read "Longshoreman" Jamieson's virulent attack, they also read "Logger" James Stevens's excellent reply. Stevens, who is the author of the collection of yarns on Paul Bunyan, pointed out that the day of the horse and buggy had passed, so also had that of photographic art. He denied that this was "Nazism" in art and pointed out that this was the kind of painting Hitler had destroyed as dangerously symptomatic of a new age.

At least this particular exhibition of reaction got well-aired in the Seattle press, and this in itself may be a healthy sign. There was, on the other hand, hardly a newspaper ripple when a school of international reputation in the field of music, dance, drama, and the kindred arts folded up after twenty-five years in Seattle and passed from the local scene, taking with it its founder, Nellie Centennial Cornish, probably Seattle's best known citizen outside the boundaries of Seattle itself. When Seattle lost the Cornish School (it still exists but in name only—the old functions are no longer there) it did not know what it lost, because it never knew what it had. In the summers for many years Greek drama was given with an authority and a completeness possible only in an institution which trains in bodily movement and speech. Students who wanted to know how Martha Graham, or Mary Wigman, Adolf Bolm, or Jacques Dalcroze taught dancing could come to the Cornish

School and learn from the source itself, or teachers fresh from the source. Drama was conducted by a man with one of the great names out of the pre-war Russian world, Alexander Koiransky, and by Maurice and Ellen van Volkenburg Browne, two of the founders of the Little Theatre movement in America. . . . Here was a school which dared to say that the gifted student in the arts must have a specialized kind of education. Yet with the passing of the older generation—people nearer the standard of the "pioneer"—this school ceased to have community support.

In Seattle it is seemingly the showy thing which will always succeed. To be proud of the fact that Greek drama is given every summer in one's community one must be in a position to know just how unusual such a phenomenon is in American life. On the contrary, the presence of a showboat on Lake Union is something that lends itself easily to pride and even to a curious kind of snobbery.

The Symphony does exceptionally well in Seattle. Recently Seattle made headlines by engaging Sir Thomas Beecham for its conductor, and Sir Thomas ingratiated himself to sensitive Seattleites by replying to newspaper reporters, who questioned his accepting a second-string symphony, that "he liked the climate." Does Seattle's support of the Symphony indicate that it is a particularly musical town? No, seems to be the opinion, it is only that Seattle has the music habit. The uphill fight to put music over as a civic activity is won and will probably never be lost again. It may, on the other hand, be a ten-year fight to put across the idea of the importance to the city of a free and culturally independent museum which dares to show any art the museum staff considers worthy—even, if need be, full nudes, which are now discouraged out of fear of church and Parent-Teacher-Association pressures. And in time, surely, prizes awarded by a competitive jury in sincere good faith can hardly be questioned by people whose success at contract bridge or real estate does not necessarily entitle them to be judges of painting.

One interesting comment on Seattle life is the space given in newspapers to what is called "society." The power which presumably lies in newspaper publicity of a certain sort is so marked that the Olympic Hotel had to establish Monday luncheons for Seattle women of social prominence to insure its success as a rendezvous, and the papers gave space to the names of those meeting to eat the unquestionably superb food. It is not at all rare to meet people who visited in Seattle at the height of this Monday-lunch-at-the-Olympic hysteria, and who were considerably irritated by being asked to go down and eat in the grill on this sacred day, since the dining room was given over to the local gentry.

A typical Seattle headline on the society page reads as follows: "Spiritual Solemnity and Glamour Blended in Church Ceremony." This is an actual headline!

A smart woman journalist, whose tongue must surely be permanently pressed against her handsome cheek, reputedly gave a Seattle newspaper a big circulation boost with her chatty discourses—pages of them—of the following general tenor: Pretty little Mrs. Jones whose figure is still perfect by Hollywood standards in spite of her four children, Jock, Tansy, Pansy and Pock, poured tea. She was wearing one of the new pompadour hats with a bold red rose right at the front of it. Mrs. Jones and her husband Willis B. (W. B. to all his friends) recently made a trip to New York. While there they visited Pete and Pat Norris in Scarsdale. Pat Norris says New York women aren't anywhere near as well dressed as Seattle ones—And so on and on ad nauseam. But no, it can hardly be ad nauseam, for although one everywhere meets women who deplore this inability to separate museum openings, previews at the Showboat, and first nights at the Symphony from columns about what was worn by whom and how, the general public must like it or it wouldn't sell. It all leads to a great deal of minor hysteria attendant on names omitted, gowns overlooked, and so on. One hears that the museum has received letters—pitiable rather than laughable—from women who indicate that they are willing to come and look at a Modigliani if they must, but they do want to know how, at the same time, they can get their new Eleanor-blue mentioned in the society page. This kind of chatty snobbishness gets tied up with any worthy cause, from Milk Funds to Watercolors, and although Seattle is not the only American city of which this can be said, it is certainly one of the more flagrant offenders. . . . Within recent months the *Post-Intelligencer* has made a praiseworthy attempt to give music, books, and painting, visiting artists and local ones, something approximating objective criticism.

It is easy to criticize Seattle because one's heart is a little sore at the promise this city had—and has—and the picture it makes today. And one can criticize Seattle full-heartedly because it is not yet crystallized, has still a chance, and thus can take it!

Seattle is enjoying a substantial boom, due in some measure to the threat of war, new activities for expansion and defense at Fort Lewis, the Bremerton Naval Base, and in Alaska. Shipyards are reopening, airplane factories like the Boeing plant are running full time. Yet for all the bustle there are still jobless men on the Skidroad, and Seattle's shantytown along the railroad tracks is second to none in America for picturesque despair.

Since the problem of seasonal labor, with the resultant restless human tides, has always faced the Pacific Northwest, it was to be expected that a genuine revolutionary spirit would have its inception in Seattle. This spirit flowered in the early days of the I.W.W., the old *Union Record*, and the far-famed Seattle general strike. Some of the most dynamic American liberals are still to be found here, quite unfairly pigeonholed as "Reds" by the more placid citizens.

Much has been said and written about the local problems of Labor gangsterism and political corruption. Far less attention has been paid to a native cultural growth, pushing its slow way toward expression among a scattered group of musicians, painters, writers, dancers, living on the city's fringes—anonymous and often poor, yet filled with the creative juices that flow into them from the magnificent countryside, still so rich in beauty and vitality. With some community understanding and support Seattle could make a truly indigenous and original contribution to American culture. The question as to whether it will or not is still an open one. Surely no city worthy of the adjective "great" can go on endlessly priding itself on a purely materialistic achievement.

CHAPTER II

Portland

Neither Portland nor Seattle bustles. There is in both towns a marked ease of gait and manner which makes one think of the answer the coast Indians gave in the old days when questioned as to their pursuits, "Cultus nannitsh, cultus mitlight"—roughly translated—"Just look around and take it easy." If, however, Seattle moves at a slow pace it moves at least while awake, but placid and charming Portland seems sometimes to be moving in a gentle dream. One might say that Seattle is a sea-coast Chicago, though not so robust or meat-fed, and Portland is a western Boston, which, as a matter of fact, it is often called.

Portland does not mind being considered a transplanted bit of New England; it even finds a certain pride in it. Portlanders may bristle just a little at being called an overgrown country town, but they undoubtedly felt a rather indulgent pride in their famous $60,000 cow pasture in the heart of the city where—near an embroidered Victorian mansion—Mrs. H. W. Corbett kept her pampered cow for many years. An annual New England dinner was a local social event, and the Unitarian Church has flourished here in the best New England tradition, with a second generation of dignified and scholarly Eliots at its head.

Older Portland people create a very definite picture of cultivation, repose, gentility, and just a hint of stagnation. But in times like these one does not mind the backwaters so much. They even provide something a little reassuring and soothing. Walking away from an hour or so with a charming white-haired descendant of the great John McLoughlin, chief factor of the Hudson's Bay Company on the Columbia River over a hundred years ago, one is apt to wonder about the big hurry that seems to animate human beings today. This gracious old lady, living among her treasures of glass and silver, her Chinese cabinets and Hudson's Bay china, admits serenely to being a "true Pyramidian," by which she says she means that she is immovable; having, in all her life, never crossed the Rocky Mountains, nor done much jaunting up and down the coast either. Yet she is content. And a not-so-old man speaking proudly of Portland's fine libraries, museum, Starlight Symphonies, famous newspapers, Sunday morning breakfasts at the Arlington Club and other Portland amenities, puts his fingertips precisely together and concludes with the old story of the man who was asked how he could live contentedly "so far away" and replied, "Away from what?"

The phrases "round the Horn" and "across the Plains" still count for something in Portland. One informant, however, whose two sets of grandparents made the two separate trips was anxious to assure me that the distinction which has been made by some of the round-the-Horn contingent, that the gentry came by ship and hoi polloi by oxen, is definitely not true. It seems a curious thing to boast of ancestors coming by the comparative comfort of a sailing vessel when among sagas of gallantry and endurance of oxen pioneers one can hear a story like the following:

A Portland grandmother set out as a young woman with her husband on the four months' trip to the Pacific Northwest. Although pregnant when she started she believed that she would reach the coast before her baby was born. But the group with whom they traveled got lost, and endured the incredible hardships of the famous Applegate Cut-off. The woman gave birth to a seven-months child and her life was despaired of. As she lay in the wagon bed she overheard the men speaking of their plight. Their food was almost gone, people were dying of hunger, and they stood now on the brink of a canyon over which they felt they dared not move with the sick woman.

She called her husband and said to him that they must go on at once, and when he told her that she could never survive the trip she replied calmly, "Why should all die because one must?" And that is a story of a Portland grandmother. For of course she did not die and the seven-months baby born on the Applegate Cut-off lived to be ninety.

The early settlers of Portland, shrewd hard-bitten New Englanders many of them, had to work indefatigably to make Portland the dominant Oregon town, for although Portland has been called "the city that gravity built" and the point stressed that the inland trade can most easily get to the coast down the ocean-seeking Columbia, towns of small significance today along the banks were not long ago her rivals. The story of how Portland businessmen outsmarted other communities like Milwaukie, St. Helens, or Oregon City need not be told here, but there were hours of worry and many a clever manipulation to fulfill the dream of Captain John H. Couch, who, out scouting for the Cushings of Newburyport in 1840, brought his ship upriver and fastened it to a tree at the foot of what is now Washington Street. "To this point," said Captain Couch, "I can bring any ship that can get into the mouth of the great Columbia River." But that Columbia River bar! One can only marvel that early settlers kept on believing in the possibility of the growth of a port town some 110 miles upriver from one of the most treacherous and dangerous bars in the world.

Already the drive, the bustle, and the fierce competitions by which so many charming Portland homes were established and Portland people given their quality seem dim and remote and even a little unreal—as they are also dim and remote and unreal in many New England towns and among many proud New England families. And perhaps it is because of this formalized and faintly smug backdrop that Portland has produced so many Promethean spirits in the years of its history. These personalities have been rebels in the realms of ideas—which has made them different from the racier types of characters which have lent flavor to other towns. Perhaps only Portland—or New England—could produce a C. E. S. Wood, a John Reed, an Abigail Scott Duniway. Just as only such places as Newburyport, Westboro, and Groton, Massachusetts; Holland, Vermont; and Calais, Maine, could have produced the ancestors of those early Portlanders: Couch, Lovejoy, Corbett, Ladd, Pettygrove.

Some Portlanders may try to tell the inquiring visitor that such colorful personalities as John Reed or C. E. S. Wood are not "typical," but it would be rather like saying that Socrates was not typical of life in Athens in the fifth century B.C. To be sure, in a sense Socrates was not a typical Athenian, but it was Athens which produced him and nurtured him to full stature, just as it was Portland which helped form the careers of such "outlaws" as Reed and Wood.

John Reed's life gave sincere pain to many honest Portlanders who were friends of his parents and grandparents, and who remember his grandmother Mrs. Green because of her parties and her gowns and particularly for her carriage, when only she and Mrs. Ladd had carriages in Portland. Jack Reed went to school "in the East" like most of the sons of best Portland families, and after Harvard became a brilliant, if erratic, revolutionary who was awarded after his untimely death the distinction of burial in the Kremlin. Portland papers could not agree on the facts of his demise and attributed it to various causes from poison to overindulgence in caviar. When Granville Hicks wrote his book on Reed he was helped in data-gathering by the descendants of some of the most honorable Portland names, and this heresy one or two descendants of equally proud name cannot quite forgive. They still speak softly of the betrayal in charming firelit rooms over the best of imported tea.

As to Charles Erskine Scott Wood, whose fame has gone far beyond the confines of the town where he lived for so many years, to this day in Portland he is represented as the Anti-Christ or as a many-dimensioned almost Goethe-like figure, depending on where you hear him discussed. (As a matter of fact, Portland would not be a bad double for cultivated, respectable, gossipy Weimar, in the days when Goethe was a chancellor and a poet and the local Don Juan.) Colonel Wood, a graduate of West Point, was a highly successful corporation lawyer and the first man of reputation to defend the I.W.W. He was a personal friend of the great Indian, Young Joseph, chief of the Nez Percés. Wood sent one of his sons to live among the Indians to learn wisdom. He "Englished" many Indian myths, wrote poetry and prose and won fame with his Heavenly Discourse. He followed all the contemporary movements in painting, made a collection for his home and helped his friends collect, did some painting himself, brought Childe Hassam out for the summer to do the murals in the old Wood house. Today, still very much alive though an old man and living away from the town which he rocked so often to its conventional base, he—like Goethe who finished Faust in his eighties—writes every day and has recently completed a long epic poem, *Circe*.

Because of her inability to accept the unjust lot of the women who were asked to endure so much in a pioneer society for so little in return, Abigail Scott Duniway set out single-handed to give women some rights as citizens. This indomitable Far Western female deserves to rank with Julia Ward Howe and Susan B. Anthony who were her friends. She began to take a firm stand as far back as the time of the Donation Act of 1850 by which 640 acres were allotted to every man and wife if married before December 1, 1851. Mrs. Duniway refused to accept her allotment of three hundred and twenty acres on the occasion of her marriage, lest she be considered just another "Donation Claim bride." Many of those brides had pretty obviously been chosen just for the government acreage with which they could provide their husband in return for his name. One reads of "brides" of the period in the backwoods "still playing with dolls," and of marriages of grown men with ten- and eleven-year-old girls, whom, in some cases, they left at home for a year or two and in some cases did not. Mrs. Duniway founded her own newspaper for women readers, *The New Northwest*, raised a family of six children, and though suffering much from ill health, traveled constantly by steamer and stagecoach up and down and across this uncomfortable dusty and muddy country preaching her gospel in the face of pulpit disapproval and social ostracism. Finally as a handsome strong-faced old woman in a white lace cap and a billowing fichu, she lived to register as the first woman voter in Portland.

Among many prominent men who did not agree with the stand she had taken was Mrs. Duniway's own brother, the studious Harvey Scott, who left a post as city librarian to become the most famous editor of that famous newspaper, the *Oregonian*. Mr. Scott, like his sister, had a forceful command of English. It was Abigail, however, not Harvey, who kept the diary on the trip across the plains, during which their mother and a little brother were buried beside the road. As editor of the *Oregonian*, Harvey Scott fought for free trade and sound money and held out for the gold standard in the "free-silver" days of the nineties. Under his editorial leadership the *Oregonian* did not find it unfitting to deal with religion as a matter worthy of earnest consideration; not just Christianity, but other religions; religion as *Religion*. Mr. Scott found the "Bible a masterpiece of our prose, as Shakespeare's work is of our poetry"—and there are Portland young people unkind enough to say that this still enduring double influence on the *Oregonian*'s style may account for those editorial "forsooths" and "gadzooks" and other stylistic anachronisms which appear from time to time to excite them to unseemly mirth. Harvey Scott was unquestionably a fitting editor of Oregon's greatest newspaper, the only one which has been published without interruption from pioneer days—having been established in December 1850.

Recently, to make money—or perhaps just to make more money—the *Oregonian* changed many of its ways. It livened up the front page, went in for pictures, decided to get along without the criticisms of books and music for which it was formerly distinguished, and in general lowered its traditional intellectual tone. The present publisher, Palmer Hoyt, one of the youngest and certainly one of the most amiable newspaper men in America, when attacked on this apparent lowering of standards, replies that—make of it what you will—when these sections of the *Oregonian* were omitted he waited for loud protests and none came. So apparently, he concludes, Portland people did not care very vitally. Yet Portland has always been a bookish town, and although the Oregonian has abandoned literary criticism, the *Oregon Daily Journal*, the vigorous "opposition" paper founded in 1902 by C. S. Jackson, does offer a weekly page of reviews of current literature. The old firm of J. K. Gill has served the Pacific Northwest with its books for years, and the city has a regional press, the *Metropolitan*, which with the Caxton Press in Idaho divides the Pacific Northwest's mounting flood of early regional classics and new novels and nonfiction, mostly of local interest.

It is still possible to be startled in Portland by coming unexpectedly upon a private collection of Cézannes, Picassos, Derains, owned by a lady of New England lineaments who will remove a fine Brancusi from a stand and place it firmly on the carpet "for better light." And one can, if fortunate, be barked at by Mr. "Tam" McArthur for an informative hour; his bright eyes under their enormous bushy brows, alert for verbal fumbles as he asks your opinion on etymological matters and tells you emphatically that there are three expressions which drive him to towering and empurpled rage. One is coastal. Why coastal? Coastal highway! Bah! Coast is enough! Another is recreational. What's wrong with simple recreation? Also route. Why route? Highway is a good solid and expressive English word. Mr. McArthur wants far less Gallicism in the English tongue and more of the good old Anglo-Saxon words. Above all in the names of Purity, Good Sense, and the Pioneer don't use the term Old Oregon Trail. There was one trail and of course it's old, but why stress that? It is the Oregon Trail. Just that! Mr. McArthur also deplores such terms as The Riviera of the Northwest, the Switzerland of America and so on. The latter phrase is sometimes applied in travel folders to the Wallowa Mountains of northeastern Oregon. The only point in common with the Alps, says Mr. McArthur, is that both are of granite. You've seen the Alps, haven't you? Yes! Well then, did you ever in the Alps see anybody on a pack trip, fishing for rainbow trout while somebody on the shore fried flapjacks over a campfire?

Mr. McArthur's *Oregon Geographic Names* is everybody's source book, and though he hastens to tell you that it has some mistakes in it he also admits to glowing with pride when Mencken mentioned him several times in *The American Language*. Mr. McArthur is a cousin of the Ankenys who lend Walla Walla such a special flavor, and I could see a similarity between Mr. Nesmith Ankeny and Mr. McArthur in their dynamism and forthrightness.

Mr. C. C. Chapman, the editor of the *Oregon Voter*, is another citizen who seems to belong to Portland. The *Oregon Voter* is just what it claims to be, an "economic, financial, taxation and public affairs review of Oregon and the Pacific Northwest." This weekly pamphlet has a paid circulation of 2,000; it never deviates a hair's breadth from the editor's tested opinions on the honesty and integrity or the unfitness of candidates for office; it is a dignified and not a muckraking sheet; it accepts no advertisements for cigarettes, liquors, or any curative drugs or food preparations; it heads its first column with such quotations as one from George Washington: "If, to please the people, we offer what we ourselves disapprove, how can we afterwards defend our work? Let us raise a standard to which the wise and the just can repair. The event is in the hand of God." Perhaps only a community like Portland, a state whose citizens have always been politically active and fundamentally argumentative, could make this periodical self-supporting.

Portland prides itself on its cultivation, and yet sometimes the outsider is apt to wonder if some change is not occurring which Portland residents do not yet realize. He sees the Portland Symphony not functioning after some thirty years as a vital part of community life, and he raises questions. Presumably need of money lay at the root of the Symphony's discontinuance, but in Seattle the Symphony is flourishing, and though Portland may say that Seattle is richer, Seattle will reply that Portland moneybags are always full and always will be because the Portland people do not take chances, and the whole town has been owned by the same names from the beginning, and probably always will be.

Portland may let her Symphony die (some argue that the summer "Starlight Symphonies" are an adequate substitute) but she will hasten to remind you that the support of her local library and museum has never wavered. The Portland library has played an exceptional role in civic life since it opened as a subscription library in 1864. It has a fine record for freedom from bigotry and has never in any way been involved in political freebootery, thanks to a self-perpetuating board which has maintained from the beginning the highest standards of library administration. In 1939 the library association gave a play to celebrate its seventy-fifth anniversary, and much was made of such details as the village mud holes through which members splashed on their way to the first board meeting. Honor was then paid to names not so well known in Portland annals as the names of rich merchants: Leland H. Wakefield, the Vermonter who made a house-to-house canvass in the fifties to raise funds for a reading room; Henry A. Oxer, the scholarly Englishman who acted as librarian, walking about in carpet slippers, smoking a leisurely pipe after lunch, and keeping track of books by a wholly ingenious system of his own. For a number of years the librarian also kept meteorological observations, for which he was paid fifteen dollars a month by the city. This may have been due to pressure from powerful Judge Deady, who remarked with some asperity in 1870: "If we were at the pains to keep and publish an authentic weather report our wholesome, temperate and agreeable climate could not be successfully caricatured and depreciated abroad, as is now too often the case."

The local art museum has played an ever increasingly vital part in community life since the day in 1892 when the Portland Art Association was organized and a museum opened on the second floor of the old City Library. By 1905 it was ready for a building of its own. It was built—the first public art museum in the Northwest—and art instruction to the public was begun at the same time. The highest praise has been given to this museum by Walter Pach and C. J. Bulliet, and there has never been here the interference from laymen which has affected the Seattle museum. Since 1932 the museum has been housed in a charming modern building.

Many Portland houses afford a pleasant contrast to the hackneyed eclecticism characteristic of so much Northwestern building. Part of the charm, simplicity, and freedom of design of these houses is due to their perilous perch on hillsides to afford their owners a view of majestic Hood, or the snowcaps of Mt. Adams and St. Helens, and the green valley through which the Willamette River wanders. Portland home owners always demand a view, and although Portlanders consider the wrangling between Seattle and Tacoma over the renaming of Rainier nothing short of childish, they do feel a personal, if less proprietary, interest in Mt. Hood. It is not unusual to see such a lead as the following on the front page of a Portland paper: "Portlanders trudging off to work early this morning, reluctant to leave a warm bed for the chilly outdoors, were rewarded for their discomfort by the sight of Mt. Hood, outlined against a brilliant sunrise."

Portland crosses and recrosses the Willamette River, so that directions for getting about in the city always involve the mention of a specific bridge.

The residence districts wind up country roads and hairpin curves. The houses give the feeling of unpretentious but very real comfort. No one splurges. It would not be good form. There are still people who would consider it the height of disgrace to have their pictures in the papers.

Seattle erected an Indian totem in its town square, but Portland put up a classical fountain and horse trough with lions and female figures, beautiful, dignified, a little stale, looking back at another world. According to the *Oregon Guide* the famous Skidmore Fountain was "the Rialto of the 1890s; the center of such life as there was. 'Meet you at the fountain' was a popular expression." There is a story about the dedication of the Skidmore Fountain which has a fine robustness: Mr. Weinhard, a local brewer, asked for permission to borrow the fire department's hose to pipe beer from his brewery to the fountain on the occasion of its dedication, so that it might initially play beer rather than water.

Portland is very conscious of its history and the history of the state. Such famous local landmarks as the Dr. John McLoughlin house in Oregon City are beautifully restored and refurnished. Mr. Burt Brown Barker, Vice President of the University of Oregon, and Dr. R. C. Clark of the same university are the only two men ever to have had full access to the Hudson's Bay Company's sacrosanct London files pertaining to Oregon. The Oregon Historical Society, an active body, has its library and its collection housed in the Civic Auditorium. The society, which was founded in 1898, has many rare manuscripts and objects in its possession: Jason Lee's diary, the old mission press of the martyred Whitmans; the sea chest of Captain Robert Gray, discoverer of the Columbia River. It also has in its possession a librarian, Miss Nellie B. Pipes, whose efforts on behalf of researchers have put her name in the gratitude section of almost every recent book dealing with Oregon history.

Portland goes a long way back for the Pacific Northwest and, although it may be yielding place now to more aggressive cities to the north, it can still coast a long time on the financial power it acquired when Captain John C. Ainsworth, Simeon Reed, Ben Holladay, William S. Ladd, and Henry W. Corbett commanded the Columbia River and the coast trade, stage and telegraph lines, mining and lumber properties, real estate and railroads. The tentacles of these financial giants reached north to Puget Sound, down the length of the Columbia, into the Inland Empire, south to the California border.

Portland has its stories to match Seattle's refusal after her big fire to keep the money for Johnstown flood aid at home. Among Portland's annals are such instances as Mr. Henry Failing's gracious but firm return of voluntary contributions from other western communities at the time of Portland's fire in 1873. As chairman of the Relief Committee he opened the local subscriptions with ten thousand dollars and Portland rebuilt with her own money.

The criticism is often made in Oregon that the great Portland fortunes have never been spent to the benefit of universities or colleges. Simeon Reed was a notable exception. The fortune that Reed, the great financier, left on his death, went in part to the founding of Reed College in Portland: an institution with high scholastic rating and such innovations in its favor as no intercollegiate athletics; no fraternities, sororities, or honor societies; complete student self-government; grades for quality not quantity; an oral examination before graduation; no attendance records; written examinations at the students' request, and so on. The college has exercised a real influence in educational circles, and from its student body and faculty have been recruited staff members for institutions on the opposite side of America; modern ones like Bennington and Sarah Lawrence, and less experimental ones like the Massachusetts Institute of Technology. But though one of Portland's leading citizens gave the grounds and another the library—in addition to Mr. Reed's initial munificence—the town and the college have never meshed. One graduate has explained it by writing: "Portland is by nature conservative and subscribes to the Petrine doctrine, 'Let there be no innovations except those which are handed down.'"

CHAPTER III

Spokane

The heart of Spokane is a hotel, the world-famous Davenport, and this is symbolically fitting for a city which has been made lively and prosperous by the people who own the farms and mines and stretches of lumber within a 150-mile radius and who come "to town" to spend their money. This they do simply by having a good time, or by building a home and investing in downtown real estate.

From Spokane east to Minneapolis and south to Salt Lake City there is no town of equal size, and so this city reigns as undisputed Queen of the Inland Empire. The Empire consists of some 100,000 square miles which include eastern Washington, northeastern Oregon, northern Idaho, western Montana, and even southern British Columbia. It is a land of quite extraordinary natural resources and some of the most beautiful and spectacular of Far Western landscapes. Into Spokane flows the trade of the rich wheat-producing areas of the Big Bend and the Palouse; of forests with the largest stand of white pine in the world; and of a country with a "multimillion dollar mining output" of gold, silver, lead, and copper. Five of the eight transcontinental railroads serving the Pacific coast converge at Spokane; highways from all directions come threading into the city, and now the government is establishing a large air base on the city's outskirts.

Spokane bustles by day and is gay by night, far into the small hours; and through the Davenport Hotel moves, from dawn to dawn, a constant tide of visitors of every variety. You may not be able quite to agree with Mr. Will Irwin who is reputed to have said—with gestures—that there are only two outstanding deluxe hotels in the world, the Davenport in Spokane and Shepheards in Cairo, but you will have to admit that the former deserves its popularity.

People tell you that the Davenport Hotel and all of Spokane have had their depressed and sluggish moments, and that the new rush is due directly to the fact that the Grand Coulee Dam is only a short ride away; but when one begins to search back into the city's history there would seem to have been here, from the beginning, some magnetic pull that brought people together in groups. Even the Indians made the Spokane Valley a gathering place because the salmon coming upriver were retarded by the falls and allowed themselves to be easily caught in great numbers. The old Indian word Spokane means literally "sun" and one is inclined to admit the Chamber of Commerce boast that Spokane is in truth "a child of the sun."

Spokane people are unusually civic-minded. The town tends to produce citizens like Benjamin Kizer, active in all regional planning councils, and Aubrey White, "Spokane's Civic Horse Trader," whose technique for persuading corporations and people to donate some fifteen hundred parcels of land to the city for parks was described at length in the *Reader's Digest* in October 1940. Spokane boasts a park or a playground within five minutes' walk of every home, and the town is so front-yard conscious that it has won the title of the City Beautiful in national contests four years in succession. You can ride over one hundred miles on parkways around Spokane without seeing a billboard. There are no slums here; no eyesores along the wandering Spokane River which flows through the city.

Spokane is proud that Seattle's labor "leader," Dave Beck, has never been able successfully to penetrate this area. You hear that a group of Spokane citizens was responsible for the recent defeat of Clarence Dill as candidate for governor and the election of Seattle's Mayor Langlie instead. As certain citizens speak sharply and critically of "coast politics" you sense a similarity between this community and certain ones in Oregon. One feels here the influence of the rural mind which, though often narrow and prejudiced, is—according to its own lights—an incorruptible mind. It may give the body politic certain curious inconsistencies but it does tend to discourage big-time chicanery.

One is amazed to find still alive in Spokane the old agitation for having the Inland Empire split off from western Washington to form with northern Idaho a separate state called Lincoln. One eminent citizen wagged a solemn finger at me in the winter of 1941 and told me to watch; the subject would be brought out again into the open very soon.

Although Spokane feels the influence of the farmer, it feels also the influence of the miner, the gambler, and the chance-taker; those lovers of the swift-paced and glittering. The visitor who penetrates more than one layer of this city comes inevitably upon curious anomalies. The people from up on the hill where the big stone mansions stand are inclined to be a little envious of Seattle, which seems to them more lively and more cosmopolitan than Spokane. The visitor who is invited to "exclusive" private clubs is shocked to have his ears assailed by the constant din of slot machines, and to see members—predominately female—working the handles with zombie intensity while the minutes tick past. Explanations that these slot machines were installed to pay off debts in depression years, and that the proceeds now go to charity, seem less credible than the theory that this might well be expected of a city which has known the gambler's spirit from its beginnings.

The flavor of Spokane's immediate past is heartily spiced with the kinds of personalities that are produced in mining country when overnight riches raised simple people to the top without allowing them time to adjust themselves to the change. The visitor is amazed, amused, and a little disappointed to discover that this side of Spokane is decidedly a *sotto voce* topic. Even the files of old newspapers have little to offer except when town characters die without issue, move away, or never get into "society." Some five years after a commonplace obituary notice the *Spokesman-Review* may dare a Sunday article on the crotchets, foibles, and fanciful activities of such a character.

You can read about Dutch Jake Goetz, a famous genial ruffian who, after the Spokane fire in 1889, set up a great tent, some fifty feet by two hundred, with an enormous range, tables for eating and drinking, and every kind of gambling game: faro, roulette, keno, and poker, for a patronage of miners and loggers reputedly ranging from six hundred to one thousand a night. This same Jake is remembered for his wedding ceremony in the mining country from which his riches came. The invitation read: "Dutch Jake's Wedding. Everyone invited. No Cards. Procession will form at 7:40 tonight. Murray Silver Cornet Band Leading; the Murray Hose and Ladder Company and Pioneer Fire Brigade, all in full uniform, civic societies in full regalia," and so on. Perhaps the most memorable part of the wedding was the band's choice of post-ceremony music. Their selection was "The Mistakes of My Life Have Been Many."

There were some pretty fancy times in Spokane in past years. Those who shared in the gaiety of the period felt that "civilization had come to the frontier." There are hints of near tragedies, however; a visiting "Chesterfield," one Arlington Buckingham Wadsworth, whose name strangely enough did not at once put him under suspicion, was unmasked just in the nick of time before carrying off one of the local heiresses. A visiting pianist named de Konski is remembered for breaking the piano at a private recital during a too spirited rendition of his own composition "The Awakening of the Lion." A "Lady Albion" wrote for a local paper in buttery phrases near the turn of the century: "The Hill is very aristocratic and receives on Wednesdays, when carriages and coupés, hansoms and gurneys, climb the spacious streets and throng the wide avenues with their fair freight."

After such verbal treacle as "the tea is brewing, while fingers like rose leaves stray softly yet busily, among the dainty cups," one turns with relief from Lady Albion to that forthright, audacious, and original character, May Arkwright Hutton.

Mrs. Hutton came west "on her own" at twenty-three, and with utmost respectability conducted a mining camp boardinghouse until she married an engineer on a local train who invested money along with a milkman and a butcher and came into the legendary riches of the Hercules mine.

Mrs. Hutton is remembered for an admirable independence of character which enabled her, as a rich woman, to go her own way no matter what the world thought of her. While acting as one of the first two women delegates ever elected to a national political convention (Champ Clark's sister was the other) she hung her washing out of the window of one of Baltimore's leading hotels and left it there over the protests of the management.

Mrs. Hutton was accustomed to express herself vigorously on all topics. While still living in the Coeur d'Alenes she wrote a book about her life over which there is still a good deal of talk and mystery. Very few copies are to be found, since Mr. Hutton bought up all he could find and a powerful friend even managed to get the city library's copy by some subtle sleight of hand.

Mrs. Hutton vociferously attacked Theodore Roosevelt for his statement that "only twice should a woman's name be seen in public—when she marries and when she dies." When T.R. came to Spokane and sat at dinner in the Davenport Hotel with men only allowed to be present (although women were permitted to take seats in the balcony and gaze on the awesome spectacle), Mrs. Hutton wrote for the papers, "I am proud of the women of Spokane who had the self-respect to refuse this invitation to place themselves on a par with the wives of the merry monarchs of old, who allowed their women to gaze upon their orgies at the round table. And I am heartily ashamed that the City Beautiful contained some women whose sense of the eternal fitness of things is so little removed in this instance from the habits and customs of blanket-Indian squaws."

Mrs. Hutton was an ardent—sometimes almost too ardent—worker for equal rights for women and for many another good cause, and when she was dead and her famous costumes of plumes and feathers and plaids and zebra skins were no longer seen in Spokane, her large-hearted husband left her a monument of which all Spokane is sincerely proud. This is an orphanage which is reputed to be the best of its kind in the whole United States.

Spokane entertains a rather possessive air toward the Grand Coulee Dam and in particular toward the Columbia Basin Irrigation Project. This section of the state has its candidate for the honor of "father" of this project, Mr. E. F. Blaine, now in his eighties and active for many years in reclamation work in the state of Washington. Spokane's claims for Mr. Blaine are equally as impressive as the claims made for The Boys from Ephrata. A Spokane citizen pointed out very emphatically that there is a vast difference between stating oracularly that "there ought to be a dam" and in actually setting forth some sound engineering ideas for its accomplishment:

"It reminds me of the time when I was a boy and my father pointed to the old fashioned telephone hanging on the wall of his store in Kansas City and said—'My boy, the time will come when you will be able to see the fellow you are talking to over that telephone.' Of course my father never contributed anything toward the development of television, but because he made that statement I suppose I should now be canonizing him as the Father of Television."

Spokane is, however, one hundred percent behind the idea of the importance of the irrigation aspects of the Grand Coulee project. Businessmen are quick and clear with their figures about the self-liquidating aspects of the agricultural lands and with their facts about soil erosion taking out more land each year from the nation than that reclaimed by the federal government since it began to work in the reclamation field.

Spokane boasts of a mythical "Spirit" also. Some argue that this Spirit in its original form is dead now and some say it is not. It is said to be this Spirit which produced the willingness on the part of citizens to dig down in their pockets "to buy rights-of-way for railroads, buy stock in new industries, buy a site for Fort Wright, put up thousands of dollars to advertise the town and surrounding country, get Grand Coulee started" and so on.

Like many other Washington communities Spokane is beginning to take a marked interest in its earliest history. The old roadways, like the famous "Mullan Road," are now being re-marked and the sites of old forts of the fur trading days are put on travelers' itineraries.

Old Spokane House, established in 1810 by David Thompson of the North-West Fur Company, the Hudson's Bay Company's Canadian rival, was one of the most luxurious of the posts of the early fur trading era. Trappers on brief holiday could dance with Indian beauties in a real ballroom, bet on horse races, drink their fill, and in general make merry in robust fashion. In 1812 John Jacob Astor and his Pacific Fur Company sent John Clarke from the mouth of the Columbia inland to found a post in the same neighborhood.

After the furs—some thirty years or so—came the gold, discovered in the roots of grass pulled up by grazing horses. The inland gold discoveries helped build up Spokane, but more slowly than the distant Oregon city of Portland, which was to benefit so phenomenally from its control of the Columbia River navigation by which all men and supplies going inland to the mines must travel. Later there were the railroads, and Spokane, needing them desperately to develop her mines, lumber, and agriculture, had many a bitter experience with their builders and promoters. The Northern Pacific had what it called "terminal rates" by which Puget Sound cities and the town of Portland paid lower freight rates from the East than did Spokane. Poor Spokane, indeed, was forced to pay haulage charges to the coast and back as far as the Inland Empire. It is not to be wondered at that Spokane citizens listened with joy to the honeyed promises of J. J. Hill who assured them his line, the Great Northern, would be happy to cut freight rates in return for a million dollar right of way. Spokane fell all over itself to provide this handsome right of way, but after the panic of 1893—which did away with Mr. Hill's rival, the Northern Pacific, in most timely fashion—Mr. Hill's memory seemed peculiarly to fail him on that promise of lower rates. Appeals to the Interstate Commerce Commission were so signally unsuccessful that when the United States Supreme Court in 1897 ruled that the commission had no jurisdiction over freight rates, tariffs shot up until it was cheaper to ship goods to the Orient from the east coast than to ship them as far as Spokane. The farmers grew so violent in their protestations that Mr. Hill held some meetings in the big grain country, where he distinguished himself by a statement that "you might as well try to set a broken ankle by statute as to reduce rates by statute. You can legislate until the barn door has fallen off its hinges with rust, and you will not succeed." It wasn't until 1906 when the Interstate Commerce Commission, through the Hepburn Act, was given power in rate fixing that Spokane began to get somewhere on rate reductions. It found itself in company with other cities in the same section of the country—the inter-mountain country—fighting a similar battle. There were years in which the railroad scandals and their acts of piety and grace were well aired in court—to the marked indifference of a great percentage of the American populace—but finally in 1918 Spokane's fight was won. Just at that time Spokane shipping began to decline. Although inland people still feel bitter about the freight rate war and are inclined to blame the coast cities for playing a selfish part in it, it is now pretty much of a "dead horse." Motor freight and chain stores have changed the entire situation.

Whatever the future may hold for Spokane it is impossible to imagine this city other than vigorous and lively. The one criticism which might be leveled at it is that community cultural life seems relatively feeble when compared to activities in the fields of commerce, city beautifying, and the marking of historic sites. The town does have a very good library with what seemed to me an exceptional staff. One is told, however, that the predominant Catholic element produces a certain censorship of books, and that this censorship has been extended also to certain movies. The town once had a symphony orchestra of which people can at least say that it was a "step in the right direction." It has an imposing list of high school orchestras, singing groups—male and female—and a lively Little Theatre.

Spokane has a distinguished newspaper, the *Spokesman-Review*, which is an institution in Spokane much as the *Oregonian* is in Portland. The *Oregonian* has been a sort of "big brother" to the *Spokesman-Review*, several veteran members of the staff having come originally from the Oregon paper. Mr. W. H. Cowles has published the paper since 1893. His two sons are now in the business in managerial capacities. Mr. Cowles also publishes the *Chronicle* and what is known as the Pacific Northwest Farm Trio: three bi-weeklies, the *Oregon Farmer*, the *Washington Farmer*, and the *Idaho Farmer*, all printed in the Spokane plant with editorial bureaus in each of the three states. One hears that in spite of a record-breaking circulation (combined daily for *Spokesman-Review* and *Chronicle*, 120,000) the papers are cordially hated. Among the various reasons given for this hatred are the *Spokesman-Review*'s "bone dry" attitude (it takes no whiskey advertising although beer and wine are acceptable); its opposition, because of fear of increased taxes, to such municipal enterprises as free garbage collection and sewage disposal, and the building of a new city auditorium; its tendency to describe all adjacent countryside as "Spokane country"; its indifference to local, school, and county elections but its willingness to "stick its neck out" on congress-men, governors, and senators.

Spokane has a local museum in an old mansion, with the inevitable Indian arrowheads, ore samples from mines with such poetic names as June Echo, Full Moon, Lady of the Lake, and some dubious "art" from old houses. Recently the city acquired an Art Center downtown, established by the W.P.A. but carried on now by the city with the help of some enterprising women and a director named Kenneth Downer who was one of the controversial prize winners in the Northwest's recent *But Is It Art?* battle in Seattle. This center, which has 625 students and waiting lists for most classes, looks very hopeful.

The visitor—observing Spokane's civic-mindedness and energy—is quite prepared to believe that when the backyards are all planted to lawn, and the historic sites are all marked, this city may turn with equal wholeheartedness toward the appreciation and the promotion of a truly vital local "culture."

CHAPTER IV

Tacoma

....

The development of Tacoma has followed a different pattern from most Pacific Northwest cities, in that it was established out of hand or "as though by imperial ukase." When every port town in the Far West was competing to become the "tidewater terminus" for the much advertised Northern Pacific Railroad, it was Tacoma which succeeded in pleasing the railroad men and eastern investors who arrived with capital in hand and set out to build it into the great metropolis of the coast.

Curiously enough this very ease of initial development—which for so long seemed to put Tacoma ahead of other Northwestern cities—may have been a misfortune rather than a blessing. For it is as though the growth of a city must follow some more slow organic law, and a town which is force-fed may prove to be rather like an overfertilized plant with a quick display of showy green and no essential substance. In Tacoma already the unprejudiced observer has seen the force running down.

Tacoma may advertise itself as the Lumber Capital of America, but actually it has become a City of Homes. This is sometimes said of Portland, Oregon, but there is a difference. Portland has a past that is deep-rooted in the state's history. Tacoma is essentially rootless. Its many "Easterners" were not typical "pioneers." They came with capital, and they were able—though transplanted—to maintain a certain way of life to which they had been accustomed in more established communities.

Robert Walkinshaw in his book *On Puget Sound* has said that there are streets on the Bluff, from the Stadium to Point Defiance Park, where it "seems always afternoon." The phrase is so apt as to be unforgettable. And when one visits the charming small estates which lie on the shores of the chain of lakes just outside the city one feels a repose which belongs to rose gardens, tennis clubs, and the suburbs of Philadelphia. Tacoma, indeed, boasts one of the oldest tennis clubs on the coast and there is an active hunt club to which nearby Fort Lewis contributes invigoration. There is always a certain significance in the early organization of leisure time in any town.

Tacoma's air of lazy relaxation (if the sun is out) and rather depressing and not quite healthy inanition (if it isn't) nicely prepare one for the kind of sightseeing which belongs to the Tacoma environs. You can get off the main roads very easily and wander about on the lakeshores, over prairies growing scrub oak and wild roses, to the little historical town of Steilacoom, rotting gently and sedately among its memories of early territorial days. You can lunch or dine, see a movie or go ice skating in the charming community center of Lakewood. And although you may want to take a quick and perhaps troubled look at the enormous expansion of Fort Lewis and the activity of planes around McChord Field, it is somehow the more gentle and leisured activities which seem fitting to Tacoma visitors.

Old Fort Nisqually, transplanted from its original site on the prairies, stands at one end of Point Defiance Park overlooking the turbulent Narrows. Within its weathered palisades are the granary, the oldest standing building in the state, built in 1843, and the gracious white house of the factor which was built in 1853. It was as early as 1833, however, that Nisqually House was established by the Hudson's Bay Company. For about thirty years a farm was maintained on the prairies of Nisqually, and long-haired Spanish cattle roamed where the encroaching fir trees now stand. From the lookout on this fort's wall one commanded, for some months in 1940, a magnificent view of the Narrows Bridge which spanned the stretch of blue water from one fir-crowned shore to another, until the autumn day when a forty-mile gale started "Galloping Gertie" waving like a ribbon and the whole midsection plunged into the Sound, to the horror of all onlookers and the dismay of all engineers and insurance men involved.

In studying Tacoma one finds seemingly anomalous factors which play against one another and tease the mind: the Weyerhauser home on the Bluff, a tourist target since it is a residence of a member of the family heading the world's greatest timber monopoly, and down in the town, not many blocks away, the offices of the most successful publicly owned utilities plant in the world. Tacoma claims the lowest light and power rates of any city in the United States and its municipal light and power system is a genuine monument to civic enterprise and to the efforts of a group of exceptionally able men.

Tacoma has the most complete historical museum in the state. Seven years before the Oregon Historical Society was founded citizens of Washington were meeting to organize their state society. The museum is an outgrowth of these first meetings held in Tacoma in 1891. Unfortunately, though full of treasures, the absence of organization in the museum up on North Cliff Avenue—probably traceable to shortage of funds—drives some visitors into a fine frenzy. They wander, bewildered, among a rich motley of objects of every description from rare Indian healing boards to dusty birds' eggs, from beautiful Haida masks to bad Greek casts, from a lock of Narcissa Whitman's blond hair to an octopus-shaped hat rack (unmarked) with eight tentacles, and from the aluminum fuel tank of the Norge, through machines for sharpening razor blades to historic cradles and fading photographs of nameless pioneers. It is in vain that one tries to determine the criterion by which these objects are accepted, and in the end one comes to the conviction, shared by many, that it has been used as a clearing house for Old Tacoma families emptying their attics to the enrichment of this state Depository. (The name is used advisedly—the very cards say "deposited by.") There are Indian collections of which the Heye museum could well be proud, and there are "deposits" by the Junior League of the unmarked etchings of Thomas Handforth, a local boy who has done good work in remote places in the world, but whose name is apparently of less significance in his home town than the name of the group which made the presentation. When the visitor gets this far, and finds Mr. Handforth in juxtaposition to a hand-tinted photograph of the Cascade Creamery's buxom milkmaids near the century's turn, he is apt, if uncontrolled, to rush screaming from the building. On the way out he may encounter the Fighting Gladiator taking off from a cupboard containing a highly catholic collection of small cream pitchers, and he will then tell you that this is not a State Historical Museum: it is the Cabinet of Doctor Caligari.

Less temperamental folk sit down and talk with genial Mr. Bonney who works full-heartedly at the job of curator and who is much too pleasant to ever be wounded with pressing questions. He sits under a photograph of Ezra Meeker who called him Willie. The photograph shows Ezra in his war garden. Although well on in his eighties at the time of the last war, Mr. Meeker set off at once to Washington to offer his services at the front. The suggestion was made that he return home instead and plant a war garden. Mr. Meeker complied and with what must have been sheer whimsy planted the whole acreage in cucumbers for dill pickles. What is more he sold the pickles, every one, from shop to shop in a wheelbarrow. He confessed that he didn't mind the hoeing but the picking got his back just a little. Downstairs in the museum in a glass case are the old covered wagon and two stuffed oxen, Dave and Dandy, who took Meeker on his famous trips across America, making the country Oregon Trail conscious.

Meeker played a part in the successful capture of the Northern Pacific terminus by Tacoma. In 1870, at the time of all the agitation for the railroads, he took east from his farm in the rich Puyallup Valley fifty-two varieties of flowers that he had found blooming in December. He presented them to Horace Greeley who wrote about them in the *Tribune*, and Jay Cooke, seeing the item, invited Meeker to sell him five thousand pamphlets of his own on the beauties and advantages of the Puget Sound country. Jay Cooke had already been doing such a job of high-pressure salesmanship that the land through which he wished to push the railroad had become known as "Jay Cooke's banana belt," and this was his opportunity to substantiate his claims for the mildness of climate and general prodigality of nature through-out the Pacific Northwest.

Most histories of Tacoma begin with stories of the Hoosier, Job Carr, who is said to have had a clairvoyant wife who perhaps guided him to put his little rowboat around what is now Point Defiance on Christmas Day 1864, where he saw—and, what is more, recognized as such—a harbor so superior that he rose in his boat and cried "Eureka! Eureka!"—though we have only his word for it. It is not recorded that Morton Matthew McCarver of Kentucky and points west, south, east, and north uttered a word when first clapping an eye on Commencement Bay, but he was pretty sure he'd made a find. And Mr. McCarver had had some experiences in finds and duds, having had a varied career which covered such seemingly unrelated activities as promoting Sacramento for Captain Sutter and introducing horseradish west of the Rockies. This is the man who has won the title of the Father of Tacoma. Mr. McCarver began by calling the little shantytown Commencement City, after the name Lieutenant Wilkes of the Navy had given the harbor in 1841 simply because this was where he began to survey. Mr. McCarver, however, under the influence of Theodore Winthrop's *The Canoe and the Saddle*, and a visiting friend with ideas, decided to call the town Tacoma, in honor of the great mountain which lies on Tacoma's immediate skyline and also on the skyline of half of western Washington. Tacoma's attitude toward this mountain has always seemed to the rest of the state singularly proprietary. When Tacoma agitated to have the mountain's name changed from prosaic Rainier to the more suitable Tacoma there was a furor which shook the state, made enemies of old friends, and led to the writing of many a scorching editorial. Rival lobbies representing Seattle and Tacoma worked in Congress. All the great and famous were asked for their opinion. Latent anti-British sentiment was aroused against Rainier as a "butchering" British officer. Importuned red men made themselves laugh-able by putting out a magazine at a convention bearing the picture of the beautiful mountain and the words, "We pray the Great Spirit Kitche-mani-tou to restore to the Indians Tacoma, meaning Nourishing Breast." Research turned up the fact that Indians had also called the mountain Chebollyp,

Stiquak, and Tiswauk. As to spelling the name *Tacoma*, there were a number of authorities on that point also, offering a choice ranging from Tahoma through Takhoma, to Tacobet and T'Kope. Finally the United States Senate in 1924 passed a bill to change the name, but Seattle was able to get the bill held up in the Public Lands Committee—and presumably that's where it still is. Tacoma got almost as much publicity out of this cause célèbre as she would have had from naming the mountain.

Whether Tacoma has really had more citizens who were vociferous boosters than other Pacific Northwest towns would be hard to determine; certainly it has that reputation—which again affords a Tacoma anomaly, since the substantial citizens along the lakeshores seem to conduct their lives with singular lack of noise. Among characters of the not very distant past was one George Francis Train, perhaps the epitome of the Booster, who carried his enthusiasm for his adopted city to such lengths that as a stunt to advertise Tacoma he set out round the world in 1891 in an attempt to beat Nelly Bly's seventy-two-day record. Train succeeded by a five-day margin. When the railroad fantasia was at its height Rudyard Kipling visited Tacoma and reported seeing a man pull a gun on another because he would not agree that Tacoma would outstrip San Francisco.

Tacoma has had more than its full share of daring men who made and lost fortunes in a hurry with schemes as fantastic as one—never carried out—for transporting ice from the mountain by means of a wooden chute. Critics who suggested fire hazard from friction were assured that moisture from the ice would prevent this. There were seeming fools who turned out to be very wise men indeed when they went against all advice and built out on the tideflats—now the center of the manufacturing district. There were many men who successfully combined a six-day week Yankee acumen with one day a week Puritan church-going. One of the partners in what was to become the largest lumber mill in the world, the St. Paul and Tacoma Lumber Company, distinguished himself by such pithy American axioms as: "See what the people are going to need; see it first; then get it and the market will follow." This same gentleman is credited with replying to a visitor's questions about the significance of the four towers of the First Congregational Church that they represented "the Father, the Son, the Holy Ghost, and the St. Paul and Tacoma Lumber Company."

When in the late eighties and early nineties nationwide depression hit America, the northwestern branch of Coxey's famous army had its rise in Tacoma. This "industrial army," endorsing locally the program which Ohio's Coxey had proposed as a panacea for the current national ills, was led by "General Jumbo" Cantwell. Jumbo Cantwell had been a bouncer in Tacoma's notorious Morgan resort, a joint deluxe which flourished in the gilded days with many gambling rooms, a Théâtre Comique with beauteous girls, and rooms in which—so it was said—loggers could with the aid of knock-out drops be easily relieved of their wallets. General Jumbo, leading off with the rallying cry of "On to Washington," left Tacoma on the afternoon of April 29, 1894, and went as far as Puyallup, some nine miles distant, where he made camp in some empty buildings. He had had the presence of mind to take up a collection from all the spectators who had assembled to see him off, and it was well worth an admission price. General Cantwell was wearing a new wide sombrero and uniform, beside him walked his big St. Bernard dog, behind him came his followers bearing a large flag presented by the G.A.R. Not all the members of this movement were rabble, by any means. There were earnest men among the six hundred marchers, of whom three hundred were pledged to go to Washington, and the others pledged to stay home and care for the families the men were temporarily deserting.

This local branch of Coxey's army had a strange and rather unhappy history in their attempt to get on eastward. Governor McGraw went to Puyallup at one time to hear their troubles and to listen to a speech from Jumbo, who said the railroads had induced this army of men to come west; now there was nothing for them to do, no work and no money in this Land of Promise, and they intended that the "foreign-owned corporation, the railroad" should carry them all back. They threatened to take over the cars of the bankrupt Northern Pacific and get east under their own steam. In the end Jumbo got there and not many others. He traveled with a vaudeville act in comparative comfort and rode into Washington behind Coxey on his famous great Percheron horse.

In spite of fairly steep perpendiculars in the graphs of Tacoma's prosperity and depressions, and in spite of the many singular characters who have lent it such color in the past, the town gives the observer today the feeling of maintaining a rather steady, somewhat languid gait. There is a small group of people which promotes amateur dramatics, a symphony orchestra, a local art association, which with the help of Carnegie funds brings modern art to the attention of Tacoma citizens. Up on the hill and around the lakes people grow roses, look at the mountain, ride, play tennis, sail, and swim. Down in the back alleys and along the waterfront one must search to find the remnants of the kind of wild living characteristic of a seaport, a lumber capital, and a railroad terminus.

SECTION IV

More Places and People

CHAPTER I

The Islands and the Land To and From

Up in the extreme northwestern part of the State of Washington where it looks as though some giant had carelessly laid out the bits of a jigsaw puzzle and then gone away and left it, there lie 172 enchanting, rock-ribbed, and tree-crowned islands called the San Juans. These islands and the channels between them bear Spanish names: Orcas, Fidalgo, Lopez, Rosario, Haro.

A Spanish mariner, one Francisco Elisa, attempting to strengthen the claims of Spain to the northern Pacific shores, sailed about these islands in the year 1791 christening them for Spanish gentry safe at a distance. The United States sent Lieutenant Wilkes in 1841 to do some surveying in these waters, and he tried to call the islands the Navy Group, and to give them names commemorating the heroes of the War of 1812. Wilkes's maps, however, were published only in a limited edition, and when six years later England sent Captain Henry Kellett for a British Admiralty survey, he ignored Wilkes's names (naturally enough since they honored some late enemies of Great Britain) and used the old Spanish ones instead. The British charts were made available to anyone with two shillings; mariners bought them, got used to them, and hence the old Spanish names have endured down the years.

Their romantic Southern names add in a way to the curious and subtle beguilement of these islands. People who once fall under the spell of these land- and waterscapes never quite shake it off. The winding shoreline with its gnarled and twisted pines reminds one of the inland sea of Japan. But there is a difference. The tawny slopes which rise from green water to be crowned with green trees show in spring the brilliant red flash of Indian paintbrush and all the rich variety of blues possible to Pacific Northwest flora. These golden slopes, like lions sleeping in the sun, are the picture the islands leave most unforgettably in the memory of those who wander them on foot.

The countryside on the settled islands is intimate and cozy with lichened rock, meadow, and lazy flocks of sheep. Although there are mountains they are far off, ringing the sky. At hand one sees a barn set in the protection of a gentle hill, old orchards moss-grown, boats rocking in the gentle airs which stir the red-limbed madronas. It is in some blending of the pastoral farming scene and the adventurous restless sea—leading north to Eskimos and Indians and west to the Orient—that there lies, it seems to me, part of these islands' binding charm. The heart feels repose but the eyes still search the far sky, the distant peak, the turn of the tides round the farthest rocky point.

Some of the first people to come to the islands as settlers were men from the Fraser River and the Cariboo goldfields; men who did not strike it rich in the Canada stampedes and who came to the islands to raise sheep and fruit in peace and contentment—if without much profit. The ownership of these islands was a matter of rather bitter dispute for many years between America and England, and the homely incidents which helped to settle the controversy in favor of the Americans are known as the Pig War of the San Juans and the Island Sheep Controversy.

Local historians like to dramatize the whole matter a little: "Just as the hiss of a goose saved Rome, so the squeal of a pig may be said to have saved San Juan." They also like to compare the Sheep case to the Boston Tea Party, since both were rows over taxation. These rural altercations did, as a matter of fact, pack enough potential dynamite to have led to war, if both countries involved had not been anxious to avoid such a major calamity.

Difficulty over the ownership of the island of San Juan began with the treaty of 1846 between America and Great Britain which set the line of demarcation between Canada and the United States at the forty-ninth parallel and along "the middle of the channel which separates the continent from Vancouver Island." Unfortunately there were three channels, not just one. The United States said the treaty meant the Haro channel, which would allow her to claim San Juan Island, and England said it meant the Rosario, which would give her practically all the islands.

The first legislature of Washington Territory had some words to say in 1854 about removing the "foreign trespassers" from San Juan Island. Taxes had been levied on the island as a part of Washington Territory and were collected in 1855 by the sheriff from nearby Whatcom County. In the meantime, however, the smart Hudson's Bay Company had brought in some thirteen hundred sheep from Victoria with Kanaka herders and an agent, Charles J. Griffin. Mr. Griffin came up against a stout-hearted American collector of customs named Colonel Isaac Ebey who objected to the sheep and said so. Even as he discussed the matter with Mr. Griffin some British bigwigs, including the Governor of Vancouver, came to the island in a company boat, and Colonel Ebey, perceiving them about to land, sent off a man on a dead run to the top of the nearest hill with the Stars and Stripes in his hand. The British had their flag in hand too and were considerably annoyed at this evidence of quick thinking on the part of an American.

There followed a good deal of give and take on the sheep question and finally Whatcom County seized and sold some thirty of the animals for unpaid taxes. This created a mild storm but no violence until, in the winter of 1859, the Hudson's Bay officer's pet pig dug up some potatoes brought in with great labor and expense from the mainland by one Lyman Cutler, and as it was not this animal's first depredation, Cutler shot the "unspeakable, common, old razor-backed shoat." The arrest of the man who shot the pig led the islanders to ask the protection of United States troops. They appealed to that tough old soldier, General Harney, who sent in Captain Pickett with a company. This young captain, who was to immortalize himself some years later by leading the Confederate brigades at Gettysburg, defied all the British forces with a splendid show of bluff and arrogance, and the strong attitude of the Yankees served to awaken both countries to the threat of a major war over an insignificant stretch of country. A temporary arrangement was made by establishing one hundred men each on the Island of San Juan at the extreme opposite ends, where they remained for twelve historic years.

The little booklet you can buy for a quarter at the old British block-house ties up the incident nicely with general world history:

"The greatest civil war of history muttered, broke into the roar of a devastating whirlwind and died away; Prussia thrust Austria from the map of Northern Europe; Italy, after her centuries of political death, was gloriously resurrected; the most splendid, glittering, hollow empire in the world was forever shattered at Sedan, and a great republic rose from the blood-soaked ashes of the commune: and still these 100 officers and men, under the Stars and Stripes, and the 100 under the cross of St. George held their lonely posts in that far off island of the lonely Northwest.

"And when in 1872 old Emperor William of Germany decided, as sole arbitrator, that the Haro channel was the boundary and that all the islands were American, the Yankee bands played out of camp the British force, which left without a murmur of rancor or hostility."

Today the former British garrison is a moldering homestead where the daughter of William Crooks will take you on a leisurely stroll past the old barracks where her family lived for fifteen years, to the old blockhouse that guarded the bay's entrance, down the green vista of the parade ground with the moss-hung fruit trees her father set out and past the tangle of lichen-bearded plum thicket along the water's edge. There is supposed to be a sign on the gate that says Admission Ten Cents, but we didn't see it and it's only to "keep out the riff-raff." Mrs. Davis gets nothing for the hours she spends guiding tourists through the green lanes and down the crumbling mossy steps. It is a labor of love because she does not want the place destroyed. She will let her dinner grow cold to go with travelers because, quite frankly, she doesn't trust them not to try to carry off a bit of the dilapidated steps or some wood from the blockhouse.

Inside her neat and crumbling old house there are knives and forks and pipes, the cribbage board, bowling balls, and cannon of the British soldiers; and a naive delightful painting of the garrison by one of the men.

Part of the charm of the old blockhouse lies in its caretaker's tart Scotch ways, her little sharp comments, "All the Crookses have notions—follies some might call 'em"; illustrating this remark with the dozens of her father's fruit trees set out when he had the dream of being an orchardist; the decaying sawmill at the water's edge; her bachelor brother's sawdust burner for the cookstove fuel. To stress her uneasiness about vandals she speaks of the disrespect shown the famous McMillin mausoleum in Roche Harbor. This is a shrine on the hilltop of a private estate, where six marble chairs are placed round a six-sided marble table, in the midst of a circle of seven pillars open to the sky, with one pillar broken in half. This is said to be symbolic of the difference between mortal and immortal concepts of life. The chairs at the shrine have the names of the family inscribed on the backs and such salient highlights of a career as "Thirty-Second Degree Mason, Knight of the Mystic Shrine, S A E, Methodist, Republican." It was on this table that light-hearted and disrespectful tourists set up a beer bottle lunch and left it in the dark of the night; and young people have been known to indulge in hilarious antics with decks of cards. Small wonder Mrs. Davis and her big beautiful collie accompany all visitors to the old garrison.

Roche Harbor offers a charming little sleepy hotel, the de Haro, ivy-grown and cozy, with old ship's lanterns shining at night among the green foliage, and lovely gardens sloping down to the water's edge, massed with roses in the summertime. There is an arbor leading to the boat landing, whose cross-beams convey to the departing traveler a series of last messages beginning with Adieu (and the appended notice, *Clearance 8' 10"*) followed by *Farewell then and if Forever, then Forever Fare Thee Well.* Not too cheering a note if one is about to set out in the teeth of a fresh breeze from the southeast.

The other highlight on San Juan Island is the old American military camp of which nothing remains but a small stone monument with the dates 1859–1872, and an enormous flagpole. Here is the best view on the island. From the hilltop you can look all round the vast bowl of the sky to the spears and peaks of the Olympics and the Cascades with the sprawling snowy bulk of Mt. Baker rising above its brothers. If you go to American Camp at sunset you ride between streams of color, the sun setting brilliantly on the right, its reflection turning to rose the snowy slopes far to the left. Standing beside the stone monument while the light fades, the wind dies, on the hidden shore the waves break and fall, the loutish sheep blat drowsily and across the road a farmer walks home with slow step, you think of the coast of Cornwall and all old peaceful and bucolic ways of life.

Orcas Island is not so rich in historic shrines as San Juan but Orcas does have the view of all views in the Pacific Northwest.

You wind up the easy grades in Moran Park to the final curve where you leave your car and climb the last gentle slope to the tower and then up the stone steps of the tower itself. You come out above the treetops into the air to find yourself master of earth and sky. In an almost complete circle the mountains rise out of the land, their snowy peaks pushing skyward: the Cascades, the Olympics, the Canadian Rockies, Mt. Rainier, Mt. Baker. Below you there lie all the rocky and tree-spired islands of this broken archipelago; dozens and dozens of bits of green land reposing, all shapes and sizes, on the blue sea. Far away are the smokestacks and factories, the cars with loud horns and the roar of machinery and traffic. Between you and them is a boat trip of at least an hour and a half. You can take a deep breath down to the bottom of your being.

People who love these islands say you must cruise them to know them. There are dozens of little landlocked bays and deep lonely anchorages which you can have all to yourself overnight or by the week, just for the taking. A man who has been exploring them for thirty years says he will be doing it for thirty more and still be making discoveries.

The islanders themselves are kindly and hospitable people, pleasantly salty like all folk who live surrounded by the sea. Their life is hidden, however; the farms lie off the main-traveled roads; you have to search to find the "characters" and wait to really know them. You come on remarkable people, gentlefolk like the Dodds at Grindstone Bay who left Long Island twelve years ago and have never gone back. There is something specially charming in their shabby old house at the end of a narrow rutty road; something intangibly heartening and delightful emanating from the chairs covered with homemade cowhide; the rope-edged nooks of books flanked with vases made of driftwood, the old stove, the old dog, the pencil sketches, and the open worn volume of Emerson. And there is Mrs. Dodd's voice, cultivated, gentle, unmarred by the nervous strains of competition and hysteria. Yet these are workers, hard workers, cultivating their land without help, fishing and hunting for their food, raising and educating two children.

Then there is Henry Cayu, one of the leading citizens of Deer Harbor, who remembers walking eighteen miles to and from school in the old days and sitting up until midnight helping his father cut shingles in the days when everyone was so poor. Mr. Cayu has been county commissioner of San Juan Island for twenty-six years, off and on. He knows his country with a wonderful intimacy. He takes a particular interest in fisheries and would like to see the legislature come to terms with Canada so that some of the thousands of pink salmon and sockeye that go past these American shores to spawn in the Fraser River might be taken by local trap-fishermen en route. Since he is by nature a mild man he is mild about the legislation against fish traps, but he thinks it wrong because it has taken livelihood from many honest people who had to go on relief, and because a fish trap, constructed Henry Cayu's way, does no harm. It is, in fact, less wasteful, he says, than seine fishing, in which the smaller fish are often killed by the ton.

Once when I was on the islands I tried to find out something about a Peer Gynt ride reputedly made by one Charlie Beale on the back of a wild buck which is supposed to have given Buck Mountain its name. All I got from old-timers was a lot of friendly laughter and the remark, "That's a new one on me. Never heard that!" The young purser on the ferry, an enthusiastic student of Pacific Northwest history, told me rather aggrievedly that the old-timers knew less than the newcomers. "They just aren't interested." He had been particularly upset to learn that there was no one to explain the origin of an anchor and an arrow made in stones and left on the hillsides—one on Mt. Constitution and one on Turtleback. Turtleback had also yielded a large stone with mysterious inscriptions which, so far as anyone knew, had been broken up and carried off, or maybe left where it was, "probably grown over by now." Since this attitude of mild indifference to their possible tourist attractions is true of the island people I did not ask about the yarn I had heard of the island hearse because I was afraid it would be denied and I like to think that it is true.

This story says that the island hearse (which island I don't know—perhaps it served them all)—was kept in somebody's prune dryer. It was a proper hearse, with black fringe and plumes and all the trimmings, and it had been bought by the island ladies because they felt that the conveying of the bodies to the grave by one Bill Long—who would dig a grave and transport the corpse in his own wagon all for the sum of five dollars—was faintly undignified. Bill had, as a matter of fact, got the job because he always went to the island funerals anyway, and it was decided that he might as well be paid for it. But Bill's wagon was so small that it necessitated his sitting on either the head or foot of the coffin as he drove it, and although he sat in a reverent posture it was considered rather intimate and lacking in proper respect. So one spring the ladies sold enough pincushions and penwipers to buy a hearse. It cost twenty dollars.

For those who want to look again at woodpiles in side yards, at rainwater barrels, old long-handled pumps, chickens feeding under apple trees, sawbucks and grindstones, wheelbarrows and ivy-covered outhouses; to catch glimpses through small-paned windows of red plush rockers, coal oil lamps, and knitted antimacassars, the San Juans are the place to visit. The islands are designed for retreat and many people from spinster heiresses to eminent New York psychologists have made them just that; and the dream of half the harassed businessmen one meets in the coast cities is "a little farm on one of the islands." After all there are 172 of them, many uncharted, and it seems likely that there are plenty of ideal sites still to be found.

Although the island of Whidby is not one of the San Juan group it has much the same nostalgic and reposeful quality.

In August at the time of the Indian boat races at Coupeville the island is at its most enchanting. It is lovely to approach by ferry from old Port Townsend, seeing the mountains rising dreamily out of the channel heat haze, with the fields of ripened hay on the island coming down to the water's edge. One drives on winding roads through pastoral country where weathered signs point to places like Clover Valley and Oak Harbor. There are sheep and cows in the fields and notices on the fences reading "Bird Dogs Boarded and Trained," or "A Friendly Glass May Cost an Unfriendly Crash."

It is difficult to believe how short a time ago warlike Indians from the north, in their great canoes each carrying fifty men, prowled these island waterways in search of slaves and loot. Whidby was the scene of one of the most terrifying of the early white killings, when Colonel Isaac Ebey, as he left a party he was giving and stepped out into the fog to speak to the men who had summoned him, was beheaded by Indians. His terrified guests hid out all night in the woods. A Captain Charles Dodd, working for the Hudson's Bay Company, recovered the Colonel's head after two years of physical risk and many parleys, in order that it might be buried with his friend's body.

The Indian races are held in the waterway in front of the village of Coupeville. Coupeville has some nice old houses and, as a grim reminder of the past, a dark blockhouse. At the time of the races there is a rather gimcrackery fair, with the local Rebekahs serving meals to tourists, and nondescript people selling soda pop and chances, while a whining carousel turns in the square. Sometimes, however, one can buy a piece of beautiful Indian work; perhaps a canoe bailer of cedar bark and cherry, soon to be classified as a "lost art" since only one old Indian in his nineties still makes them.

The races themselves are worth the trip for just one moment of pure beauty, when the long, incredibly slim canoes, painted in different colors, holding eleven Indians each, flash across the blue waters; the brilliant tips of pointed paddles catching the light; each boat using an individual rhythm. So low are these canoes built that they seem merely a projection of the torsos of the eleven Indians who kneel dipping their swift paddles in and out of the water.

You may go to Whidby Island by Deception Pass, one of the most popular of all coast view spots, where people leave their cars to walk out on the sloping rocks to gaze in long silence at that varied picture of curving beach, tree-crowned tawny slope, rocky promontory, and swift blue channel, so characteristic of island scenery.

Near the Deception Pass bridge is one of the most delightful of small Washington state parks. Left very much in its natural state, it is never crowded and makes an ideal overnight camp spot. Its unusual feature is a freshwater lake in close intimacy to the sea. One follows a winding footpath through the woods, crosses by charmingly designed rustic bridges to the calm lake with its birds and rushes, where, just over the sandspit, the restless sea chafes at the shoreline.

If you've time for dozy travel in any old dinghy, or dreaming on solitary shores, there are plenty of aimless trips around the old town of Anacortes (once a hopeful rival of Seattle's).

Inland, the country near Marysville, La Conner, and Mount Vernon has many spots of lasting enchantment. The land is dairy country: flat green fields, rolling blue hills, here and there sharp spears of mountain breaking the plain. You can climb through any careless forest to where the great rocks wear thick coats of lichen, the wild rose grows small and delicate, and succulents display their minute and complicated patterns. Here it is possible to lie on a mossy bed and look down a hillslope to a lonely lake with lily pads and a bit of an island. Across, one can see houses for dwarfs in distant valleys. Toward evening there are cowbells, and mists begin to steal round the rocky cliffs of the lakeshore with the subtle suggestiveness of old Sung landscape paintings.

The town of La Conner dozing on the flats of Swinomish Slough had ambitions once. It went so far at the time of the railroad rivalries as to solemnly warn J. J. Hill that he had better get the right-of-way across the flats "before it was too late" to secure the great trade-route, "New York–La Conner–Yokohama."

The people who go to La Conner today are not the kind to interest empire builders. They are apt to be artists seeking retreat, or anthropologists studying the Swinomish Indians, or earthy people growing bulbs and seeds. Not that La Conner is a "colony" or ever will be, but it does have some peculiar charm blended of old ivy-grown houses and misty plains, giant rocks, and distant salt water beyond the marshes, which is appealing to the eye and the spirit. Just to drive through it, however, is to see nothing, suspect nothing—not even the presence of Indians who still dance beautifully and sometimes awesomely at the time of the winter and summer solstices and at the dates of the treaties with the whites.

If you go to the islands by the Chuckanut ferry you will pass through Bellingham. Bellingham is closely related to the islands since they were nominally a part of Whatcom County during their most troublous times. Bellingham is a pleasant and prosperous city with lots of highly advertised adjacent scenery, well worth the advertising: the snowcapped peaks of Baker and Shuksan, the Whatcom Primitive Area, the Heather Meadows of the Mt. Baker National Forest beloved of skiers for their sunny slopes and powder snow. The city itself has Chuckanut Drive, winding along the edge of high bluffs from which one looks out on breathless beauty of landlocked blue waters, rocky ledges, wind-shaped trees, and a skyline of hills and peaks in every tone of blue from misty gray to deepest indigo, dominated by the great hump of Lummi Island.

The city is surrounded by beautiful drives along lakes and through twenty-three public parks. It is only an hour and a half from Vancouver and within easy ferry distance of the old English city of Victoria. Twenty-three miles to the north at Blaine stands the famous Peace Arch of the American Canadian border which Sam Hill the "Road Builder" conceived and Marshal Joffre of France dedicated in 1922. Wags may amuse themselves with one of the inscriptions which reads "Children of a Common Mother," and the arch itself has a rather too chaste and Grecian air for its setting, yet one cannot but be impressed by the thousands of people who travel here annually to view a stone structure commemorating a century and a half of peace between two countries living as neighbors along a three-thousand-mile boundary without a single fortification its entire length.

Bellingham was started by men in search of lumber in conjunction with power and transportation. Indians guided them to Whatcom, "noise all the time"—the falls from which the county later took its name. Nothing much of note happened to Bellingham until the summer's day in the early fifties when men looked up from their peaceful labors and saw a boat black with people bound for the gold rush on the Fraser River in Canada. Then the town became "The American Gateway to the New Found Treasures of Fraser River" and lots on the old waterfront sold for five or six hundred dollars. Later they couldn't be given away!

The next great boom was the railroads. Bellingham, like many another town, hoped to be selected as the tidewater terminus for the Northern Pacific. It advertised itself as the shortest route to India, if the railroad would use the Skagit Pass. Its hopes were blasted. Visionary dreams of this period were followed by collapse and panic, not only in the Northwest but all over America. Out here in raw new country, however, there was little in the way of resource to which the people could turn. There followed the period when "the shingle reigned supreme. . . . During the long hours of winter darkness nearly every home was transformed into a shingle factory, and the hand-drawn shingles passed almost as currency at a standard value of five dollars a thousand. . . . The forests were ruthlessly slaughtered and one of the richest heritages of Whatcom County was sacrificed below the cost of production to a great extent, but the shingle not only kept the rain from the floor, but the wolf from the door during these hardest of hard times."

Today Bellingham looks toward the development of the rich mineral resources in the Skagit Valley, into which the man-made Ruby Lake of Seattle Light's Skagit project gives transportation. Whatcom County itself is highly mineralized and Bellingham has the largest coal-producing mine in the state. There is chromium and iron ore in the adjacent country as well as lesser known ores like molybdenum. The completion of Ruby Dam has made power available to this district and it confidently expects to boom.

Whether or not it booms it remains a pleasant place for its citizens. The Western Washington College of Education is located here, and the townsfolk have demonstrated the quality of their leisure-time interests by the organizing of music clubs, by the excellence of their public libraries, and by a theater guild of distinction which maintains its own playhouse.

If you approach or leave the islands from the south you will pass through Everett, a made-to-order town. In 1890 a group of Eastern capitalists, including John D. Rockefeller and the firm of Hoyt and Colby, formed a syndicate to establish a manufacturing city which they would plan and control from the outset. Having selected an ideal site where mountain rivers met tidewater, they planned to build a city of lumber mills, planing mills, paper mills, shipyards, and many related industries.

By 1907 Everett was already proudly advertising itself as the City of Smokestacks. It had been made a tidewater terminus for the Great Northern when all the other towns were scrambling for this same prize and "men were prospecting for townsites along the shores of Puget Sound just as they prospected for gold among the granite peaks of the Cascades."

Yet somehow Everett missed the fulfillment of its bright arranged destiny. It is sad but true that many people associate its name with a massacre which took place on its waterfront in 1916 when a boatload of I.W.W.s from Seattle was turned back at the pier with shooting, bloodshed, and drowning. Whatever the provocation on either side it was a dark indictment of a community which—in common with all other American communities—should have offered the rights of free speech and assembly.

Sometimes on rainy wet nights Everett achieves a sombre beauty. Jagged lights from the mills shine in the moving waters and the sky is ominously flushed with the breath of burning piles of waste. On the air there lies the good scent of sawdust, of tidewater and river, and in one's ears there is the clear clean roar of machinery.

CHAPTER II

Spirit Dancing

About eight o'clock on New Year's Eve we took the road just outside the town of La Conner, which leads to the Smoke-house of the Swinomish Indians. Five of us had been invited by a University of Washington anthropologist to watch these Indians welcome in the New Year.

The Swinomish Indians still dance regularly during the months of the winter solstice, unheeded for the most part by the white world, except the neighboring farmers on the flats who hear in the night their distant drums throbbing steadily under the soft slur of the rain.

At the entrance to the reservation we stopped the car to look briefly at an incredibly bad modern totem pole with its aboriginal designs surmounted by the carved wooden face of President Roosevelt, complete with nose glasses—a tribute to a recent housing project for the Indians. The sight of this totem did little to encourage five skeptical whites in the belief that they were about to see "spirit" dances which would awe and amaze them. As soon, however, as we had stopped in the frost-rimed grass outside the long Potlatch house, could hear the insistent blood-beat of the drums striking against the thin walls and see the long slope of roof dark against the pale sky with the sparks flying up from the smoke holes toward the snapping stars, we were all instantly in the mood to believe any promises of strange and beautiful things.

Inside the long building, some one hundred and thirty by forty-five feet, was a congregation of roughly a hundred Indians seated on benches. Three enormous fires of crisscrossed logs burned on the hard dirt floor. We were welcomed by Andrew Williams, an important Swinomish Indian who manages with surpassing aplomb to combine his duties as Shaker minister with such ancient and traditional practices as spirit dancing and healing.

We were given seats near one of the blazing fires, and the wide flat wooden bench behind us was indicated as a place where we might relax or even take a nap if we got tired during those lapses when the spirits leave their victims alone. A little boy came along with rough wooden sticks, two for each of us, with which we were invited to join in beating any rhythm that appealed to us. All the seated Indians held sticks also. We made a small contribution to the gathering and were publicly thanked by Andrew, while all the other Indians present turned faces of utter impassivity toward us.

Soon long, red-stained cedar poles, about twelve feet high, thin and round and hung with plumes of shredded bark, were brought into view. Andrew was going to "run" the poles. We had already been informed that his power to animate these mysterious foci of energy was considered fairly phenomenal in these degenerate times when Indians have lost much of their ancient power over inanimate objects.

Andrew did not hold the poles himself. Two other Indians did; one old, one young. Andrew, with black grease makeup on the lower half of his face, and a red scarf knotted round his forehead, slowly began one of his songs. As "Shaman" or medicine man, he has earned the right to sing a number of spirit songs. When he started to chant, three drummers took up the rhythm, and as he sang and the drummers beat, the clack-clack of the wooden sticks began to sound out sharply in the firelit room and the long, thin red poles began to move inexorably up and down, and then around the fiercely burning fires. The poles moved at times with a terrible force, obviously making the attendant Indians act their will. It was the poles which ran the Indians round the Smokehouse—always counter clockwise. At one point the poles, turning toward the wall, began to beat wildly in the direction of the costumes hanging behind the benches, until a middle-aged woman got up and calmly took down the headdresses and the embroidered shirts. The Indian explanation for this protest on the part of the poles was that their powers did not want the symbols of other powers (expressed in the costumes of other dances) to be displayed during their activity. As soon as the interference from the costumes was removed the poles turned, with the Indians, and began again their swift circuit of the hall.

Anyone who has ever successfully played with Ouija boards or table tipping can picture the movement of these poles. They are apparently filled with some powerful abstract force which shakes and animates them. In the beginning of the "running" the Indian's hand is lightly clasped round his pole, and within that light clasp the pole jumps up and down seemingly under its own power. Not many Indians can hold them and get results. An old man who had a particularly lively pole that night tried, when exhausted, to give it to another Indian, but this Indian was helpless. The pole died. And yet, as soon as the old man's hand was on it, it began again to move. Someone suggested that the Indian who had tried to substitute for the old man might have been under the influence of liquor. If he was he would have no power with the poles.

Poles, similar to the ones we saw that night, and wooden rings and boards in the possession of these Indians are claimed to have powers of divination. It is asserted that in one authenticated case the poles discovered a buried sum of money.

Joyce Wike, the anthropologist who took us to the winter solstice dances, has been accepted as a "white daughter" by the family of Andrew Williams, and it was due to her that we were able to understand the implications of many of the curious and provocative things we witnessed among the dancers that night. The most impressive part of the spectacle was the apparent agony of the Indians' reception of the "spirit." The dancer's pain seemed to begin in the abdomen, to move up through the chest, and finally force its way out of the throat in cries which often began feebly and confusedly and grew in strength and clarity as the drummers caught the rhythm, the sticks took it up, other voices rose in the chant. One old man—apparently not having expected to take part, since he was wearing no makeup—was suddenly seized. Although it seemed really a "seizure" it came on slowly, and he accepted it with dignity, with an air almost of resignation to some painful and inescapable duty. His suffering was obvious and appeared to be acute. Tears ran down his face. His groping hands cupped themselves before his abdomen, before his breast. As the cries began to come out of his throat a woman member of his family stepped up beside him, removed his hat, tied a red scarf around his forehead, and began slowly to help him out of his coat. When he still could not get the song clearly, and the drummers stood waiting and ready, the woman leaned forward as though to catch it and she gave it in a voice of penetrating sweetness. Then the old man rose and with the drummers accompanying him he made the circuit of the room three times, now singing at last fairly easily.

Andrew's daughter danced and in this we were all particularly interested, having heard the story of the reluctance Emma had to overcome to accept the role of a "Smokehouse dancer." To young Emma this was "old-fashioned." But it was in vain that she resisted her hereditary powers. (Spirit dancers run in families.) She finally gave unmistakable evidence to her parents, during a period of sickness and psychic disturbance, that she was to be a singer, for she "breathed" like one. The nature of the sighs of a person still uncertain whether he is meant to be a dancer, or what he is supposed to dance and sing, can often indicate to experienced singers what power it is that seeks to come through him. Even then it is not always easy to get the power into expression.

Thus with Emma Williams, as Wike says in her monograph on these dances: "It was a hard job, for Emma's songs were all 'mixed up.' Andrew, her father, knelt on the floor, singing, to travel with his power down Emma's path of life, down the long straight trail which is her life. He looked at the life through his spirit's eyes and saw what was the matter."

The thing chiefly wrong in the beginning was that one of Emma's powers was being blocked by two other powers—all wanting to sing. Only after much effort on the part of her father and all the other Indians who possessed that same spirit power did she come through. Now when she dances in her cedar headdress, gently, softly, and with faintly agonized cries and disturbed breathings, one can still see something of the convulsive agony of the obligation she has accepted to take part in this ancient ritual; to accept what we would call "possession."

The struggle between the ideology of the contemporary white world and the old tribal world of their ancestors can still be witnessed among these Indians, even among some who do not dance. Near us a woman, who had risen and sung, suddenly sat down, began to weep and cross herself. There were two possible explanations: either she was a Catholic and the momentary yielding to an old primitive drive filled her with guilt and penitence; or as a Shaker—and they also cross themselves—she wished to refer the possession to God, as a manifestation of divine power.

In getting the particular power which forces him to express himself in ancient rituals of song and dance, the singer has usually been visited by some vision, perhaps of a former ancestor who had the same spirit long before and who shows the new dancer how to paint the face, what costume to wear, and so on. Sometimes the power comes through an owl, duck, chipmunk, or some other creature. In Wike's monograph there is, among descriptions of various ways in which neophytes acquire their powers, one line which points the anomaly between the everyday lives of these Indians and such aboriginal vestiges as seeing spirits. An Indian describing the tutelary power who visited him and instructed him said: "I watched it like in a movie."

A few of the costumes worn on New Year's Eve were elaborate and beautiful. One man, who danced and ran more beautifully and fiercely than any other, had a long black shirt with dangling wooden ornaments—small war clubs—sewed to it; a design of a bird painted in white on the front; fur boots, a great headdress of cedar bark concealing almost all his face except his constricted mouth held open with all the teeth exposed. This man leaped high into the air. His elevations could well have been envied by many a trained ballet dancer.

On concluding their circuits of the room the dancers do not at once relax. They sit, making cries, breathing hard, convulsively moving their hands before them. Sometimes the power will again force them to their feet and once more around the floor.

First dancers or new dancers usually "come in" with frenzy, have to be held with a strong band around the waist while dancing to prevent them from injuring themselves or falling into the fire. One woman danced, held thus during the evening, but on inquiry we learned she was not a new dancer; it was only that "her husband came in drunk and that disturbed her mind."

To dance when drunk is considered a desecration. And deeply disturbing as these dances are, even to white onlookers, there is seldom anything orgiastic in them. I was told, however, by a man who stayed until morning at one of the Treaty Dances (ceremonies honoring the treaties made with whites at the time of the Indian wars on Puget Sound) that he saw at the end of his night's vigil a dance so horrible and frightening that he rushed out of the Smokehouse and will, so he says, never return. This was performed by a group, dancing with wide-open mouths and every tooth exposed so that it seemed to him as though they dripped with blood. When he described the dance to Dr. Erna Gunther, head of the Anthropology Department at the University, she said this resembled one of the Cannibal dances of the Northern Indians, although she had never known it to be danced so far south.

Indians come from far away to see the Swinomish dances. We fell into conversation with the family beside us who had come all the way from Wenatchee in eastern Washington across snowbound and icy Stevens Pass to spend New Year's Eve watching this famous dancing. The young Indian woman beside me felt most intense admiration. "Yes," she said, nodding her black bobbed head above the baby asleep in her arms, "they sure got something here, all right!"

CHAPTER III

Olympic Peninsula: Big Trees—
Sacred Elk—Ghost Towns

The Olympic Peninsula is a little world in itself. Although only eighty by one hundred miles in area it has such a wide variety of ways of life, types of people, and range of scenery that there is nothing in America to which it can be compared. Even its climate helps to set it apart for the peninsula enjoys the distinction of possessing the record rainfall for America not many miles from a freak section so dry that irrigation has to be used for farming.

There are four counties on the peninsula: Grays Harbor, containing the largest towns, Aberdeen and Hoquiam; Clallam County with old Port Angeles, named by the early exploring Spaniards and full of history; Jefferson County with Port Townsend and some of the raciest ghosts of any Northwest community; Mason County with little bustling Shelton which successfully weathered the change from big timber operations to pulp mills. Away from these towns, along the lakes and rivers and mountain trails, the forest paths, the sheltered bays, the open beaches, lies one of the most complete recreation areas in the country. It is this recreation area which has been so much in the newspapers of late, due to the establishment of the Olympic National Park of 898,000 acres and the resultant bitterness and animosity toward the federal government among certain groups of Northwest citizens.

Even though the fight is seemingly lost for these people, maps of the peninsula are still thrust under even the most indifferent nose, and before long the nose isn't quite so indifferent. The man with the maps is too much in earnest and too sincere and too tired. After a little conversation you hear yourself saying, "But it's ridiculous!" To which the man replies roughly as follows: "Sure it's ridiculous! It's crazy! But it's done! We're done! Remember the Roosevelt elk, sister! Shed a tear! Sure, they're increasing so fast that there should be a bounty on them, but they're Wildlife, remember, and that makes them more important than the future of some 104,000 citizens whose lives are going to be affected by what we aren't afraid to come right out and call an arbitrary, wasteful program in the name of conservation."

If any hexing ever goes on among peninsula folk one of the victims will certainly be Rosalie Edge, chairman of a National Conservation Committee whose emotional pamphlets on the land which was about to be snatched from innocent unborn generations by wicked lumber barons and wasteful unprogressive local citizens helped put over the Park program. Peninsula people like to point out that museums in towns like Newark, New Jersey, displayed this propaganda all unwitting as to its real meaning to the folk in the part of the country where that land lies. They describe such highlights of Rosalie Edge's local visit as a "fake faint she pulled at the sight of one of those Beautiful Forest Giants being dragged past on a truck—probably some snaggle-topped old tree well past its prime." They like to ask you with sardonic emphasis if you've read her little pamphlet, *Man's Friend: The Crow*. "Never shoot such a gentle benefactor!" And they laugh wryly as they tell you that anyone who knows the peninsula knows that the Roosevelt elk which will soon be "as sacred as the cow in India" are becoming a pest. In the winter of 1941 a band of elk actually held up traffic on the Aberdeen-Raymond highway (U.S. 101). Also these elk, which have been pictured as being happiest in the forest primeval, do not enjoy food-gathering there anywhere near as much as in a good piece of logged-off land "where they can see what they're getting." Naturalists have found that a certain variety of maple—not found in dense woods—attracts elk "like candy attracts children." In the *Olympic Peninsula Answer to the Wallgren Bill* the writers contend that there is, in certain districts, overgrazing on the part of these elk, constituting a serious food hazard to the rest of the game population. Then, just to thoroughly confuse all issues except the major one that most of the arguments for the establishment of this big park are foolish, you are told that Ignar Olson the Quinault guide and packer says that predatory animals will now have a better chance to destroy the elk, as the park area in which "varmints" like cougars are safe is thus enormously increased.

As to the matter of "nature's cycle" in the forests—a phrase beloved of ardent conservationists, referring to new trees growing out of the remains of prostrate fallen ones—in hearing it discussed pro and con one comes inevitably to the conclusion that the facts about the "natural cycle" of timber growth are extremely hard to get at. The experts row among themselves and there are many who contend (with pictures to back them up) that out of a fallen Douglas fir giant there will grow—not another Douglas fir—but a hemlock; which, if true, upsets quite a propaganda applecart. It is because hemlock will seed in shade where firs will not, and the "Clear Cut" adherents hold that since fir will not propagate in the forest shade, the only way to get a good stand of young firs is to cut them clean so that an even age stand can grow up.

People in newspaper rooms and Chamber of Commerce offices offer to show you government bulletins with hemlocks growing out of a fallen fir. ("Not that the government knows the difference!") They'll tell you that fir will reseed itself on burned-off land. Trees, they assert, when they reach their prime, die like humans, and if they're taken out just before they begin to die they let other firs come up; but if they get too crowded then hemlocks, *not firs*, appear. And they all say, sure there used to be waste in logging operations and there probably still is some, but the Forestry Department and the lumber companies were getting along fine; they had a good work cycle under way which was conserving big trees, preserving "playgrounds"; and also freeing a certain percentage of timber for industrial uses.

They end bitterly: "States haven't any rights left. The government's got all the money. . . . Any squawk is supposed to come from the Big Interests, when actually it's the little fellows who are feeling the pinch. But the people won't fight. They don't know what's what anymore."

Sober citizens on the peninsula point out that the four counties of Washington affected by this bill stand to lose $85,000 annually for school and road funds from curtailment of the lumber industries. No possible tourist industry can ever compensate for such a loss—particularly since the season is estimated at a two months' maximum, due to excessive rainfall during the greater part of the year; a rainfall which has created this green forest jungle, through which old-timers find it very amusing to picture happy Easterners lazily wandering, communing with nature.

The most vigorous and dramatic protest on the peninsula came from Mr. John Huelsdonk and some of his neighbors on the Queets and Hoh Rivers. Mr. Huelsdonk, "The Iron Man of the Hoh," walked into this country years ago carrying a cookstove on his back, and he starved and sweated and endured loneliness because of his love for this land. Now a stroke of Mr. Ickes's pen has dispossessed his children along with a great many other folk—and Huelsdonk made some banners and led a contingent of protesters to Olympia to see the governor. They went carrying such signs as, "Stalin Took Finland, Hitler Took Poland, Don't Let Ickes Take Our Homes Away from Us."

There are many people who feel that the final solution of the Olympic Peninsula controversy—a solution which set aside the mature judgments of regional conservationists—is a threat. How, they ask, can states in the Pacific Northwest continue their present living standards, or take care of the new influx from the drought area, if more and more sections of land are withdrawn from commercial development? What's to stop this drive for parks? Already a campaign for setting aside a vast area in the Cascades is under way. Although the amount of timber lost in this "locking up" of land for posterity can be estimated, who knows—they say—what potential mineral wealth will remain unused, undiscovered, now that this acreage has become permanently a national park and thus untouchable except by act of Congress?

Local Grays Harbor people remember the days when the big log boats sailed out of their harbors "with logs piled so high the skipper couldn't see over the tops of 'em—loaded with 'Jap squares' bound across the Pacific; coming back in time—after Japanese cheap labor had had a crack at it—as sandalwood boxes or something fancy—just good old Washington cedar."

Aberdeen's most famous citizen, to the world at large, is a sea captain. This is Captain "Matt" Peasley, whom Peter B. Kyne has used as the hero of his Cappy Ricks series. Captain Peasley's colorful speech and famous yarns of the days when he sailed the *Vigilant*—built right in local yards—to every great world port are a constant source of local pride and entertainment.

The book *Marching Marching* which won the *New Masses* prize for the best proletarian novel of 1935 had an Aberdeen setting. It was written by Clara Weatherwax from "The Hill" where the first families live. If it made a local stir, the stir has been forgotten. Ideologists among the working class in Aberdeen are apt to take less interest in literary arabesques than in techniques of direct action; as when the Finns rose and destroyed the Communists' Hall after Russia marched into Finland in the winter of 1939. The Hill People will tell you that Clara's book didn't cause any stir at all because everybody knew that she just made it up out of her head; she'd never seen any of the people she described. Not but what there were people like that around the waterfront—or any waterfront for that matter—but Clara Weatherwax with her face like a valentine and her neatly parted hair never saw any of them or heard any of those words she used either, and so people were just amused and thought she was pretty smart to fool Easterners that way, and collect a prize so easily. Of course, to be sure, she knew the technicalities of mill and lumber operations; raised right in the middle of it how could she help it? But the idea of the "buzz of sawmills" sounding in her ears from birth on—as the *New Masses* blurb asserted—well, that was just a source of hearty laughter among family friends.

If you go to the Olympic Peninsula for a brief holiday you'll have a choice to make. If you want the average tourist's experiences then you'll keep along the famous Olympic Loop trip and treat yourself to highly advertised mattresses and excellent food at places like Lake Crescent or the Olympic Hot Springs. If you're in search of something less stereotyped and more rigorous, abandon as soon as possible the paved highways, and almost at once you're safe from crowds. When you look at the map of this extreme northwestern part of the state of Washington you'll know why. It's wild land; land of green jungle, snowpeak, and lonely waterways. In all directions lie those collections of bumps and rays which indicate mountains on maps—an almost circular group whose center is Mt. Olympus: Diamond, Octopus, Trinity, Constance, The Brothers, the peaks Sugar Loaf and Windfall—there are some fifty of them within a narrow radius.

The Indian names on the peninsula seem richer in soft running sounds than almost anywhere else in the state. Dosewallips, Quillayute, Duckabush, Lilliwaup. One is astonished when Sappho turns up, cool and enigmatic at the turn the road makes coastward; or something as prosaic as Forks, where in the midst of wilderness one does not expect to find—and finds—an excellent drugstore and good thick malted milks. Clallam County once had the town of Psyche also, but the baffled natives finally converted it to Pysht, which it remains on the maps.

Port Angeles is a little town with a good feeling of aliveness about its streets. It has an old and honorable history. The Spanish in the late eighteenth century gave it its name because of the beauty of the sunsets—so says legend—and they are still unsurpassed here.

Port Angeles claims to be the only town in America that was once also a "national city"—the other being Washington, D. C. These are the only two cities in America where the national government actually bought land and set it aside to make a city. During the Civil War a man named Victor Smith came out to act as special agent of the Treasury Department and Collector of Customs (in those days of smuggling from Canada this was quite an important job); and Smith secured the passage of an act in Congress which would set aside the public land on which Port Angeles was located, to be used for the purpose of creating a city, sales from these land lots to be turned over to the government. So filled with delight over Port Angeles was he, that he moved the customs house bodily from Port Townsend, although the citizens of the latter place resisted manfully, secreted the keys and refused to hand them over, only giving in when the guns of a cutter were trained on their community. These rebels lived to see the customs house returned to them after a flood in Port Angeles had carried the building out to sea, where Indians boarded it, looted it, and set the records afloat. Victor Smith involved himself, in a short space of time, in curious and picturesque difficulties so that he was recalled by Lincoln; an act which created a breach between the president and his secretary of the treasury, Mr. Salmon P. Chase, who was Mr. Smith's good friend.

It's not far from Port Angeles to the unbeaten paths of the Peninsula, lonely camp spots where you can sit in solitude on a beautiful shore, look off to a distant mountain, hear no noise but a stream or the tide, look above the driftwood fire to where the Big Dipper slides down the sky almost within reach.

There are any number of peaks within easy distance which you can climb to look on glaciers; on deep timbered gorges; upland meadows where deer and elk feed; off westward to Cape Flattery thrusting into the roaring blue waters; east to the winding channels of Puget Sound, to Mt. Baker and Mt. Rainier.

Away from the paved roads, where gas pumps are only part of the grocery store at the corner of a dusty road, you find yourself in country with plenty of history but very few traces left to observe. All the way down to Lake Ozette and back you're apt not to see a soul. Even the Indian reservation is deserted. The last member of the tribe has joined the Makahs at Neah Bay. This "last of the Ozettes" is Jim Hunter. Mr. Hunter says that the extermination of the Ozettes illustrates what often happens to the innocent bystander, for the peaceful Ozettes were on the main line of travel for those bitter enemies the Quillayutes and the Makahs, and en route to a raid either tribe would stop off and get itself nicely whipped up for murder and plunder by a little practice on the Ozettes. Finally the Ozettes got tired of it and when a squall drove some raiding Quillayutes back into Ozette Bay, the Ozettes set them up to a great feast and, when they were properly drowsy with food and fire-heat, fell on the sleeping raiders and murdered them all. Their bodies were laid on the beach disemboweled, their heads were stuck on tall poles, which stood for years on the beach as a silent warning to all comers.

Jim Hunter also remembers the whale killings at Neah Bay which have lasted well down into the present. The Indians hunted the great sea monster in their canoes and it was a highly dangerous procedure. After a whale was sighted the canoe was brought within six feet of the mammal so that the harpooner could thrust in his lance. Then the men at the paddles carried the canoe out of reach of the fiercely lashing tail and prepared for the wild rush toward the open sea, dragged by the harpoon rope. Whenever the whale rose to spout, more harpoons, equipped with balloon-like bladders, were thrown into the animal's body to prevent its continued diving. There was no way to kill the great creature except slowly by hundreds of darts and even the Indians sensed the cruelty of this killing and can still remember that "its cries and moans of pain were almost like those of an agonized human being."

The town of Neah Bay, farthest out-thrust of the American continent, hasn't done anything fancy to lure the tourists—nor is it likely to—yet its past is far from commonplace. It was in 1790 that Spanish explorers founded the settlement of Nunez Gaona and lived here until 1800, when the Indians rose and massacred almost the entire settlement. Some few survived, it is said, and lived on as slaves, accounting for a fancied resemblance to the high-featured aquilinity of Castilian cavaliers seen to this day in certain Indian faces. The old adobe bricks from the Spanish buildings are still findable, and not many years ago it was reported that an old wooden crucifix, supposedly clasped in the hands of the priest who died at his church door, was found in a rubble of stone and dust.

Neah Bay Indians were fierce once, and they and the Clallams fought many a bloody fight. Today they seem peaceful enough. Their boats ride lazily at anchor in the half-moon bay. All about their village lies an untouched wild and lonely land of great beauty; small coves of hard-packed white sand with good loot of strange shells; great rocks flung out into the sea on which one may walk when the tide retreats. Camping in the darkness on the point, one can sometimes see a moving band of lights far out on the water. This will be a boat bound the shortest way to the Orient. Then one remembers why the Spanish came to this unlikely and forbidding shore and tried to attune their warm natures to a life of rigor and deprivation.

There is a wonderful place to camp on a completely deserted bay called Port Crescent. The beach is a semicircle of white sand, a mile long, lined with bleached logs from some ancient "blow." When the tide is out there lie revealed a few posts from what was once a dock, for Port Crescent gave promise of being a city some forty years ago. Along the shore, among the groves of giant cedar with their outswept limbs touching the earth, are sites for homes where homes were never built. Here are dozens of "view lots" and hidden retreats where the trees shut out everything but the sky, and wild roses grow to tree height. On the out-thrusts of land at either end of the long curve of white beach curlews and gulls sit all day, and beds of kelp swing hypnotically in the sea wash. This, one thinks, is the perfect place for a resort. Pray Heaven no one ever makes one here!

Just around the western headland from Port Crescent there's another beach, Agate, utterly different in character, fierce and wild, with no sand and a shelving slope covered with agates, jasper, and many strange stones. There are gnarled trees, and bright lichen gardens underfoot among them; some tiny cabins for rent and polished stones for sale. Around these two beaches are scattered a few old homesteads, isolated a great part of the year when the winter rains begin.

The Olympic Peninsula is noted for its seafood. The famous Dungeness hard-shelled crabs come from a beach where the Clallams in 1862 succeeded in massacring a band of fierce Haidas from the North who were out on a commercial trip with their families and had no thought of war in their minds. It is on the Olympic Peninsula also that the wild oysters grow so abundantly. You can go down with a sack at Waketickeh Creek, for instance, and pick them up as fast as you can stoop for them, where they lie among the stones they so much resemble. On the peninsula are also great herds of deer and elk; and driving over the Elwah River at salmon-running time you see the fish moving upstream by the hundreds. Once we saw giant dogfish, in pursuit of the salmon, landlocked by a shrinking river and churning fiercely many feet below us along the banks.

It's hard to do justice to the Olympic Peninsula. It's too big, too beautiful! You can know it all your life and still not finish with exploring it. It offers all possible comforts and amenities in such inns as the one at Lake Quinault and it offers every kind of mountain-climbing thrill and woodman's discipline. You can shoot the Quinault River in an Indian canoe and fish on gentle Lake Sutherland. The Indians are said to have called this lake Naketa after a beautiful Indian maiden for whose sake the gods created the lake when she was torn to death in the forests by a wild beast. "The birds appear above it every autumn and call 'Naketa, Naketa' and in answer a gentle ripple passes over the water."

The waters that wash the northern boundary of the peninsula are called the Strait of Juan de Fuca—a name going back to a Greek sailor of the sixteenth century who had taken a Spanish name while in service to Spain. Juan de Fuca is considered by many to be a wholly legendary character and by others to be merely a shameless liar who claimed he sailed through this stretch of water in 1592. He described the country pretty accurately but put off latter-day historians by a bit of careless fiction to the effect that "the land is very fruitful and rich in gold, silver, pearls, and other things like Nova Spania."

Along the indentations of the peninsula's winding coastline, there are plenty of ghost towns and old homesteads sinking into the earth, poignant reminders of high hopes and big plans, financial skulduggery, simple stupidity, exhausted resources. The ghost towns all have a similar look. The few houses still occupied have bare windows usually filled with giant plants. This one often notices: how when there is no life left in a house, no young blood, only an old woman with her recollections and an ailing husband, then the geraniums become gigantic, the begonias are fabulous, the hen-and-chicken plants multiply with indecent haste. And so it is also with the wild blackberry bushes in these abandoned Northwest towns. They grow like trees, and one often sees an old ladder propped up against them. They seem to feed monstrously on some imponderable death.

Yet in deserted Irondale there were signs of new life, a family with a little store—a few pitiful candy bars and a gasoline pump; a boy with a fresh bright young face and the flat sandy voice of the midwestern prairies. People from the drought area, we suspected, but we did not ask, for this is often embarrassing, even to children. Already they know the stigma of being a "migrant." This little boy looked happy enough, and indeed it must have been a happy place for a child, with the beach, the salt water, the hillslopes and hilltops, valleys and streams, all within easy reach of his wanderings. But what of the year ahead, and the one after that, when they've found that few people detour like ourselves to look at old ironworks; when the gas pump stands idle for days on end?

There are other towns around here, not quite so forgotten as Irondale but sliding slowly downhill. There's Port Ludlow, where the old company houses wear a dim New England air in their direct clean line; where the great docks now lie empty, the streets are deserted, and the big hotel with its yard full of holly, oak, and maple has its doors locked, its windows shuttered; the high-ceilinged rooms which have seen so much of good living will probably never be opened again.

Port Townsend was lively once also, yet now it is merely the place from which one takes a ferry to the islands. If you're early, or the ferry is late, you can climb up on the bluff above the town and see the old streets somewhat as they used to look in the days when any town might still become the Queen of the Sound, and Port Townsend had the highest hopes of any. In 1890— when railroads were again inflating the ambitions of Northwest communities—real estate transfers filed for record in Port Townsend reached the amazing sum of $4,595,695.93. A town grew up which could have easily taken care of a population of twenty thousand. Then came the collapse!

A nautical friend of mine likes to moon over the magnificent harbor, and try to picture it as it must have looked in the 1890s during the depression, when shipowners laid up their ships by the hundreds and Port Townsend had a bone yard of handsome square riggers from all over the world. The harbormaster entertained grave fears that the bay was "shoaling badly by reason of the large number of tin cans and beef bones the various ships' cooks were heaving overboard."

A descendant of a pioneer Port Townsend family, Mr. J. G. McCurdy, has written *By Juan de Fuca's Strait*, describing the boom days of this community when it was a hangout for every kind of adventurer and desperado to be found on the waterfronts in rich new country. The sober citizens, living high on the hill, used to lie in their beds and hear tinkling music from old pianos and accordions on the waterfront entertaining the roisterers far into the night at The Whalesmens Arms, or the Dog Corner. When some of the old saloons were torn down, many were found to have trap doors which opened onto the beach, well above high-tide mark; a handy way of getting rid of troublesome fellows, or perhaps of dropping them into the arms of men seeking a cargo of sailors in a hurry, without being particular how they got them. Not only was Port Townsend a refuge for smugglers bringing in opium, whiskey, wool, and Chinamen, it was also a popular rendezvous for the strong-armed ruffians who made a living by shanghaiing men for sailing ships. One of the most prodigious of these "runners" was a man by the name of Sunderstrand. He finally got his comeuppance when a sailor he had beaten—having nursed his grudge all the way out to Australia and back—walked into a sailors' boardinghouse in Port Townsend one night and proceeded to sever Sunderstrand's neck and arm muscles with a sheath-knife. Sunderstrand did not die but he was forced to take up the less demanding occupation of fishing for a living.

Mr. McCurdy's book has descriptions of other legendary evil characters of the period when shipping reigned supreme. Men like "San Juan Tripp" distinguished themselves by bloody shooting affrays in the street. Poker Jack Quayle when already wounded thrust his clasp knife some seventeen times into the prostrate body of a former friend. Both were acquitted. Pure case of mutual self-defense! (There was only one hanging in Port Townsend, but "practically the whole town, including many children assembled to witness it.") Gentleman Harry Sutton, a Bostonian of good family (there were a notable number of Bostonian gentlemen fallen into evil habits in the early days in the Far West) who was well educated "and almost effeminate in manner" began his Port Townsend residence as the editor of a newspaper but degenerated by slow degrees until he was running the Blue Light saloon. And it was there that he murdered a former friend before witnesses, and though handsomely imprisoned with carpets, good books, and an easy chair, he made his escape by water one dark night and was never seen again.

Time and circumstances have mellowed Port Townsend. One might almost say, embalmed it. In addition to its racy lore it has some rather pleasant relics of a less desperate past. In a quiet street there stands the Tree of

Heaven, gift of the Emperor of China, sent from Peking as one of a pair intended for the citizens of San Francisco who had royally entertained one of the Emperor's sons when he was on a mission in the sixties. The ship bearing the trees was blown off her course and finally limped into Port Townsend in bad condition. So courteously was the crew treated that the captain took it upon himself to present the town with one of the sacred trees.

On the capitals of the Federal Building, gazing out to sea, are the faces of the Indian Duke of York, his wife Queen Victoria, and other red notables—placed there by suggestion of the pioneers. The streets of Port Townsend knew intimately the picturesque Duke in his suit of blue blanket cloth, trimmed with stripes of red from an old petticoat, which his dutiful women had designed and made for him. This chief stood by the whites during the Indian uprisings on the Sound and most old-timers do not feel that he deserved Theodore Winthrop's chastisement which led the young New Englander to write home proudly to Massachusetts, "Yes, I have kicked a king."

In the lobby of the Hotel Central you may still see a large stuffed cougar which stood for many years in the front window of a paint and wallpaper store across from a Chinese shop. At one time a little Chinese boy lay sick in an upstairs room and a delegation of Celestials visited the cougar's owner to ask him if he would mind turning the stuffed animal to face in the opposite direction since they felt that the creature was casting an evil spell on the sick child. The owner complied and the child recovered.

There were a good many Chinese in Port Townsend at one time. Chinese New Year was a great occasion and it is pleasant to think of them flying their bright disc-shaped kites against this beautiful skyline with the white mountains shining across the strait.

Going to or from Port Townsend you may go by way of Port Gamble and look upon a charming little village which has managed to retain its quaint New England air through many a deflation and many a boom. Laid out by men from Maine in 1853 it was once an important Puget Sound city. History books list the Battle of Port Gamble, which took place during the Indian Wars of the 1850s; and although only twenty-seven of the Northern Indians involved were killed and twenty-one wounded, it was a strategic turning point, for it discouraged these fierce Northern tribes from joining the Sound hostiles.

On a summer's afternoon Port Gamble dozes charmingly inside the walls of its sedate old houses; its chaste white church spire points heavenward, and the lulling snore of a distant mill sounds as lazy as a bee's hum. Yet the residence part of the village probably looked just this innocent and aloof when waterfront activities were at their most glamorous and sordid; when a shanghaiing dentist put up a large sign which warned all sailors, "Remember there are no dentists at sea! Don't start on a long voyage with bad teeth." During a promised "free examination," a timely administration of ether made it easy to add the victim to some ship's list.

CHAPTER IV

Capital Towns

OLYMPIA

Capital towns are strangely restless and diffused communities. Perhaps they seem without core because every four years there flows through them a wholly new citizenry brought in by changes of administration. Yet hidden and almost lost in the towns of Olympia and Salem there may still be found fragments of quite another kind of life.

Olympia was for many years the leading social community on the Sound. Eminent visitors came here rather than to such rough unlettered upstarts as Seattle. Personal recollections of those early days evoke a picture of a life so gentle, cultivated, and almost idyllic that one likes to linger over its description. There were local musicales, charades, minstrel shows, and elaborate tableaux setting forth such themes as "The Presentation of the Jewels from Rebecca to Rowena."

Every house of quality had a Chinaman famous for his cooking; and the cake boxes and the cooky jars were always full, waiting for guests. In summer, life centered on the beautiful little bay called Budd's Inlet—the same delightful body of water on which the homesick first governor's wife used to drift in her canoe listening to the Flatheads singing the chants of the Catholic church in the old mission at Priest Point. A descendant of one of those first Olympia families has left in the book *Tillicum Tales* a description of scenes on this bay in the long northern twilights from May to September:

"It was an enrapturing sight on a summer's evening, dotted with boats from the landing to the falls at Tumwater, with sailboats in the distance, with one of our gorgeous sunsets casting a glow over the water, and the sound of music greeting the ear. . . . Immediately after dinner young and old strolled down to the landing and embarked. Many families owned a boat and it was the custom for the entire family to go out for a 'row on the bay'; the rowing was often drifting, the boats keeping near each other, while we sang whenever we got together on the water, around a camp fire, or in a home."

The first newspaper in the territory, the *Columbian*, was published here; the first women's club was established in this little town and important women visitors like Julia Ward Howe came to speak. Mrs. Howe found the place so enchanting that she even bought a tract of land near Tumwater, planning to come back there and spend her declining years.

Tumwater, near Olympia, was the oldest American settlement on Puget Sound; founded by Michael Simmons who decided to come into this country in spite of the threat that England would eventually own all the northern lands of what was then called Oregon Territory. Tumwater Falls leaped and fell down a lovely wild glen, well into the turn of the century; but now the town looks as commonplace as any other and is chiefly visited because of the modern brewery which the Schmidt family built; and which still uses the pre-Repeal slogan of this beverage, "It's the Water."

Mr. George Blankenship can tell you about the "bad Indian" Yelm Jim, whom his father, as sheriff, used to shackle heavily and bring out to the house to watch the baby when the mother had to be away. He remembers about Old Betsy, the good Indian. (Every town and most families had a pet Indian; Seattle, for instance, had the "Princess" Angeline, daughter of the chief for whom the town was named, who sold Indian baskets on the sidewalks of Second Avenue and is now reproduced in dolls for tourists.) Mr. Blankenship remembers also Betsy's bad daughter, Julia, who lived scandalously with a white man named Oyster Jack; believed to have taken her on because he thought she knew of a grave with gold and stones buried along with the corpse. Julia, when drunk, liked nothing better than to join the Salvation Army as it came down the street on a Saturday night past the saloons full of loggers. The memory of her piercing yells to the accompaniment of the genteel boom of drum and tinkle of tambourine have been preserved in a local sea captain's poem:

> *Hear the drumbeats with the yells—louder yells;*
> *What a world of sentiment their melody now tells.*
> *What a pounding, pounding, pounding*
> *On the quiet hour of night*
> *While the stars that oversprinkle*
> *All the heavens seem to twinkle*
> *While a-looking at the sight.*
> *Keeping time, time, time*
> *In a sort of runic rhyme*
> *To the pulsatory beating that so musically wells*
> *From the yells, yells, yells, yells, yells*
> *From the sounding and the pounding as she yells.*

When you go back at all into pioneer reminiscences of a town like Olympia, you can't escape "poetry." Writing it was once a pastime. One of the poems that almost anyone on Puget Sound could recite in the early days is *The Old Settler* by Judge Francis Henry which is always read at pioneer meetings:

> *For one who gets riches by mining,*
> *Perceiving that hundreds grow poor,*
> *I made up my mind to try farming—*
> *The only pursuit that is sure.*
>
> *So rolling my grub in my blankets,*
> *I left all my tools on the ground,*

And started one morning to shank it,
For a country they called Puget Sound.

Arriving flat broke in mid-winter
I found it enveloped in fog,
And covered all over with timber
Thick as hair on the back of a dog.
I took up a claim in the forest,
And sat myself down to hard toil;
For two years I chopped and I niggered,
But I never got down to the soil.

I tried to get out of the country,
But poverty forced me to stay
Until I became an Old Settler
Then nothing could drive me away.

And now that I'm used to the climate,
I think that if man ever found
A spot to live easy and happy,
That Eden is on Puget Sound.

No longer the slave of ambition,
I laugh at the world and its shams
As I think of my pleasant condition,
Surrounded by acres of clams.

Those last four lines are quoted as often as the famous lines of Judge Cushman of Tacoma who asserted that during hard times the people of Puget Sound relied so exclusively on the products of the sea—particularly the many varieties of clams—that "their stomachs rose and fell with the tides."

All this sort of life seems very remote, peaceful, and curiously rich when one listens to it being recalled by an old man with a lively memory and a merry twinkle. Now when Mr. Blankenship walks on Olympia streets the familiar faces are ever more scarce. The scurrying people from the six imposing semi-Greek buildings which house this growing state's manifold activities do not know who he is any more than they recognize the spry old lady waiting on a corner for the bus to Cloverfield Farm as the last surviving child of the first governor of the Territory—Kate Stevens Bates.

This delightful little old lady, with her roots deep in New England (one of her father's ancestors was a founder of Andover, Massachusetts, and her mother was a Hazard from Newport) lives in the farmhouse of her famous brother, Hazard. She likes to talk of Hazard who distinguished himself in a variety of ways: by going as a lad of twelve alone with an interpreter to make a treaty with the Gros Ventre Indians; by being the first to climb Mt. Rainier; by writing a complete life of his father, General Isaac Stevens, who lost his life at Chantilly after making his mark in the new Northwest.

Mrs. Bates remembers very keenly the day on which she learned that the state administration, under Governor Hartley, was tearing down the first home of the Stevens family in Olympia. She tried ineffectively to save it; feeling—what many belatedly history-conscious people now feel—that it was an important historical landmark. This state also tore down the old building of good simple lines in which the first legislature convened. People in power at one time in Washington had little patience with symbols of the past.

Mr. George Talcott, who designed the seal of the state in 1889, is still running a local jewelry store. His story of how the state seal was made sheds light on the quality of happenstance that has undoubtedly surrounded many similar historic moments. The committee on seals sent in something pretty complicated in the way of a design, showing the port of Tacoma, sheep in the valley at the foot of Mt. Rainier, the mountain itself, and some wheat fields. The Talcott boys hadn't had much experience in cutting state seals but one of them quickwittedly suggested that the growth of the state might outmode this particular picture. (After all, there were some other ports!) With the base of an ink well and a silver dollar, Grant Talcott drew two circles, printed between them the words, *The Seal of the State of Washington, 1889,* licked a postage stamp and placed it in the middle with the remark, "That represents the bust of George Washington." The design was accepted. Grant did the lettering and George the embossing of the picture. It was a rush order and George had a sick headache. He thinks a better job could have been done under more "normal conditions." The picture they used for Washington himself was copied boldly from an advertisement for Dr. Janes' Cure for Coughs and Colds.

SALEM

Salem, Oregon, has a family. That family is the Bush family. Salem and the Bushes made a duo that could not be split apart in the minds of Oregonians of another day. There are facts about the Bushes and their ways that shed light on a kind of spirit which once flourished in certain Oregon communities. Miss Sally Bush kept forty woodland acres intact, not far from the state capital, where she could raise the flowers to decorate her brother's famous bank, and pasture her cows as Mrs. H. W. Corbett pastured hers in Portland.

When in the spring of 1940, at the age of eighty-three, Asahel Bush II retired from active business, selling, for a reputed $1,200,000, the bank his father founded some seventy-odd years before, the magazine *Time* dealt at length with the Bushes under the heading "Oregon's J. P. Morgan sells out." This Asahel II was the son. Asahel I left the state of Massachusetts in 1850 at the age of twenty-six, bound for the Pacific coast. He was already an attorney and a printer and he had the presence of mind to take with him a printing press on that 15,000-mile trip round the Horn and up the roaring western coast. Asahel founded the *Oregon Statesman* in Oregon City, but moved it to Salem in 1853 when that town became the capital. From the beginning the paper was famed for the spirited verbal swordplay of its owner and editor. Mr. Bush was, indeed, a master at a kind of flamboyant vituperation which came to be known as The Oregon Style. Men took their politics hard in those years. "Lickspittle and toadies of official whiggery" might be taken as a fairly mild sample of Mr. Bush's forthright style of attack.

By 1862 in spite of, or because of, his tongue, Mr. Bush was rich enough to retire from the publishing business. At the age of forty-four, under the persuasive urging of William Sargent Ladd, the Portland banker, he emerged from retirement to found the banking firm of Ladd and Bush. The bank then became his life. Old Salemites can tell you (among their more kindly tales of him) how he looked up from his deathbed at the age of eighty-nine to ask, "Is everything all right?" Receiving an affirmative reply he admonished, "Keep it so," and died. Asahel II never forgot his father's last injunction. For years he is said to have taken over delinquent loans himself rather than have them appear as dark spots on the bank's records. Within recent years the bank published *The Ladd and Bush Quarterly* which must certainly be considered unique among the publications of banking institutions. It contained a smattering of local historical matter; memories of days when Oregon winters were cold and local blades skated on the slough with their beards blowing back in the wind; such literary gems as a poem entitled *Mystical River* dedicated by a father to his daughter on her eighteenth birthday—"Adieu! Adieu, a last goodby, The myrtle groves of girlhood sigh"; and a general miscellany of fact and fancy with such well-placed reminders as:

"With direct connections in practically every banking point throughout the Willamette Valley we have excellent facilities to collect your out of town items with exceptional dispatch."

When the New Deal went off the gold standard, Asahel II astonished the U. S. Treasury by turning in $350,000 in gold. An arch-individualist, he refused to close his bank during the enforced 1933 bank holiday. He went into the street himself to urge any frightened people to come and collect their money if they wanted to. When, under pressure from federal officials, he had to close the front door he left the side door open anyway.

This is the kind of arrogant and somewhat pernickety individualism that Oregon produced in the old days, along with a cooperative community effort that seems almost a contradiction. General Nesmith lost the Senatorship in the seventies because he wouldn't interrupt a poker game to come up to the Democratic caucus at the Statehouse and the boys who were not in the game took this unkindly. Men were admired and even loved for their ability to deal deadly thrusts in that "editorial duello" of the Oregon Style which never under any circumstances led to libel, but only to a sharpened attack.

Old Mr. Bush the first was admired for the style of his hat which he wore for forty years without change, "always new and becoming, totally unlike that ever worn by any other man, since no other man has been able to discover where it is obtained." Perhaps his hats and his tall standing collars of the post-Civil-War style came from a special stock in some New England town. Even Salem's pet Indian, old Quinaby, asserted his independence by dying from the effects of gluttony after a Christmas feast to which white friends had invited him. Quinaby was the last picturesque survivor of one of the local Indian tribes which "the great sickness" wiped out by thousands in the nineteenth century.

Salem is the home of the oldest university west of the Rocky Mountains, Willamette University, originally called The Oregon Institute and founded as early as 1844. Before there were roads or houses or boats for the rivers or guns to fight the Indians the settlers had established an institution of higher learning.

Most of the early settlers in the valleys of the Willamette and the Tualatin and among the Waldo Hills were a proud and self-respecting lot, with high and visionary ideals reflected in the names they chose for their towns— Philomath, Lebanon, Sublimity, Bethany. They considered themselves far superior to the settlers of California who "settled down there because they couldn't settle up where they came from." Nonetheless during the forties the gold rush to the south lured many away from the hard life of pioneer farming. A few returned, however, bringing back their riches to help build up such towns as Salem.

Salem was in the beginning a missionary community. It was founded by Jason Lee who came out from New England in 1834 to act as Methodist missionary to the Flatheads. The town was given its present name by these early men of God who chose a Biblical name similar in meaning to the Indian name for the place, Chemeketa, or Place of Rest. The old home of Jason Lee still stands and the site of the Jason Lee saw- and grist-mill is marked for people with a bent for history. This was the first structure to be built in the settlement. The machinery for it came round the Horn, up the coast to Fort Vancouver, and then upriver to Salem in Chinook canoes.

Jason Lee, whose knowledge of grist-mills was presumably less than his knowledge of the Old Testament, at first set the millstones incorrectly and the mill spat out the wheat instead of grinding it.

Salem was in 1861 the scene of a disastrous flood when the Willamette, swollen by rains of unusual violence, came roaring over the town, setting back its growth for almost ten years. Today Salem is a charming town with tree-shaded streets and a group of new state buildings dominated by a capitol which has dared to desert Greek eclecticism for a style at least approximating the "modern." In the main foyer are murals depicting the early highlights of Oregon history: Captain Gray landing on the Columbia; Dr. John McLoughlin welcoming settlers at Fort Vancouver; the Lewis and Clark Expedition stopping among the Indians at Celilo Falls; and a typical wagon train of 1843. Near the capitol stands the handsome library building, a credit to a state which (with certain notable and painful lapses) has on the whole, from the beginning, held before its people high ideals of education and self-government.

CHAPTER V

River of the West

··

Recently, in speaking of the Grand Coulee Dam, a man in Spokane said with a note of almost angry triumph in his voice, "Well, at last, the state of Washington seems to be able to show the world that Oregon isn't the sole owner of the Columbia."

Oregonians are inclined to assume calmly that the mighty River of the West, which forms the boundary between the two states, is exclusively an Oregon landmark. The identification of this state with the river arises from the facts of early history. Even before it became the great artery of life in this distant territory, it was the river of mystery, the "Oregan" or the "Oregon," rising in unnamed mountains and flowing through a fabled landscape, hearing, in Mr. Bryant's parlor verse, "no sound save its own dashings." Years after Captain Gray, the Boston fur trader, had made his way upriver, naming the stream the Columbia after his stout little boat, the French Canadian *voyageurs* used it for carrying their cargoes of furs to Vancouver for the Hudson's Bay Company to distribute all over the world. Guiding their *bateaux* through the dangerous white water and the calm blue stretches, they flung against the barren palisades and the fir-crowned hills the gay words of their famous boating song,

Rouli, roulant, ma boule roulant
En roulant, ma boule roulant.

After the *voyageurs* some of the early home-makers tried to get to the green Pacific slopes down this waterway—so treacherously calm-appearing where they first came upon it in the dry interior. In 1843 pioneers, worn out with months of trekking across the waterless plains, stopped on the shore to make flat boats. At first they were deliriously happy to be carried along by the current in the clear air, the bright sun. But as they came downstream to the rough passages rain began to fall, it turned cold, one boat was overturned in rapids and several people were drowned. Many more might have perished from cold and hunger had not old John McLoughlin sent help to them from Vancouver. He had bonfires lit on the shore, gathered all the available blankets, prepared hot tea and thus made for himself another black mark on his ledger with the Hudson's Bay Company. For this mighty monopoly did not want American settlers hospitably welcomed to the land of Oregon.

Through the Columbia's richly varied landscape in the sixties and the seventies there passed miners, thieves, harlots, and businessmen, on their way to the gold mines of the Inland Empire. At the height of the gold discoveries the demand for boats was so great—with as many as 1000 people a day landing in Portland from San Francisco, all demanding passage upriver—that builders were brought from the Mississippi, from California and British Columbia to fill rush orders for that high-binding monopoly the Oregon Steam Navigation Company. This was the great day of steamboating on the river, when graceful stern-wheelers and side-wheelers—of an elegance quite unusual in such rough land—made the trip from Portland to Lewiston and back.

"It was a magnificent steamboat ride in those days," writes one who remembers it. "The fare was sixty dollars; meals and berths, one dollar each. A traveler would leave Portland at five A.M. on perhaps the *Wilson G. Hunt,* reach the Cascades sixty-five miles distant, at eleven A.M., proceed by rail five miles to the upper Cascades, there transfer to the *Oneonta* or *Idaho* for

The Dalles, passing in that run from the humid, low-lying, heavily timbered 'west-of-the-mountains,' to the dry, breezy, hilly 'east-of-the-mountains.' Reaching The Dalles, fifty miles further east, he would be conveyed by another portage railroad fourteen miles more to Celilo. There the *Tenino, Yakima, Nez Percé Chief,* or *Owyhee* was waiting. With the earliest light of the morning the steamer would head right into the impetuous current of the river, bound for Lewiston, two hundred and eighty miles farther yet, taking two days, sometimes three, though only one to return. Those steamers were mostly of the light-draught, stern-wheel structure. They were swift and roomy and well adapted to the turbulent waters of the upper river."

There are still old-timers like Judge Fred Wilson of The Dalles who can remember this colorful period, when "men talked steamboats, they lived with them, the coming and going of the boats were the crowning activities of the day; the captains and the engineers, the pilots, mates and pursers were the best known men about the town." They remember well the beauty of line and the interior decoration of the *Daisy Ainsworth*, with her Brussels carpets, glittering chandeliers, and shining silver service. You can still hear the romantic tale of the young river captain who was entrusted with taking the *Daisy Ainsworth* upriver by night in 1876 with a load of cattle. Mistaking a light he saw on the shore for a port signal, the unfortunate young man wrecked the beautiful boat. Children in The Dalles went weeping to school when they learned that they would never hear again the whistle of the *Daisy Ainsworth*. The poor young captain went into a decline and died of what the doctors called tuberculosis, but the old river men opined it was really a broken heart. There are a number of versions of the misplacing of that fatal lamp. One asserts that the watchman at the Upper Cascades, thinking that the boat could not possibly be due for hours, took his lantern and walked up the track a quarter of a mile for a cup of coffee, carelessly leaving the light burning directly in line with a rocky ledge. This famous river yarn provided Nard Jones with a handy piece of villainy for one of his characters in *Swift Flows the River*.

When the days of the gold rush were over, the Columbia began to be used for shipping wheat from the rich soils of the Inland Empire, and that was the day of another river beauty, the *Harvest Queen*. Along with such famous boats as the *Harvest Queen*, the *Carrie Ladd*, and the *Lot Whitcomb*, one must remember also the heroic little side-wheeler, the *Mary*, which played so unforgettable a part in the Indian massacre at the Upper Cascades in 1856. The *Mary* was only eighty feet long, and nothing much for looks, but she made her way upriver with bullets crashing into the pilot house so that the steersman had to crouch by the wheel and steer as signals were called, and she never stopped until she got to The Dalles where there was a garrison.

Red men, antedating any of the tribes known today, passed along this mighty waterway and left a record of their passage in pictograph and petroglyph on the walls of the gorges. Some Indian names still cling to a few of the landmarks and there are Indian legends associated with almost all the outstanding physical features. Heartbroken wailings of supernatural origin are still said to come from Castle Rock, that curious steep landmark on the Washington side which was once an Indian lookout, unscaled by white man until 1901. This wailing, most noticeable "when the Chinook blows soft and damp from upriver" is the voice of a heartbroken Indian maiden who fled here to escape the wrath of her father who had killed her lover and threatened her child. The remorseful chief climbed up to beg his daughter to return, but never got back himself. This gigantic rock has an unexplored cave and the spears and arrowheads found in the neighborhood are unlike those usually found on the river shore. There is an Indian myth that the rock is filled with ancestors turned to stone. Perhaps some day the cave will be explored, ancient bones discovered, and its secret revealed.

There were a number of Indian burial islands in the river. The most famous was the big Memelose Island—now almost covered by water since the building of Bonneville Dam—where there stood the stone monument to Vic Trevitt, the old-timer who asked to lie here among his red friends. One of the smaller burial islands of volcanic rock was the scene of a myth which W. D. Lyman relates in his book on the river. This myth tells of the death of a young Indian woman's lover. She grieved so terribly for him that she was finally called by the spirits to come to visit him. Her father paddled her across the river and left her on the island where she spent the night blissfully with her lover in the world of the dead. In the morning to her terror she found herself in the embrace of a skeleton. She fled from the island but was called back again and again to repeat the experience. She finally conceived and gave birth to a wonderful child, part spirit, part human. She was told not to look upon it for ten days, but she could not resist the temptation. The child died and her visits to the world of the spirits came to an end.

It was a good many years after the creating of such myths as these that Indians along the river saw their first white men. Some welcomed the newcomers in a friendly way and some tried to prey upon them. Some of the more thievish used to lie in wait at the Cascade Portage and demand bounty of all travelers until 1896 when the government built locks. When Lewis and Clark came down the river they found the Indians fishing at Celilo Falls, standing at posts which had been handed down from father to son for generations. The Indians still have "exclusive and perpetual fishing rights" here, but how much the Bonneville Dam is eventually going to affect the salmon run is not yet entirely determined. They may in time give up fishing as they have given up the gathering of the wapato roots in the slough where the Willamette meets the Columbia. Here the squaws used to strip naked and dislodge the edible roots from the soft mud with dexterous toes. They spent whole days in the water and brought home their canoe loads at night.

Inland one moves toward the Columbia through swinging green and yellow lines of wheat or dark lines of furrows, with wagon roads going nowhere over the stripped hills. Sometimes—too often for a "booming" country— one sees buildings in ruins and a scattering of rabbit hutches, that last resort of a desperate man whose land yields him no fruit. Coming to the river, the hills, fruitful or barren, rise to cliffs and monumental walls, tumbles of ancient basalt to provoke the fancy with half-formed images. In midafternoon these ancient walls hold their shadows close-pressed, while the hot sun picks up bright glitters in the sand, grass tufts and bleached twigs of sage taking on sudden brilliant significance. Then the river winds into a flat plain and loses its fantastic walls, the clouds float tenuous and opalescent in a far hot sky, like clouds over a southern sea. Occasionally there comes the grateful respite of dipping down from the high, hot—or if it is winter, the high, cold, and windy—bluffs to the river's edge and to little sleepy towns left over from the days of boat traffic, like gentle Arlington dozing among its cottonwoods.

Slowly the green cliffs begin to appear. The pulse of the ocean beats far upriver and moist salt airs affect the landscape. Out-thrust wooded ridges define the shorelines, a rhythmic monody as far as the eye can see, sometimes east and west for more than thirty miles in either direction. On either shore of the river lie enchanting valleys. One at the base of Mt. Adams on the Washington side, one toward Mt. Hood on the Oregon side. For some eighty miles east of Portland one travels the famous Columbia River Highway. This was a great feat of engineering in its day, and the building of the Vista House by imported Italian workmen in "modified Tudor" to honor the pioneers was an event of great moment. A trip to the many beautiful falls—Multnomah, Horse Tail, Wahkeena, Bridal Veil—has been for many years a "must" on every Portland visitor's itinerary.

Much of the credit for the building of this highway goes to Samuel Hill, "the Roadbuilder," whose cold stone mansion on the Washington shore has recently been opened as a museum. Not far from his house stands the replica of Stonehenge which he built in one of his famous outbursts of "visionary" energy. Samuel Hill is said to have built his great house in this treeless yellow landscape because tests had led him to believe that here were to be found the most health-giving winds in the world. The house is chiefly remembered as one of the much publicized stopping-places of Queen Marie of Romania on her famous junket across the United States in 1926. At this time the house was dedicated as a museum, but it was not opened to the public for some years. Now, however, any traveler may park his car in the flat bright light that strikes these barren walls above the great river, and go into the curiously naked-appearing stone structure to view Mr. Hill's ideas of museum treasures. These treasures consist of such incongruities as a collection of formidably ugly Byzantine furniture from the summer palace of the Romanian Royal family near Bucharest, a silver filigree wedding set from Balkan royalty (gladly relinquished one feels sure), the Queen of Greece photographed in Arnold Genthe style, mistily glamorous in a large black hat, set down for no apparent reason in a case of prehistoric Greek pottery, coronation robes from Graustarkian principalities, and so on. There are innumerable pictures of Queen Marie in various roles and disguises: Marie as Nun, Marie as Madonna, Marie as Her Majesty, Marie in peasant costume leaning on an ancient cross. There is a room blessed by Cardinal Mercier and "the Pope himself." There is also, on the authority of Loie Fuller, the dancer, and in her own words, "an engraved portrait of the Cardinal which touched his face before they put him in the bier—a sacred relic indeed."

In addition there are some fine Tanagra pieces, some good Rodins—watercolors, sketches, and sculptures—and downstairs in the basement a collection of ancient Indian material from local graves and diggings—stone tools, arrowheads, clothing, pictographs hewn out of the rock wall. The Indian exhibit is well patronized. So is the amazing "Library" which displays the backs, fronts, sides, and insides of standard classics bound in conventionally tooled leather. It is filled with people shaking their heads humbly and drawing in their breath. The locked cases tauntingly point out that "Good reading inspires right thinking" and that "Good books are an eternal blessing, therefore acquaint thyself with them."

Surely incongruity can reach no sublimer heights than it does in the Maryhill Museum. And yet in this very incongruity one can see a picture of American culture: clouded with European values (often the more tawdry and temporal), idealistic, humble, easily awed, prone to make borrowings without thought of context. Sam Hill is a man worth contemplating: the Roadbuilder, the Quaker and high liver, the friend of royalty, and the apostle of peace, on whose burial crypt are the words: ". . . amid Nature's unrest he sought rest." Essentially he was a simple man and a well-wisher. When he was taken to view the ruins of Stonehenge by Lord Kitchener he was so moved that he at once had it copied in shockingly bad machine-hewed stone and set up on the shores of the Columbia as it supposedly looked when constructed in the age of the Druids. It was to serve as a War Memorial and a symbol of peace, and the reasons given for this extraordinary display of inappropriateness move one only to pity: "Impressed with the thought that after 4000 years the world still made human sacrifices to the Gods of War as did the Druids, he felt that it should be a powerful 'Sermon in Stone' for future generations. Dedicated early in 1918 it is believed to be the first American War Memorial and placed in it are the names of the soldier dead of this country."

There are people unkind enough to suggest that the Bonneville Dam may prove to be just such a useless monument. This $75,000,000 hydroelectric project, built where the Columbia is about to issue from the gorge it has cut through the Cascades, is part of the federal government's great Columbia River plan, which includes also the Grand Coulee project and eight others planned by the army engineers for the future. Together these two great dams now tapping the flow of the Columbia are going to generate one-third as many kilowatts of electricity as were generated in 1940 in the public utility plants of the whole country. And who is going to use this energy? ask the skeptics, willing to admire the ingenuity of the construction, and the neat green and white picture made by the government's village at the dam, but waiting for the rush into this region of promised big industry, even while they hope that they will not live to see it.

Many simpler-minded people who do not understand any of the complexities of hydroelectricity stand by the hour at the fish ladders to watch the ingenious devices by which government engineers are luring the salmon upriver in spite of man-made dams and locks. The fish ladders at Bonneville are really a series of sixteen-foot pools, each pool a step in a stair, each step one foot higher than the last, and up these climb the salmon in all sizes and conditions, going home, after two to six years in the ocean, to lay their eggs and die. Richard Neuberger says that "Frank Buck never tried harder to get a Bengal tiger into a cage" than the government engineers have worked to lure up the stairways of their ingenious system the hundreds of thousands of salmon that pass the dam at spawning time. Now it remains to be seen whether the fisheries experts farther upstream can strip the salmon artificially of their eggs and still keep the fish coming; for there is absolutely no way to get them over the barrier of the wall at the Grand Coulee. Here man must step in and play the role of nature.

River towns may well take on new character if traffic on the Columbia picks up as it is expected to from these two dam projects. The old town of The Dalles, which played so significant and colorful a part in the days of the stern-wheelers, may become active again with the dredging of a ship channel from Vancouver, on the Washington side, to Bonneville Dam, making marine transportation possible 189 miles above the mouth of the Columbia.

The Dalles has a peculiar charm created at least in part by memories and weathered relics of the past. The museum in one of the old pseudo-Gothic buildings of the garrison is full of a jumbled miscellany of objects from other centuries. Two exceptional Indian carvings may be seen here, one of a fish-man and one of a deer's head, with the ancient coloring still showing faintly around the eyes. This is the work of people much more sensitive to form and craftsmanship than any local Indians have been for generations. Here also you may see fading photographs of graceful riverboats. And there are some of those little elaborately framed pictures of moss, shell, and fungus—with watercolor sketches in the background of palaces and sailing ships—which so poignantly remind one of lonely ladies with tireless hands. On the wall is one unforgettable bit of fancy: a delicate construction of "oat straw and binding twine" called Castle in the Air, built lightly to catch the breeze like a Calder "mobile" of this century, done by some nameless farm woman.

The Dalles once measured its days by the whistles of the riverboats. It boasted the sumptuous splendors of the Umatilla House, one of the most famous of Far Western hostelries when, says an old resident, "men played poker and chewed tobacco, but they paid their debts, were kind to the poor and considerate of the unfortunate." During the sixties and the seventies the town swarmed with life, not all of it from the river; for out of The Dalles, southward and eastward, moved freight wagons and stages, men on foot and muleback, bound to the mines and the stock ranges of the inland country. When the gold rush was at its height the government erected a mint at The Dalles, but the mines were rapidly exhausted and the mint abandoned.

The town takes its name from a fancied resemblance between the walls of the narrows and the flagstones (*dalles*) in the village streets of the French

Canadian *voyageurs*. The town rambles over its rocky perches with a pleasantly informal air. It was once a great gathering place for the Indians, and Lewis and Clark marked it as such, while pausing here to make "some selestial observations." Here also York the Negro danced for the red men to the fiddling of Pierre Cruzatte. The men caught a seal and had some salmon trout which was pronounced the finest fish they had ever tasted.

The town of Hood River has also grown in lazy ambling fashion up and over the terraces of the Columbia River. It lies between the turbulent Hood River and the stream called Indian Creek. From its heights—which are connected by steps with the lower town on the river level—one commands magnificent views of snowcapped Mt. Adams and Mt. Hood.

Hood River claims to have inaugurated the apple industry on the Pacific coast, shipping the first carload to New York in 1900. When word began to circulate of the fortunes to be made in Oregon fruit, the town had one of those spectacular booms which have marked all these rich western valleys where beautiful cherries, pears, and apples are grown. Hood River claimed at one time a University Club of several hundred members. Life here had a quality not unlike that of Medford, where a similar class of people came to live the life of gentlemen farmers. Of course not all the farmers were "checkbook farmers" by any means. There is a long grim tale of hard work and endurance, sweat, backache and heartbreak behind the smiling picture of prosperity which many ranches in this valley present today. There was even an importation of industrious Japanese laborers to help clear out the great trees, dig up the stumps, cut, slash, burn, and at last till the soil into its present semblance of a natural green garden. Today at harvesttime Hood River is one of the best places in which to observe the migratory worker and his undernourished, round-bellied, and pinch-faced brood of children.

Hood River residents are keenly aware of the magnificence of the natural setting in which they live their lives. Mt. Hood is treated rather like a deity to which one must regularly raise the eyes in worship. Once a year natives of the town and the surrounding country make an expedition to the top of the peak, meeting at dawn on the east flank of the mountain to begin the sharp ascent. Portlanders have always had something of a finger in the pie of Hood River's development, partly because of the mountain which they too worship from their viewsite. As early as 1889 Portland capitalists built Cloud Cap Inn—the first mountain hostelry in the Pacific Northwest—and memories of trips to Cloud Cap form a tender part of Portland recollections. Dr. Thomas Lamb Eliot, who served as pastor of the Unitarian Church in Portland for fifty years, took a great interest in the scenic beauties of the Hood River country, making a gift of acreage between the gorge of Indian Creek and Hood River where one may go to see all the native trees and flora growing in exuberant untouched profusion.

"This is what we mean by Oregon scenery," says the local booster waving his arm with majestic and forgivable arrogance on Observation Promontory. His sweeping gesture takes in the gorges of the Columbia and Hood Rivers, and a landscape grandly and breathtakingly symphonic in its variations of mountain, hill, valley, and stream. To the south above the checkered green pattern of the orchards rises the glittering spear of Mt. Hood, and across the great Columbia one sees the golden hills of Washington, blue in the distance, roll to the foot of serene and snowy Mt. Adams. Good for Mrs. Coe! one thinks, remembering the early postmistress who refused to accept community mail until the name Dog River—commemorating the eating of a dog here by a band of starving immigrants—was dropped as a postal address. But too bad it was that she could find nothing better to take its place than a repetition once again of the name of a man so wholly unrelated to local history, a name which does nothing to point up the quality of the countryside. Far better the name Waucoma, given by the Indians to their tepee village, established here at the meeting of the rivers when Lewis and Clark visited them in the autumn of 1805.

CHAPTER VI

Oregon Coast

Although the Oregon coast is as varied scenically and socio-logically as any stretch of country you could find any where, it has come to be lumped in people's minds as one thing, a certain type of experience. "You must see the Oregon coast," natives always say and then they proceed to tell the stranger about places and people and things as different in all respects as the inn at Neahkahnie and the Reeds who run it, the barbecued crab prepared by the red-haired woman at Netarts, Brigham the king of the sea lions and his harem, unexploited marine gardens to be visited at low tide, or Tillamook cheese factories and the sign which reputedly hung for years at the town's entrance, "ALL THAT WE ARE OR HOPE TO BE WE OWE TO UDDERS!"

On the Oregon coast the world tends to drop away and you can enjoy that delicately nostalgic sense of solitude born of the wide view coupled with the reassurance that at your back there lies an old barn in the lee of a great rock, or a house of the soft weathered gray created by salt and fog. When in the evenings the great bands of saffron fog move in from limitless distance and surf booms dully along miles of white sand and wave-carved cliff, it is good to be able to turn the eyes inland and see an old man leading his goats home along the mist-hung roads; or to look into a farm kitchen where a woman lights a coal-oil lamp beside a wood-burning range.

Despite the good highways which run the length of the Oregon coast (sometimes annoyingly winding if one gets behind the big log trucks) and despite also the comfortable inns, overnight cottages, and other signs of the twentieth century, the traveler is able to get, over and over again, the feeling that he is exploring new land. A year or so ago on a gray day in late autumn, looking down from a hilltop not far from Humbug Mountain, we beheld a schooner wrecked on the shore, and men who from our height seemed pygmies gathered around a beach fire. Two had waded out into the shallow water to capture a floating barrel, and the five-master lay wallowing in the breaking surf. It was some minutes before we knew just what "time" we were really in.

Spanish names crop up the whole length of this coastline, from Heceta Head, with the old lighthouse and the great sweep of magnificent view, to Cape Blanco, the farthest western reach of Oregon, with a name going back to the expeditions of Vizcaino in the sixteenth century.

Almost every Oregon beach has its tale of treasure; there are ancient kitchen middens, scenes of aboriginal clam bakes, haunted lighthouses, scores of old-timers with tales ripe for telling. There are still remains of diversified Indian cultures to attract the ethnologist, the anthropologist, or the simple yarn collector. Some Coos Bay Indians still remember the rich dream life of their ancestors, when they were avowedly guided by spirit powers, and among these scattered fragments of a once dynamic race, anthropologists like Melville Jacobs from the University of Washington have done some interesting dream and myth research.

It is not difficult to re-create the picture of life in Newport in the late sixties, the seventies, and the eighties, when people from the inland valley of the Willamette made it their ocean resort. Here they came to build houses of that architecture, both decorous and drippy, which characterized the Victorian era. Here they rocked, facing the Pacific, on the verandas of the Abbey, Fountain, or Ocean Houses, and from here they made five-day jaunts to San Francisco by boat. The shore of Yaquina Bay nearby was the scene of a macabre and beautiful piece of Surrealism when Lieutenant Phil Sheridan, with Indian permission, pushed a cemetery of Indian burial canoes, with their contents, out to sea. It was done just at sunset, and the receding tide carried the weathered canoes with their bones and skulls and the skeletons' favorite lifetime possessions out to the open ocean. On the strategic spot cleared by this action Lieutenant Sheridan then built a blockhouse.

At Manzanita one reads or hears about Sacajawea coming, papoose on her back, to view the giant whale which Lieutenant Lewis had reported washed up on the beach. It is said that permission to view this great sea monster was the only personal request she made in the two years she accompanied the Lewis and Clark expedition, and that as an old woman her memory of the "big fish" was her most vivid recollection, and one she never tired of describing to inland Indians.

At Manzanita one may also see in a local "museum" fragments of the much debated Nehalem beeswax, one of the unsolved mysteries of the Oregon coast. The sands of Nehalem have yielded an inexplicable harvest of a substance appearing to be beeswax which has puzzled native Indians and whites for well over a hundred years. Some ten tons of the wax have been found buried in the sand, several blocks inscribed with what are said to be "mysterious hieroglyphics" and others stamped with the familiar Catholic I.H.S. and I.H.N. The most likely explanation seems to be that this is the buried cargo of a Spanish ship, bound to a Catholic mission in the New World, blown off its course in a storm and landed here far to the north.

Neahkahnie has its tale of mysterious treasure also. Many people have searched for the box of gold which an Indian legend says was buried here by unknown bearded men. These men came ashore with the box, dug a hole, drew lots, and killed a member of the group to bury with the treasure to keep the superstitious Indians away. They then set sail and were not seen again.

Altogether the whole Oregon coast is country for loitering, for lazy conversings with soft-voiced, easygoing people in general stores and at gas stations. You cannot hurry here. You want to get out of your car many times and wander through moss-hung forests which lead out on bare hills, russet with low-growing huckleberry, where trees grow with delicate defiance out of rocky ledges and great isolated promontories rise starkly from white sands. These single mammoth rocks, so characteristic of the coast, offer sanctuary for seabirds and make sunsets almost too dramatic by their dark presence against the sky.

Old towns like Port Orford are rich in memories of the past. There was a time when local cedar "as white as white pine and of a peculiar fragrant smell, almost equal to sandal-wood," was in highest demand for the saloons and grocery stores of gilded San Francisco. Later this same cedar, with its "straight grain, lightness, and tensile strength" was used by Sir Thomas Lipton in the construction of his cup challengers. The little New England inn, called the Knapp Hotel, used to carry a lamp nightly in its upper windows to warn ships off the rocky coast. Many a shipwrecked sailor has found a welcome here and great men have slept in its old rooms: William H. Seward bound north to visit the recently purchased Alaska, Jack London while writing *The Valley of the Moon*. Port Orford had a newspaper published in a woodshed before it had a clergyman to make marriages, but the local inhabitants seemed to get on well enough under the kind of "contract" marriages that the Hudson's Bay Company worked out for frontier conditions.

Along this old shoreline other taverns of stagecoach days, like the Arizona Inn, serve travelers still; and the land lying to the shoreside has many beguiling roads beckoning the wanderer off the concrete with such provocative signs as Lone Mountain Valley or Cape Blanco Catholic Church. This latter is a ruin where, in the Poe-like terms of the *Oregon Guide*, "bats cling to the altar and the glass in the painted window frames is shattered."

Communities range from neat white-painted Gardner, built and kept as much as possible like a Maine village by a homesick young "down-Easter" who came here to manage a lumber business, to bustling Marshfield on Coos Bay where the lumber schooners load the loot from the coast range forests. There is Florence where the rhododendrons grow in thickets high above one's head, and people make spring pilgrimages to view them, and there is Yachats (called Yahats) where fishermen stand all day on the great rocks casting their lines into the whirling spray. At Bandon, for many years considered the most beautiful coast town until the disastrous forest fire of 1938, the hills in the spring are covered with Irish furze which Lord George Bennett, an Irish peer who settled here, imported from his native land. Lookingglass Valley, near Coos Junction—named because the green grass seemed to an imaginative explorer, Hoy B. Flournoy, to reflect light like a mirror—is the real setting for parts of H. L. Davis's *Honey in the Horn.* "The country's full of characters," people tell you. They recite strings of names, usually prefixed with the adjective "old"; a term which implies mild eccentricity, lovable vagaries, and an exceptional memory.

The communities nearer Portland, like Seaside and Gearhart, have a special place in the last century memories of older city folk. In Seaside that famous early capitalist of Oregon, Ben Holladay, entertained visitors—come north from San Francisco—with royal feasts; and here was also the house of his almost legendary daughter, the Countess.

When you get as far north as Astoria, town of the coffee-drinking Finn fishermen, you can look on many historic spots dedicated to memories of the Lewis and Clark and the Astor expeditions. Here is the place to sit—after a supper of fried clams—in a corner window of the hotel that overlooks the harbor, reading your Washington Irving or any old book of memoirs with descriptions of the famous bar of the Columbia River which played so large and so doleful a part in the accounts of early mariners. Travelers, anxious to get out to San Francisco, often hung about for days, seasick and dispirited, waiting for the captain to decide that tide and wind and lifting fog favored the run for the open sea. Above the town, on a hill which commands an outlook of river and ocean, stands the Astor Monument. On its circumference, painted by a special process to withstand the fierce sea winds, you may read the pictorial record of the discovery and settlement of this country. If you visit the monument with Merle Chessman, the editor of the *Astorian Budget,* you will hear with what surprise the present John Jacob Astor learned, on a brief recent visit, that he was actually the first of the name to visit the settlement which his great-grandfather founded in 1811. Merle Chessman shakes his head with pity every time he thinks of John Jacob Astor IV, his private car, his fear of publicity. "What a life!" he says. "Whew!"

Perhaps, however, if one were to choose a single Oregon coast town for study or simple enjoyment, Gold Beach would offer the most complete range of experience. For here there is the coast itself—a fine sandy stretch, usually deserted since the townsfolk face the hills and have had little truck with the beach since they took the last gold from it and the pioneers named the place—and there is also the Rogue River. This famous fishing river moves down out of mountain solitude, harboring along its craggy banks many a curious recluse. The tourists who come to Gold Beach are for the most part fishermen, a democratic lot. Not that Gold Beach would pay much attention to the whims and foibles of any possibly haughty outsiders. Gold Beach goes its own way and the world be damned. Here is surely one of the last stands of frontier independence, self-sufficiency, and homely eccentricity to be found in America.

Gold Beach is an unincorporated town which is also the county seat of a county without a railroad. It manages to get along without a mayor, and although it has a Chamber of Commerce there are no officers (the lone member signs himself a "trustee"). When the W.P.A. established a center here, it flourished remarkably. Gold Beach is the smallest community in the country supporting an institution of this kind. Everyone takes a vital interest in the project. The townsfolk put on with great gusto such plays as *You Can't Take It with You* (this is a way of living with which they would be completely in tune) and they even went so far as to give an Artists' and Models' Ball. Some villagers took up weaving, others law, and still others sketching and botany. When a flower painter arrived to make a record of the flowers found in the vicinity (even the flora here are singular) tough riverboatmen stopped their temperamental craft on the treacherous Rogue and clambered up slippery rocks to bring back specimens of rare plants. The center itself, though housed in a rather barren building, has an admirably clean and uncluttered interior, and here local and visiting shows of everything from travel posters to woodblocks are set forth to the obvious pride of the community.

Right across from the courthouse with the fanciful tower which the local builders added just because they had the extra lumber, you will find the general store of Bullhide Moore. Mr. Moore is a genial gentleman of large proportions about whom everyone tells tales, the favorite being how he is accustomed to shoot right across the main street (just a few inches above the highway traffic) to the opposite hill in an attempt to keep dogs away from his sheep, and how he almost "got" the proprietress of the Sunset Inn, out on the slopes picking wildflowers for her tables.

You go up the Rogue River in a special type of boat developed by local ingenuity to make transportation on this stream a year-round possibility. These boats literally scoop their way through the gravel up the roaring, rocky, and, in many places, uncomfortably shallow river. People occasionally take this trip just for the thrill of it, although in winter it is nothing to be taken lightly when the waves wash right over the boat. In summer the trip is fairly peaceful. Hogs root for freshwater clams along the shore among the reeds, buzzards dip and soar about the crags, gentle streams, unexplored, move down cool fern-crowded glens.

Once well upstream the world drops completely away. You can sit on the weathered porch of a neat old house dignified by the name of "hotel," with the river flowing out of sight at the foot of a bank, an old dog sleeping on the sagging steps and an old horse dying dreamily in a pasture. The handsome proprietress who has just fed you a "pick-up lunch" of some fifteen delicious and utterly unrelated varieties of food, whistles *Juanita* in the kitchen and her beautiful shy children come and go about the place. You think this is surely the retreat to seek if the world gets any worse. But when you leave she comes out to ask you about "conditions." She speaks of the radio. You've forgotten they exist. "Things are changing," she says. "Oh, not here—not yet," but she notices it in Marshfield, over the mountains where they go occasionally for supplies. "People's eyes are different." She supposes it's "all this war talk." . . . Look your last at all this, you say to yourself, going down the steep path, smelling balm and hearing the doves cooing.

In Agness you may have a happy moment on a forest path when you meet an old prospector with his grub bag on his back and his eyes deep with accustomed solitude, wearing on his right ear a bright shiny-new city earphone. To hear bird calls with, one concludes, knowing he is bound beyond habitations and humans.

It seems utterly fitting to find across the river at Agness two people like Arthur Dorn and his wife, with their "two hundred mile backyard," raising all their own food, living completely remote from the world after many years of being very much in it. Arthur Dorn is working on translations of Buddhist sutras. He can speak of profound things if the mood is on him, or the ear receptive; or he can retell a Hathaway Jones yarn with a circumlocution worthy of the master himself.

One cannot really imagine Hathaway Jones emerging from any other kind of country; fabulous Hathaway with his unknown antecedents, his cleft palate, his mysterious and terrible death, whose imaginary exploits illustrating his own courage, strength, and ingenuity have made him one of the immortal yarners of the Pacific Northwest.

Hathaway was proud of the distinction of being the biggest liar in the country and, on hearing once that the Portland *Oregonian* had bestowed the honor on someone else, threatened to institute suit against the paper. Hathaway felt no embarrassment about his speech impediment. He referred to it quite freely. One who knew him intimately says, "He told me one day that his Pa got quarrelsome and hit him in the nose with a shovel. This was what caused the trouble. He said his Pa was older than he was at the time."

Hathaway was said to be the last man in the United States to carry mail with a mule team, and he lost his life in a fall over a cliff, while riding along one of the precipitous trails of this country. Hathaway had a story he liked to tell which was not unlike the prophecy of his own end. In this story he was riding along on his cayuse, Baldy, one night, when Baldy suddenly stopped and wouldn't budge an inch. Hathaway tried for an hour to move him but he remained obdurate. Finally when his master got abusive Baldy sighed despairingly, stepped ahead, and plunged promptly down into nothingness. Hathaway, considerably shocked and pretty well scared, managed after a moment or two to collect his wits enough to pull up Baldy. But it was a near thing. They were already within two hundred feet of the bottom of the canyon.

Hathaway had a gift for metaphor. "Makin' more noise than drivin' a four-horse team through the woods draggin' a bull hide" might be taken as a fair example of his phrasing. Not only was Hathaway's own prowess amazing (it was nothing for him to kill a bear so large that it rendered "375 pounds of grease") but around him nature too became phenomenal. He planted potatoes in land so fertile that one day when without thinking he carelessly pulled a weed out of a hole the potatoes started popping out so fast that he had to plug it up to keep from losing all his crop. This brief activity of the potatoes did, as a matter of fact, lift up the whole garden area about three feet.

Perhaps Hathaway's two best stories, however, are the one about the year of the big snow when he lost his watch, and the rock he found to fit in the center of his fireplace:

One winter snow started early on the Rogue and came down so fast that Hathaway, hunting in the hills, couldn't walk out to his cabin and had to sit down and slide from the hilltop to the riverbank. On the way down he lost his watch, which was a real pity as he had intended timing the slide. Next summer he was up hunting in the hills again and sat down under a tree to rest. He became aware of a ticking sound near him which he finally located up the tree under which he was resting. He got up, climbed the tree, and there sure enough was his watch, still going. That was how he knew how deep the snow had been that winter. He climbed sixty feet up that tree.

When he was building his house he left a space right in the center of the stone fireplace for a rock of a certain shape and size which he fancied would look right. He couldn't find a rock to fit the place anywhere, and had just about given up, when one day out hunting he came on a big rock which seemed to him to have possibilities as to shape. He rolled the rock down the steep hillside, saw it roll up the opposite side, down again and back again—a pendulum swing. Satisfied, he went away down the Rogue, fished all summer, came back in the autumn and there was that rock still rolling. One quick look at it convinced him that it was now the right size. He hastily put a log under it, stopped its descent, took it home, and it was a perfect fit.

CHAPTER VII

Southern Oregon: Pelicans, Pears, Spade Beards, and Cavemen

Unlike in outer aspects, the towns of southern Oregon are all as one in their local pride, their ambition, and their common interest in the intelligent exploitation of the remarkably scenic part of the state in which they lie.

This section of Oregon has its own distinct flavor. Relatively late in its development, and in certain ways spectacularly swift in its growth, it has been known to complain bitterly, and publicly, against the domination of the city of Portland, alleging that Portland would rather see itself grow ever larger and more powerful than to have Oregon as a whole expand and produce competitive communities.

The largest of the southern Oregon towns is Klamath Falls. Lying in high, dry, and bracing air at an altitude of over four thousand feet the town has grown to a population of more than sixteen thousand, practically since 1915 when the railroads began to open up the country. There is something rather special about the place. The visitor realizes it from the moment when he sees his first pelican floating against one of the great cloud forms rolling up from the inland.

The white pelicans—those amiable mirth-provoking birds—nest in the reeds on the shores of the nearby lakes, and are to be seen everywhere around Klamath Falls from March to September, lending the landscape a picturesque air, causing tourists to cry out in amazement, and encouraging the growth of a host of unlikely stories. Among these stories are the explanations that their presence here is due to the rains of toads to which this part of Oregon was once subject; or that they were brought in to patrol the streets in early days when the millions of harmless but rather disconcerting snakes unexpectedly thrusting their heads through the board sidewalks were a local menace.

Around Klamath Falls lies a country which abounds in curious phenomena. It is here that one gets a guide to go out into the adjacent Lava Beds, a weird playground created by the last great lava flow which occurred here in such "recent" geological times as five thousand years ago. This vast wasteland, which extends also into northern California, consists of some 250,000 square miles of caverns, bridges, cinder cones, underground galleries with Indian picture writing in red and yellow ochres, frozen waterfalls, and many still unexplored caves.

The town of Klamath Falls itself has a series of hot mineral springs, one of which discharges about 800,000 gallons of water daily at a temperature of two hundred degrees. These natural hot springs are used to heat houses and public buildings. They supply two municipal pools and are drunk by many for their health-giving properties.

Though Klamath Falls is a relatively new town, bits of its history go far back into Oregon roots. Two of the great early names in the state, those of the Applegate brothers, Jesse and Lindsey, are associated with this region. The brothers explored here in the 1840s and were pleased enough with what they saw to organize a Klamath Commonwealth to settle the area. The gold rush of '49 to California, however, carried away all prospective settlers, and there was no pioneering in the Klamath Basin until the sixties.

The local Indians were particularly fierce, and the massacres of immigrants were among the most terrible of any. Someone called this section of country "The Dark and Bloody Battleground of the Pacific," and the phrase stuck. An army post was established for protection of the settlers in 1863 and the Indians were put on reservations, but this did not prevent the outbreak of the Modoc War of 1872 and 1873—one of the last and costliest of all Indian wars. A small band of about fifty Modocs under the famous renegade, Captain Jack, held off a force of between nine hundred and twelve hundred white soldiers, at a cost of over half a million dollars.

Trouble had arisen because the Modocs resented being placed on a reservation with their hereditary enemies the Klamaths, and attempted to go back to their old home along the shores of Tule Lake. The young chief, Kientpoos, or Captain Jack as he is always called, and his sister "Queen Mary" left the reservation, and when the soldiers set out to get them to return, Captain Jack cannily retreated into the lava beds and there this highly photogenic war was fought.

In Colonel William Thompson's *Reminiscences of a Pioneer* there are descriptive passages which make exceptionally clear under what difficulties the white men were working in attempting to find Indians in this fantastic landscape. Colonel Thompson made an apt phrase for the *Army and Navy Journal*, saying that the Indians in the lava beds were "like ants in a sponge." Although he avows in his book that the scenery is beyond the power of language he includes a description by an anonymous observer which does pretty well by the subject:

"A black ocean tumbled into a thousand fantastic shapes, a wild chaos of ruin, desolation, barrenness—a wilderness of billowy upheavals, of furious whirlpools, of miniature mountains rent asunder, of gnarled and knotted, wrinkled and twisted masses of blackness, and all these weird shapes, all this turbulent panorama, all this far-stretching waste of blackness, with its thrilling suggestiveness of life, of action, of boiling, surging, furious motion was petrified—all stricken dead and cold in the instant of its maddest rioting—fettered, paralyzed and left to glower at heaven in impotent rage for evermore."

As in most major Indian conflicts there were heated opinions on both sides as to the justice of the Indians' cause. General Canby, who was all for peace, was murdered in cold blood under his own peace flag by the Modocs, and the wooden cross that marks his martyrdom still stands where he fell. Although Captain Jack was eventually hanged with a group of his followers at Klamath Falls, he has become the hero of an historical novel bearing his name. The Modoc War also had its red heroine, Winema, a niece of Captain Jack. Winema was married to a white man and acted as interpreter between the whites and her own people. When the Modocs went on the war path she risked her life to warn the Indian superintendent of their intentions.

The flavor of the town of Klamath Falls is still that of the frontier, though it boasts of three hospitals, twenty-three churches, five theaters, two daily newspapers, two weeklies, a radio station, and a municipal airport. It claims a trade population of 75,000 people from an area extending over one hundred miles in three directions, and it is this large trade population which gives the town its lively Saturday night air and makes the audiences at the Buckaroo Days festival in July and the Klamath Lake regatta in June a significant cross-section of western ways of life. The first of these festivals which presents cowboy events such as riding, roping, bulldogging, and the racing of wild horses, celebrates the days when southeastern Oregon was still big range country. Fragments of this vanishing way of life may be seen in the land lying to the east where cattle and sheep still flourish. The Regatta has, in addition to surfboarding and swimming meets, log-bucking and log-cutting, which pay tribute to the kind of activity still going on in the land of the giant ponderosa pine. Klamath County claims some twenty-four billion feet of pine timber tributary to it.

Here also one may see the magical results of irrigation. The Klamath Irrigation Project contains almost two hundred thousand acres under irrigation, and the Klamath Basin contains over three hundred thousand acres of irrigable land. Klamath County prides itself on its potatoes. Booster pamphlets show them popping mammothly from open sacks: Klamath Netted Gems. It is said a trainload a day goes out of the Basin coastward throughout the year.

Even the local Indians are still picturesque and vigorous and retain many of their primitive ways of life. The songs of the Klamath Indians have been preserved by Albert Samuel Gatschet, an ethnologist who worked among them in the last century, and by Leslie Spier who published *Klamath Ethnography* in 1930. One may read echoes of an older and simpler way of life celebrating the days when the animal played a more intimate part in human existence:

> *An old frog woman I sit down at the spring.*
> *I the black-spotted snake am hanging here.*
> *This is mine, the black snake's gait.*
> *Lo! thus I the lizard stick my head out.*
> *When I the lizard am walking, my body is resplendent with colors.*
> *The land on which I, the female lizard, am treading belongs to the lark.*
> *What game did you play with me?*
> *Now the wind gust sings about me, the yen-fish*
> *I, the tsawas-fish am singing my own song.*
> *Here I am buzzing around.*
> *I, the bug, I bite and suck.*

Klamath Falls yarners can still tell tales of banditry, cattle rustling, and cold-blooded murder in the days when rugged individualists died with their boots off only if a friendly bystander would comply with the request to remove them ere the victim breathed his last. Nearby communities offer such stories as that of Twisted Foot, the prodigious grizzly, who measured three feet between the ears and whose paw left a track the size of a Mexican sombrero. Twisted Foot was one of those whimsical Oregon bears who would do anything for a pal. He often helped his friends among the cattlemen with their butchering and was reputed to have killed over $500 worth of cattle for one of his more intimate buddies.

Second in size among southern Oregon towns is Medford, a charming and prosperous community which does not mind advertising itself as "The Pear City." Medford streets have such a neat, well-groomed air that one must get above the town and look down on it to really see the kind of country from which it has grown. On a summer's day from the beautiful pine forests of

Prescott Memorial Park, atop Roxy Ann Mountain, one can look onto the heavy dark green of pear orchards, onto fields of alfalfa and clover, shimmering in the heat cupped here by the encircling peaks of the Siskiyous and Umpquas. Below is the fertile valley of the Rogue River, through which gold seekers pushed their way southward to California in '49; some of them remembering enough of the look of the green valley to come back later and test its fertility. As early as 1836 a band of French Canadians from John McLoughlin's post at Vancouver came scouting through here.

Because fortunes have been made in Medford in fruit, and because the adjacent countryside is a sportsman's paradise, the town has acquired a rather unusual cosmopolitan air. There was a time when the fruit boom was so phenomenal that the magazine *Sunset* asserted that Medford in 1910 had more motor cars, more cash registers, and more typewriters per capita than any other city in the United States.

During the boom days people from all stations in life invested in land in this richly favored valley, confidently expecting to put in orchards and live off the profits through a comfortable old age. One story of this period of inflated hopes sets the characteristic tone of Medford anecdotes. A young man of good family came out from the east to invest his modest patrimony in land. He planted his trees and sat down to wait. When his money began to dwindle he decided to invest in some extra-fancy cockerels which he planned to fatten and sell in the Portland markets. Discovering there was no market for his birds the young man found himself too poor to buy further provisions for his flock. Unable to endure the sight of the starving fowls he began to kill and feed them one at a time to their fellows. When he was down to his last cockerel, he dined on it. Then he went to the barn and hanged himself.

Fortunes in Medford fruit are still being made by people who know how to advertise and to make up smart packages. The recent development of the "holiday gift box"—with fancy wrapping, advertising, labeling, and so on—has taken up much of the slack caused by the loss of foreign markets. Like other Pacific Northwest fruit valleys, however, the blights and the beetles give many growers a year-round headache. Yet nothing can take from this enchanting valley those ideal climatic conditions for the growing of fruit which gave it its first impetus. Fruit here has a growing season forty odd days longer than most other fruit districts on the American continent; and this encourages exceptional growth, beautiful coloring, and fine flavor.

Medford is very civic-minded. When the citizens began to realize the importance of a good road to nearby Crater Lake and the legislature's appropriation of an initial one hundred thousand dollars was not upheld by the state supreme court, Medford people went ahead on their own. "Nearly $100 a minute" was the result of their first hour's effort at collecting funds for the road. Medford is apt to go ahead and get things done. In 1929 the city established Oregon's first municipal airport in a position so strategic that it has become a regular port of call for United Air Lines transports and for army and navy aircraft as well. The government now maintains an army servicing staff and a weather bureau and the port is being used in the current civilian training program. Medford is often held up as an example in city planning, having founded a city planning board in 1923; and it has an exceptional health service in which its citizens take a lively interest. It has also had, however, one of the major Oregon scandals of recent years centering around local politicians and newspaper men in the early thirties, a tale including murder, suicide, and insanity which Lincoln Steffens is reputed to have called "the most significant story of small town corruption in America." Its cool handling of this inflammable material won for the Medford *Mail Tribune* under Robert Ruhl the Pulitzer Prize in 1933.

One often hears, "Medford is full of Easterners." Sometimes this is said proudly and sometimes regretfully. "Too many remittance people in Medford," someone is likely to remark. (Anyone with an income from intangibles who comes west to live may still be called a remittance man and mildly looked down on by old-timers in the Pacific Northwest.) One is told that these Easterners set the social pace and have an allegedly "exclusive" club which causes a certain amount of local heartburn, but reading Arthur Perry's *Ye Smudge Pot* in the Medford *Mail Tribune* the visitor concludes that local flavor is still pretty local. The smudge pot which appears in orchards in the early spring when the frosts are apt to be treacherous seems a suitable name for Mr. Perry's column. This has been an institution since 1911 and contains a nice blending of dry, yokel wit, homely provincialisms delicately flavored with rural nostalgia, and tart but unmalicious gossip.

"A baseball game played in old man Jones' pasture broke up in the seventh inning in an uproar when Joe Spivis slid into what he thought was third base."

"Len Carpenter of the ranch set is back from wintering in California, prepared to enjoy the summer heat, but not stay in it."

"The first mustard greens of the year are reported by epicures and gourmets. They appear at the end of the pig backbones, and just before the start of the fried chick season."

What's all this about the Easterners and their local Colony Club, one wonders after reading of Mr. Jim Denkens of Beagle who, on a trip to town for a haircut and tooth-pulling, stops to deliver himself in Mr. Perry's hearing of: "The deer has the best recollection of all four-legged creatures and would be a holy terror in the timber if the Lord had only given him a fighting heart. The wildcat has a sense of humor but loses it if kicked in the short ribs. A bald-headed eagle will starve before he will eat a bluejay."

In spite of all the "Easterners" Medford is still indisputably "Oregon."

Just a short "piece" away from Medford the old town of Jacksonville dozes among its flamboyant dreams of gold and greed. Jacksonville is one of the few Pacific Northwest ghost towns which died with an air. It is full of such "firsts" and "seconds" as first bank in the state, first brick structure, second oldest inland church west of the Rockies. Legend says the Methodist church was built with one night's takings at the gambling tables (gamblers were always generous to parsons) and that bad men went to church not infrequently, dropped their nuggets into the collection box, and listened to the melodeon which had come round the Horn, then over the high mountains on the backs of mules. Quite by accident gold was discovered here in the early fifties by two men who operated a pack train between Yreka, California, and towns in the Willamette Valley and the newly settled Rogue River Valley. In a few months a community had sprung up and by 1859 Jacksonville was the richest town in the state. The old scales which stand in the window of the bank weighed some of the $20,000,000 that passed through the bankers' hands. There are buildings bullet-scarred from the Indian wars along the quiet streets. The Old Barn housed the relay horses on the California-Oregon Stage Line, and such celebrities as President Hayes and General William T. Sherman put up at the United States Hotel. This is the birthplace of the late William Hanley, "the sage of Harney County," friend of cowboys, coyotes, millionaires, and kings. In the yard of the old Hanley home stands the famous willow tree planted by his mother when he was born and about whose age Bill Hanley was always so cagey; admitting only that he was as old as the tree, and the tree as old as he.

There was a time when Ashland, the "City of Spas," enjoyed seeing itself referred to as the American Carlsbad, and took pleasure in pointing out that its mean average temperature was 51.8, that of "Florence, Italy, 58.8." This was before Ashland became outstanding by virtue of its own enterprise and could advertise itself as the only place in the world where an outdoor theater gives Shakespeare exclusively.

Annually, in August, Ashland takes on an Elizabethan aspect. Butcher boys in sixteenth-century garb get their pictures taken for rotogravure sections drinking Ashland's famed Lithia water from public fountains. All the men grow spade beards and compete for the yearly prize for the best achievement in this line; and those who refuse to attempt a beard must submit to public punishment in the stocks. Thousands of people sit under the August stars and watch *Twelfth Night* or *Midsummer Night's Dream*, costumed by the Southern Oregon Normal School, with local talent and young actors from as far north as the Cornish School in Seattle and as far south as the Pasadena Playhouse, who support themselves doing odd jobs when not on the boards. There are such other Elizabethan activities as archery, bowling on the green, and folk dancing. Not since the first year, however, has the committee felt it necessary to add such extra attractions as a carnival and boxing bouts. In the first season committee members nervously added the latter so that they would not go too hopelessly in debt. To everyone's amazement, and amidst public rejoicing from the local intelligentsia, the boxing bouts went into the red, and Shakespeare had to make up the shortage.

The town of Grants Pass—always called Grass Pants by comedians on the small town vaudeville circuits—keeps alive in its name the memory of the passionate feelings in isolated Oregon villages at the time of the Civil War. Although Ulysses S. Grant, when a young officer in the army, was in Oregon in the early days, the town was not named because he passed through it—a legend one is sometimes told—but because men who were building the pass over the mountains for the California stage route learned, while at their job, of General Grant's capture of Vicksburg.

The town is a supply center for fishermen trying their luck in the Rogue. It is the heart of a rich irrigation district, and of a lumbering and mining area. Two hotels display the many varieties of ore to be found in the countryside and the town boasts as well the famous collection of semiprecious stones of Eclus Pollock.

To advertise its nearness to the Oregon Caves, Grants Pass businessmen formed a social and service club called the Oregon Cavemen in which "the members impersonate their primal forebears." Symbolically the Cavemen of Grants Pass feast on dinosaur flesh and drink the blood of the sabretoothed tiger. Their ancestral home is in the subterranean recesses of the nearby Mountain of Marble, and there, at the caves' entrance, the tourist may, if he chooses, buy pictures of dentists and lawyers, doctors and merchants, fittingly garbed as Chief Big Horn, Clubfist, Flamecatcher, or Rising Buck, keeper of the wampum.

Roseburg lies along the gracious, languid Umpqua River and appears as placid and slow-rhythmed as the stream beside which it has grown up. Paul Bunyan and Babe the Blue Ox stopped to rest on the steep pitch of Nebo Mountain across the Umpqua, which must have given them a superb view of the river with its rocky sides growing ferns and mosses, of fine timber ripe for cutting, and perhaps of white painted riverboats now no longer seen. Prior to Bunyan's mythical visit David Douglas, the Scotch botanist who received hospitality from McLoughlin at Vancouver in the 1820s, and who named the Douglas fir, discovered on Sugar Pine Mountain the tree of that name for which he was searching. He was traveling south at the time with Hudson's Bay traders.

Although the town has an annual rose festival and prides itself on its gardens, it was not named for the flowers which bloom with such unbridled profusion in the month of May, but for an early settler named Aaron Rose who came into this remote valley in 1851 and probably deserved the honor for the solitude and loneliness he must have endured here before other settlers arrived.

SECTION V

Highlights on the Last Horizon

CHAPTER I

Tales, Tall and Small

The Pacific Northwest is a land of mighty mysteries.

When geologists set out to account for the appearance of this part of America as they see it today—and probably only geologists really see land—they have to create an ancient geography of their own with mythical islands like the Shoshone and the Siskiyou, and mythical mountains like Mazama and Multnomah. These long-vanished signposts become very real in trying to unravel the origins of this fabulous country. Even the layman can stumble on fossils of mammals; shells from ancient seas, now found inland among high mountains; the ferns from old lakes; and the scattered tombs of rhinoceros, elephants, peccaries, and pre-historic relatives of the hog, tapir, and horse.

The natural wonders of this country stimulated the Indian imagination to explain them with tales of angry gods, punishment, battle, reward, and magic. Even the early white man, in the myth-making pre-sleep moments after a hard day's work and a big dinner, produced some better than average-size yarns. Many additions to the Paul Bunyan saga came from the effect on the human imagination of these great impersonal landscapes, and also no doubt from the prodigious physical labors of which men in those days were capable. Among the correspondence of early Seattle settlers, quoted in *Four*

Wagons West, one reads the following: "My father and I took a contract for getting seven thousand telegraph poles and five thousand boat poles; these we packed out of the woods to the water on our shoulders. We rafted them by hand alongside the ship as there were no steamers to do our towing." The very idea of throwing these great logs into the water by handspikes and towing them by little skiffs to the mills seems almost incredible today. The stories of Bunyan, the mythical giant, had to be stretched almost to breaking-point to top everyday feats of ordinary men.

Where the Indians tended to attribute awe-inspiring natural grandeurs to the work of deities, the white man played with the notion that the landscape had been made since he arrived and was often his own handiwork. Joe Meek was fond of remarking that he came to Oregon when Mount Hood was a hole in the ground; and old-timers in the Puget Sound country like to say they were here before Hood Canal was dug. Sometimes Paul Bunyan is credited with digging this canal as he came along, negligently dragging his mighty pickax. As a matter of fact Hood Canal is not a canal at all, but a mighty arm of the inland sea, lying in the bed of an ancient glacier.

Sometimes Indian myths have a provocative way of re-creating past geologic history. The most familiar of these is the tale of the Bridge of the Gods, which at one time spanned the Columbia. This was a natural stone arch under which the canoes of the tribes living along the river used to pass until that fatal day when the gods of the great mountains to the south and the north grew angry at one another. Then the earth trembled; rocks, smoke, and fire were hurled between the quarreling deities; the great stone bridge collapsed, and the river was forced to follow a new channel.

And now listen to Professor Warren D. Smith of the University of Oregon in a *Geological Travelogue* recently issued by the state: "Geological examination of the terrain indicates that there was a tremendous landslide or succession of slides on the Washington side of the river. Millions of tons of rock broke away from Mt. Hamilton and Table Mountain. As a result of this slide the Columbia was forced out of its old channel and now follows a new course south of the old one."

Of course not all Indian myths are historically accurate. Some are more on the fanciful side. There is a particularly engaging Indian explanation of how Medical Lake in eastern Washington got its medicinal properties: Fighting Panther was in love with an Indian maiden whose name was Mary. He took a trip to Fort Colville to buy perfume, soap, hair oil, and other sundries for his sweetheart. On the way home he met his rival, Big Bear, and they had a fight near a lake. During their encounter they both fell in and were drowned. Fighting Panther's purchases fell into the lake with him and gave the waters their beneficial properties.

There are still some tantalizing geologic mysteries in this country which the coolest scientific thinking has not been able fully to explain. One of the most interesting is the enigma of the Palouse soil, an extraordinarily fertile earth in southeastern Washington, found lying on the bare platform of the last lava flow. None of the theories such as "decayed basalt, dissected by drainage and kneaded by the winds" or "wind-blown loess of the Pleistocene Age" are fully adequate, according to the historian, George W. Fuller. A gentleman in Portland, Mr. A. "Whiz" Whysnant, has a theory about the Palouse dust which is very much in the vein of the late Charles Fort. His theory is that sometime aeons back the earth drew into its atmospheric orbit a dark nebula, an accumulation of dust in interstellar space. Gravity pulled the dust to the earth and it fell in the Palouse country, just as the gigantic Oregon meteorite fell years ago in the Willamette Valley. Perhaps that extra-special flavor of the bread from the wheat of the Palouse country is due to its having been grown in stardust.

There is also the "rare phenomenon" of the Yakima River. The Yakima River, with what appears at first sight to be inexplicable whimsy, pursues its course with total disregard for the topography of the country through which it moves. The river stubbornly flows south through some seven mountain ranges running east and west. The explanation is that the river was there before the mountains and was not deterred from its first course simply because "surface movement and erosive action" were here matched with such precision as completely to cancel each other through the slow passing of many thousands of years.

In the seventies, when the Northern Pacific railroad was being built, engineers noticed a curious phenomenon in a stream called Crab Creek rising near Medical Lake and flowing over the Columbia plain. At its source, where it was hardly more than a brook, there were many trout, fingerlings by the hundreds. A few miles to the west the stream disappeared in sand and rock, coming out to the surface some distance below with larger trout. For one hundred miles the stream appeared and disappeared in the earth, showing, in each stretch of open water, trout of almost graded size. In its lower reaches "half pound trout went in schools," and the engineers had a lot of arguments as to how the trout got there, and as to how the right-sized fish got in the right-sized streams. The question is still unsolved.

These are Washington mysteries, but Oregon keeps pace with mysteries of her own. There is myrtlewood, a tree said to be found only here and in the Holy Land, which leads one to play with ideas of floating "islands" or land fragments which caught on to the newly formed coastline. Most baffling of all Oregon phenomena is the famous House of Mystery which stands halfway between Grants Pass and Medford in southern Oregon and has puzzled the most skeptical scientists. Here on a circle of ground some 125 feet in diameter, inexplicable phenomena can be noted at all times and have been fully reported in the newspapers. No one can stand erect in this circle, but must lean toward the magnetic north in order to keep in balance. Two men of the same height standing on two cement slabs, perfectly level with each other, one inside and one outside the circle, show a four-inch difference in height. A broom knocked over in the house falls in the opposite direction from which it leans. A ball tossed over the fence comes back to the tosser. A guide backing away from the spectators on a level board appears to grow taller. Light intensity meters on cameras register less than fifty percent of normal in this mysteriously disturbed area.

Indian artifacts dug up in the land of fossils are often tantalizing. There have been specimens found of the sculptured heads of monkeys, made of basalt, eight to ten inches high. Thomas Condon, the grand old man of Oregon geology, believed them to be mortars used by medicine men, and the theory has been advanced that some migration of natives who had seen monkeys came into the Columbia valley in the remote past.

Many times in word-of-mouth yarning one encounters fragments of old tales about the presence of "white Indians" or of mysterious white people of unknown origin. An old Indian up the Rogue River in Oregon had a tale from his very old mother, long dead, of the passing through the land in the mists of ancient time, of an emigration of whites who lived for a time among the Indians and eventually went from them to the north across a high plateau (long since vanished, but said by geologists to have once actually existed in this part of the state). The story of these mysterious whites was kept alive among the Rogue River Indians for generations. It is recorded that they received the first white men of the present time with expressions of great joy and were unwilling to take pay or accept gifts in exchange for any services.

In a book by Jack Splawn, the famous character of the Yakima country who died as late as 1917, I found this paragraph in a description of a trip he made with cattle overland north into Canada on the old Cariboo trail:

"During my wandering through the mountains after my cattle, I came one day to a camp of golden-haired Indians with fine features and the most musical language humans ever spoke. Their throat sounds were like the notes of the forest birds around them. There were several lodges, about forty in all. I never saw them again, nor learned anything further about them."

The same Mr. Splawn, a good hardheaded old-timer, has a way of dropping throughout his ambling chronicle alluring hints of stories of which one would like to read more. One night Mr. Splawn was camping out at the head of the Cle Elum River. He had with him an old Indian guide and as they sat around the campfire after their night meal, they both heard the hoot of an owl. The old Indian said quietly that this was not an owl, but the voice of a Stick Indian. Stick Indian was a term sometimes used to refer to Indians who lived in the forest; but these particular Stick Indians were a wild tribe of dwarfs which inhabited the high rugged mountains of this region. The old guide stood up and addressed the owl in the bushes, saying, "I, Mowit, come bringing a white man into this country. Don't do us any harm." The hidden Indian gave two hoots and they were not molested.

These Stick Indians were believed, by the Yakima tribes, to be the ghosts of departed warriors. They were supposed to have mysterious powers of endurance and disappearance and even, some said, to possess wings, in order to reach the craggy peaks of the Cascade summits around the headwaters of the Skagit and Chelan Rivers. Hunters of wild goats, forced to stay overnight in the upper reaches of these mountains, often claimed to have heard their eerie voices in the night.

Many of the first whites in this country seem to have had a sort of shamefaced respect for the Indians' power to see ghosts, to fast and have visions and prophesy the future through dreams. Over and over again in print one comes on oblique or direct references to that "big dream" of a great medicine man or chief, of the eventual coming of the pale face and his people's slow destruction. The poignance of the way in which this dream came true seems to have deeply touched the feeling of even the most hardened cynic.

Among Indian mystics none has had more influence than Smohalla, a Priest Rapids Indian from the banks of the Columbia who became to his tribe in fairly recent times a sort of cross between Gandhi and Evangeline Adams. Smohalla first won fame by a rumor that he was making bad medicine—which is to say that he was practicing voodoo—against Chief Moses of the next tribe along the river. Moses lay in wait for Smohalla, gave him a good beating, and left him for dead. Smohalla recovered enough to crawl to the river's edge, where he found a canoe and floated down to Umatilla. Here he was picked up by some whites and cared for until he was well. He then set out on some remarkable travels which led him as far away as Mexico. In time he returned to Priest Rapids, not as a world-traveler, but as a reincarnated spirit sent back by the Great Chief to guide his people. He guided them by means of trance and dream.

Smohalla was all for retaining the primitive Indian ways of life. His people ceased to raise sheep, hogs, chickens, or vegetables. They went back to the old diet of fish, game, roots, and berries. They even gave up their horses. In every way they resisted civilization and Smohalla boasted, "My young men shall never work, for men who work cannot dream, and wisdom comes from dreams. We will not plow the ground, for we cannot tear up our Mother's breast. We will cut no hay, for we dare not cut off our Mother's hair."

Whether Smohalla was a genuine mystic or a very successful charlatan he managed to influence enough Indians to make it hard for the whites to get what they wanted—which was Indian land. To this day some eastern Washington and Oregon Indians are designated as Dreamers, the name given the members of Smohalla's cult.

Smohalla was able to fall into convincing trances during which he frothed at the mouth. Other Indians also seem to have practiced these arts sometimes with telling effect. Even now—degenerate and enfeebled as Indians are in the Northwest country—they seem able to tap mysterious powers.

Some of the native Indians of the Washington coast developed in the eighties an indigenous "Shaker" religion not unrelated in practice to the white Shakers of the Eastern states, although the Indian religion grew up quite independently. These Indians dance or vibrate in rhythm to heavy bronze bells, work themselves into ecstasies, thrust their hands through candle flames, and give other convincing proof of possession. The Shaker religion grew out of old shamanistic practices. There are eyewitness accounts of power entering with such force a cedar board held in the hands, that the performer was dragged in and out of the fire and finally out of the house, and the two white men who came to his rescue were dragged helplessly into the river along with him.

Like Smohalla the founder of the Shaker religion, an Indian named Slocum, also "died" during an illness and came to life again. This is, anthropologists say, an old pattern in the history of possession among the Indians of this area. Shakers claim to be able to heal the sick and to do so they pantomime the removal of the sickness from the patient's body just as the old medicine men used to practice it.

Indians still believe that an enemy can cause death by practicing black magic. Within recent years in Pendleton, two Indians were given life sentences rather than death by a white jury for their confessed murder of a squaw whom they solemnly accused in court of being a witch.

One story of death from black magic tells of Chawitzit, an Indian chief and friend of the first whites around Bellingham who was "voodooed" by an enemy and in spite of the best shamanistic practices died, as he had prophesied to his white friends.

Indians believe that the dead can come back if they want to, and there are plenty of stories of the return of the *memelose*. The word *memelose* is a familiar one to the tourist who reads road markers because on the way up the Columbia River a bronze tablet points out to him the remains of Meme-lose Island, an ancient Indian burial ground in the middle of the river (now almost covered because of the change in the river level due to the Bonneville Dam). Some time since, however, the Indians had ceased to use it as a burial ground; too many white curio hunters, ghouls, and scientists had been picking it over for souvenirs or specimens. Some enterprising river dwellers had even made a business of furnishing boats to visit the island—in spite of Indian protests. It is said that the last island burial was the funeral of "Princess" Virginia Miller in the late twenties. The Princess chose to be buried, not in tribal buckskin, but in a silk dress and a Persian shawl, which came from Asia in a sailing vessel two centuries before and was acquired by her ancestors from a trader in exchange for furs.

James Swan has left a story of Indian ghosts at Shoalwater Bay. He had gone to bed in the same room with an Indian when the dogs sleeping in the house suddenly rose and made a great fuss—barking, tail-wagging, and jumping about as though greeting old friends. Swan was sleepy and annoyed and put the dogs summarily out of the house. When he got back into bed the Indian asked quietly, "Did you not see the *memelose*?" When Swan replied no, the Indian identified the visitors as two Indians who had been killed nearby some time before. "The dogs," said the Indian, "can see the *memelose* and they were jumping around because they were so glad to see their old friends again."

Indians often insist they get help from the dead, even in these times. In 1941 an old Indian woman on Vancouver Island told an anthropologist of friendly ghosts who helped an Indian collect wood: A knock sounded at the door. "Come, get the wood, we piled it up." The Indian would get into his canoe with the ghosts, whom he could see quite plainly. "His eyes are real open. Dead people tell him things that are going to happen." One day the Indian was out on the shore picking up this ghost-collected wood and throwing it onto the bank. Suddenly those who were watching saw him begin to dodge and protect himself as though warding off blows. He fell to the ground, fell over on his face, then on his back. It didn't take the Indians long to figure out what had happened. The ghosts thought their friend had been throwing the wood at them. The Indian doctor said, "Come on and help. I'm going to fight those ghosts." They took charcoal, the worst enemy of ghosts, went to the graveyard, and started throwing charcoal at them. It was "just like shooting them." . . . Trouble died down at once. The Indian had real bruises. It isn't reported whether or not the ghosts went on doing little handyman chores for him after this episode.

The Indian respect for the dead was universal, and the superstitious awe in which corpses were held accounts in part for the successful crossing of the plains of a communist-religious group bound for Aurora, Oregon, in the dangerous fifties.

Back in Bethel, Missouri, from which the Aurora colony started, little Willie Keil, the son of the founder and leader, fell sick and died just a few days before the group set out on the long trip westward. Little Willie had been promised by his fond father that he should be the first person of the group to enter the Promised Land; that he was to ride in the first wagon when they reached their destination. His father kept his word. The corpse of the little boy was placed in alcohol in a lead casket and the wagon train started on the long grilling trip across the continent with the casket at the head. The Aurora colonists crossed at the period when Indian uprisings were rife and many wagon trains had been attacked and many people murdered, but their group traveled unmolested. Word went out by the red telegraph of the strange train of whites, led by a *memelose*, and this was enough to impress the superstitious and mystery-loving Indians. This band of very fine, if mildly fanatical, people sang all the way across the plains, and being Germans they sang good music—ranging from Bach's *Ein' feste Burg ist unser Gott* to *Du, du liegst mil am Herzen*. The news of a band of triumphant singing people following a casket for months across the plains kept the Indians at a respectful distance.

The Pacific Northwest has produced some genuine philosophical mystics, or perhaps one should rather say, people who were born with that particular bias and who found it fostered in a land where the mysteries and beauties of the earth are so forced upon one's consciousness. Looking out long enough on mountains and tides, or vast stretches of desert, produces, in time, a reverse action; the eyes look in; the human being begins to seek his own meaning in such an impersonal and rhythmic universe.

Down a back road, facing the blue and white steadfastness of the Olympic Mountains, and the restless swing of the waters of Hood Canal, there lives an old Norwegian who might stand as prototype for all genuine Northwestern mystics. Here is a man who has worked hard all his life at homely tasks; a man whose hands show the jobs to which they have been put, and whose face is colored by exposure to many varieties of weather. He lives in a house that shows signs of a former prosperity. Inside there is wood carving, some by the owner and some by a friend, of Scandinavian myths and myths from the Far East, such as the Night and Day of Brahma. There is also a complete library of Scandinavian literature and an amazing collection of religious books. The owner, John Storseth, has written a book of his early days in Norway, his coming to America, and his life in the Pacific Northwest. It is written in gentle and slow-moving prose, rather like the early Knut Hamsun; all of it shimmered over with his special philosophy, the sense of himself as a poor creature about whom, none the less, all life revolves. This is a triumphant assertion to thrust in the face of tides and snowcaps!

Speaking of himself in the third person he writes:

"But I, as I said before, that have known Johannes all my life, I do not yet know where he comes from, nor do I know where he aims to settle. Perhaps he does not know himself.

"He says that in the whole world you cannot find a single one like himself. To me he looks like so many other Johanneses I have met, but to this sort of explanation he has a deaf ear. He is the only one. About him everything transpires. The earth and all the planets are created for his benefit, he imagines.

"If there only had been something to him, but that there is not; small and plain looking he is. Fragile he has always been. It has happened several times that he took sick from a gust of wind touching him. The talk that all the planets course around such humbleness sounds ludicrous, and is, no doubt, due to his own imagination."

And later in the book he writes:

"Everybody expects much from the new time that we think we have. Really we do not know much about it. No one can tell when the new time started, and no one can tell when it will end.

"It is only the 'now' that counts and the 'now' has no beginning and no end. Time comes and goes like a dream. Only the 'now' is a reality. It is so short that it cannot be measured, and at the same time so long that it takes in the whole eternity."

People flash on and off the screen of this far western picture arousing brief pity, wonder, condemnation, awe, before drifting into the darkness again.

From Oregon Cow Country this: "One day early in June a widow drove up in a covered wagon, with a wore-out team and two little boys and a girl. They had traveled to the end of their finances and now they wanted to sell their canary bird to raise some money."

The women are perhaps the most fascinating because when women are torn up from their roots their activity becomes wholly unpredictable. In an old diary, written while crossing the plains with the early emigrations, is a record of a woman who must have gone well beyond her limit in physical endurance. She aroused singularly little pity from her fellow travelers and none at all from the woman who reports her action in pithy phrases:

"September 15. Laid by. This morning our company moved on, except one family. The woman got mad and wouldn't budge nor let the children go. He had the cattle hitched on for three hours and coaxed her to go, but she wouldn't stir. I told my husband the circumstances and he and Adam Polk and Mr. Kimball went and each one took a young one and crammed them in the wagon and the husband drove off and left her sitting. She got up, took the back track and traveled out of sight. Cut across and overtook her husband. Meantime he sent his boy back to camp after a horse he had left, and when she came up her husband said, 'Did you meet John?' 'Yes,' was the reply, 'and I picked up a stone and knocked out his brains.' Her husband went back to ascertain the truth and while he was gone she set fire to one of the wagons that was loaded with store goods. The cover burnt off with some valuable articles. He saw the flames and came running and put it out, and then mustered up spunk enough to give her a good flogging."

Whether she had really bashed in the head of her son John the diarist does not say. One is inclined to doubt it, while understanding to the full how after weeks of dust, mud, jolting, sick children, bad food, mosquitoes, horse flies, lack of sleep, and constant uncertainty, one could turn to pyromania and murder with relief.

Within very recent years the state of Oregon produced a singularly intricate and dramatic character who progressed by successive stages from a lumber camp in Oregon to publication in the *Atlantic Monthly*, friendship with its editor, Ellery Sedgwick, accepted kinship by the d'Orleans family of France, and life at the court of the Maharana of Udaipur. This girl, Opal Whiteley, whose life story and diary have been the theme of many heated and unresolved debates, helps convince one of the impossibility of historic accuracy on any subject, when within such a limited range in space and time the "truth" about a single life can be so lost.

Opal Whiteley, whose diary *The Story of Opal: the Journal of an Understanding Heart* was a literary sensation when published by the *Atlantic Monthly* in 1920, was born, according to the Whiteley family, in Colton, Washington. She is, however, claimed as an Oregon product since she grew up in that state. She attended the University of Oregon just prior to the publication of her diary, and it is said that her entrance examinations were waived because of her unusual knowledge of such subjects as biology, geology, and astronomy. Opal went on from the University—after only two years there—into the teaching of nature classes for children in Los Angeles and while there planned the writing of a comprehensive book on nature to be called *The Fairyland Around Us*. She solicited and received, it is said, small grants of money from the Carnegie and Rockefeller funds and admiring testimonials from such people as Nicholas Murray Butler, Gene Stratton Porter, and Theodore Roosevelt. Finally she thought to quicken interest in her ideas by taking the manuscript to the *Atlantic Monthly*.

She raised the money for the Boston trip and presented herself to Ellery Sedgwick who was not interested in *The Fairyland Around Us* but was interested in Opal and in what she told him of a diary she had written as a child which had been torn into fragments in a fit of rage by one of her sisters (a "foster" sister in Opal's opinion). Sedgwick persuaded Opal to send out west for the fifty or sixty boxes of this diary of over one hundred and fifty thousand words, and for months in Boston she pieced together this curious document, setting forth a child world inhabited by such characters as a lost "angel father and angel mother"; Lars Porsena of Clusium, a crow; Michael Angelo Sanzio Raphael, a fir tree; and Peter Paul Rubens, a pet pig. This diary reads strangely self-consciously in the 1940s, and it is difficult to understand how it could have created the literary sensation it did in 1920 when the *Atlantic* published an abridgment of it in six installments.

Opal's private story, apparently believed by Mr. Sedgwick, was that in some mysterious way she had been substituted for a real Whiteley (presumably while on her way to a small community in Lane County, Oregon); that she was actually the child of Henri d'Orleans and a daughter of the Maharana of Udaipur. The identification of Henri d'Orleans, whom she refers to in the diary as the mysterious "angel father" was pointed out to lie hidden in such singularly mature literary exercises as an acrostic found in this seven-year-old's journal. The acrostic, in which the first letters of the listed flowers were discovered to spell Henri d'Orleans, runs as follows:

"I did sing it *Ie chant de fleurs* that Angel Father did teach me to sing of *Hiacinthe, Eclaire, Nenufar, Rose, Iris, et Dauphinelle et Oleandre, et Romarin, Lis, Eglantier, Anemone, Narcisse et Souci.*"

Some hardheaded Oregon cynics like Elbert Bede, the editor of the Cottage Grove *Sentinel,* who knew Opal in Christian Endeavor days and who has written his account of her for Alfred Powers' *History of Oregon Literature,* feel pretty sure that Opal did some homework on that journal as a mature young woman with a knowledge of college French. Bede also points out that Opal looked surprisingly like the rest of the Whiteleys—who just never could explain what had come over Opal apparently—but even he admits to puzzlement on some subsequent details of her life. He cannot explain how she embarked for Europe with a confidential document said to have been signed by our secretary of state and by Sir Edward Grey of England who became acquainted with Opal through Mr. Sedgwick; or how Opal was apparently countenanced by the mother of Henri d'Orleans and financed for the trip to India where she was accepted at the court of one of the leading potentates.

In September 1933 the information reached Oregon that "an American lady" (no name was given) had seen Opal Whiteley in India. "Half a troop of cavalry came toward her at a fast trot, lean, brown men on coal black horses, all gay and gleaming with brilliant trappings. They were escorting a gleaming carriage." They turned out to be the house cavalry of the Maharana of Udaipur, ranking prince of Rajputana. The woman in the carriage was recognized by the American to be Opal Whiteley, whom she had known well in this country. When this word reached Ellery Sedgwick, he is said to have written to a number of maharajas inquiring as to the truth of it (although Opal had already written him of her visit to India and sent photographs), and he had "official" replies from two courts verifying the fact that Opal was living in the Udaipur palace and had received "royal honors as a royal princess." A British officer of high rank also wrote him describing how the Lancers were turned out in her honor and that she was taken on a tiger hunt on an elephant supplied by the prince. Further testimony of the truth of this tale is said to have come from a Dr. Rushford Williams, a foreign clergyman at the court of the Maharaja of Patiala. The last real flurry in the Oregon press about Opal comes from an article in the *Oregonian* of August 2, 1936. This is an interview with Ellery Sedgwick in which he said that he continued to keep up a correspondence with Opal, and that she was at the time in Oxford, England. He had concluded from her references to "the sisters" that she was in a convent. He repeated once again that he still believed her diary to be genuine.

It seems safe to assert that the mystery of Opal Whiteley will never really be cleared up.

CHAPTER II

Paul Bunyan's Larder

Not long ago the *Believe it or Not* column of the newspapers carried a picture of a rather undernourished and unkempt man eating with evident relish what was said to be "an old pioneer Oregon delicacy, fern pie." This seemed hardly credible to me until I saw that the *Oregon Guide* also listed this pie under pioneer edibles, without, however, stating which ferns were used to make what would seem to be a singularly unappealing dish. I can't but believe that fern pie was only resorted to in times of dire need. A woman resident of the Northwest in the sixties wrote in her diary that miners always made a point, in telling tales of hardship, of being reduced to a diet of "ferrins," which, on inquiry, she discovered to be boiled ferns.

There was almost literally nothing on, or in, the earth, the water, or the air of the Pacific Northwest of which the Indians did not make use, and many of the early white settlers learn to depend on in their diet. I don't know that the Indians actually ate fern tops, but it is not unlikely since they ate fern roots (there were three edible varieties); the cat-tail flag, which whites also learned to like, sliced in vinegar and eaten raw; the root of the seashore rush which uncooked is said to resemble the Jerusalem artichoke and when baked a mealy potato; tree moss prepared in a variety of ways; camas root for bread and many other now neglected delicacies. Over two hundred different varieties of plants native to the land were used by the Indians as food or medicine.

Procuring food was an important part of the life of the early pioneers of this country. To the west there were always fish to be caught, many varieties of wild berry in season and plenty of gamebirds, but in the desert to the east one might think procuring food was something more of a task. A dryland pioneer, however, has something to say that would seem to indicate old-timers on the plains could take care of themselves quite as well as the folk on the coast:

"There's no need for anyone to starve to death in the open. In addition to the regular wild life bill of fare there are snakes, frogs, snails and other delicacies like grasshoppers and such, just lying about ready to be utilized. I've eaten horse meat, mule meat, camel meat, dog meat, and well over one hundred rattlesnakes. Rattlesnakes are really fine eating. I first learned this from the Indians. I've eaten everything on the Indian menu, including rattlers, grasshopper meal and hawk-squab potpie."

This old settler is very clear on the details for preparing rattlesnake:

"To prepare a rattlesnake for the table, one cuts off the head and then slips the skin off down to the tail. The skin slips off just like a glove from the hand. The next thing is to slit the belly and take out the 'innards' which is just one long intestine on which the fat appears as fretwork."

And finally he is very eloquent about its flavor:

"The body of the snake is virtually all meat and tender. . . . To cook, one cuts the prepared carcass into sizeable chunks, washes it in a salt brine and lets it dry. It is then fried in bacon grease, pan fat or oil and served hot. The meat has no odor and tastes like the flesh of a cotton-tail rabbit but is better flavored."

Among prime frontier delicacies not to be had any more are beavers. Trappers were very partial to the meat of a fat beaver, particularly beaver leg, roasted and sliced off cold, which was considered equal to the finest pig. Then there were beaver tails cut up in chunks, with the bones removed, the "meat all tender and jelly-like" eaten with hunks of smoky bread. In Lewis and Clark's journal there is a detailed description of how to catch a beaver which seems quite astonishing, involving the performance of a very delicate surgical operation on one beaver, in order to remove the "bark-stone" to use as bait for a brother-beaver; and in addition a good supply of such unusual frontier culinary equipment as cloves, nutmeg, and cinnamon. The spices and the scent of the castor brought beavers from miles away.

A story survives of a Christmas season at Shoalwater Bay in Washington Territory in the fifties when game among the oystermen—shipping cargoes to luxurious San Francisco—became mysteriously scarce and everyone was pretty tired of the staple diet of salt salmon and potatoes. The old cook refused to be downhearted. There were always crows, he said, and crow was good, so was eagle, so was owl. He reasoned in this manner: "'A crow,' said he, 'is good because it has a crop like a hen; and eagles, hawks and owls are good, for although they have no crops, yet they do not feed upon carrion.'" Someone shot two crows and the cook made what he called a "sea pie." No one found it edible, the birds being extremely tough. This old captain also cooked upon occasion lynx, seal, otters, gulls, pelican, and even went so far as to bake a skunk, but since he hadn't properly cleaned it he was forced in the end to throw kettle and contents into the river, sighing as he did so that it was a pity "when it was baked so nice and brown."

Certainly there are other dishes indigenous to the Pacific Northwest at which no gourmet could quail. Consider, for instance, the geoduck. On Puget Sound, the habitat of the geoduck, there's a favorite story which any old man digging on a beach is bound to tell you:

"So I says to this Eastern feller—he was goin' on about the size of the crabs and the salmon he caught and the taste of Olympia oysters—how'd you like to go geoduck huntin'? Geoduck, says he, never heard of it. What kind of a duck is it? he says. Well, I says, it's peculiar to these parts. Don't grow nowhere else. We'll have to wait for a low tide and then I'll take you. Why the low tide? he asks. Well, I says, you'll see and don't bother to bring your gun. I'll bring one for you."

At this point the old man doubles up with laughter and any bystanders always laugh too, for a geoduck "gun"—now forbidden by law to protect these sole survivors of some more heroic age of sea life—is nothing more nor less than a length of stovepipe, with handles attached near one end, which is rammed into the sand to prevent the big clam from escaping.

The geoduck "clam" can measure more than three feet in length with the siphons extended, and getting him from the sand to your table is an art, a science, a feat of skill, and an arduous ordeal. You wait for a minus-tide; midwinter, early summer, provide the best. You then put on hip boots and you squish out, way out, through the beds of sea dollars and sand collars, gigantic snails and starfish and crab, to the very edge of the waterline and then you start walking. You are told to keep your eye peeled for the projecting heads in the sand, just the sand color and usually concealed with a bit of seaweed. These are the necks. The trick is that a projecting periscope of neck in the sand can as easily be a horse clam as a geoduck; the former are not good eating and the latter a feast. The way you tell the difference is by swiftly bending over and feeling the projecting side of the neck before it can be withdrawn—often with a delicate geyser of water right in the amateur's eye. If the neck feels hard on the sides it's a horse clam. If it's soft and the neck goes down with unbelievable speed, it's a geoduck. You then shout and everyone gathers and begins to dig. As soon as the hole is deep enough one member of the party kneels and tries to get hold of the neck. He holds this while the others dig around his hands and pray that the walls of the hole won't keep caving in. Finally, amidst a spray of sand, mud, water, and curses, up comes the great shell with its projection of neck, and it's a geoduck!

On sunny days the geoducks come up and lay their necks out flat on the sand for a good airing, and one is told that in the early days ladies didn't go out on the beach with the men hunting these creatures, because the geoduck, when viewed in its natural state, seemed vaguely indecent.

Puget Sound and Hood Canal abound in sea life. One of the great food favorites is the hard-shelled crab which lives far out beyond low-water mark, may be trapped with a homemade contraption of chicken wire baited with clams, or picked up with a fork in a narrow channel in the in-coming tides. These crabs must be tossed back into the sea unless they are at least six and a quarter inches across, and they must be male—their sex being easily determined by the phallic pattern on the reverse side of their shells.

There are restaurants in Oregon and Washington which specialize in barbecued crab. This is the large crab boiled and served with hot curry sauce and great chunks of hot garlic bread. The waitresses tie a large napkin under the patron's chin and he quietly goes to work breaking up the shell, poking out the meat, dripping and drooling and having a wonderful time. One invariably overeats and is reminded of a sign which once hung in Portland in front of the Old Thompson House: "*Hyas Muck-a-muck, and No Airs! Call in and see Old Thompson and get the Wrinkles Taken out of your Belly.*" (Hyas Muck-a-muck is Chinook for Plenty to Eat.)

Some of the old recipes are of a richness no longer quite so palatable in these unrobust times. A favorite recipe—kept "secret" for many years—was Cap'n Doane's famous Olympia Oyster Pan Roast. People traveled miles to eat it in Doane's Chop House in Olympia. To make it you must have the delicate tiny Olympia oyster, a "freak" oyster indigenous to certain shallow coves of Puget Sound; oysters which stubbornly refuse to grow anywhere else. They are never eaten on the half shell but are eaten raw in cocktails or in cooked dishes like the famous pan roast, for which the recipe is here given:

Put one pint of Olympia oysters in their own liquor into a small stew pan, and bring to a boil. In another pan melt one half cup of butter, three tablespoons of catsup, one tablespoon of vinegar, a dash of Worcestershire sauce and cayenne pepper to taste. Add this dressing to the drained oysters and allow them to simmer for only one more minute. Serve on toast.

A pioneer delicacy, curiously effete and almost Oriental in its subtlety which Oregonians were wont to have as dessert, is the flower of the blue elderberry. You pick the clump of beautiful flat white flowers and you put it wherever it will get cold enough to become very stiff. When stiff you immerse it briefly in a thin waffle batter, dip it swiftly into deep hot fat, only until crisped, and eat at once.

Puget Sound Indians who lived almost exclusively on fish learned to balance their diet with native greens and berries. When herring were running, the Indian tempered the oily diet with the astringent green shoots of the wild raspberry. The richness of the feasts of the salmon days he balanced with salmon berries from the green ravines. If you've ever eaten *Salmon Sluitum* cooked the Indian way you may understand how easy overindulgence could be.

You make a good fire of any hard wood. (The Indian considered alder a necessity since alder smoke gives the salmon an added flavor.) The fish are scaled and have their heads, tails, and fins removed. The backbone is also carefully removed—without cutting the salmon—by making an incision down each side of it on the flesh side, not the skin side of the fish. The fish is then flattened out and in this position two wooden skewers are thrust entirely through it, one near the place where the head would be, and the other near the tail. These skewers must have about a ten-inch projection because they stand upright on the ground supporting themselves against a four-foot-high crossbar of wood, with sawhorse ends, which is placed above the coals. Thus, leaning on the crossbar, the salmon cook two and a half to three hours, so that the oils are driven by the heat back into the fish. Their only seasoning is salt, plus the alder smoke and their own inimitable flavor.

Pages could be written about the many uses of the varieties of black-berry, huckleberry, elderberry, whortleberry, and salal that riot over the slopes of the Northwestern coast. For many years the old recipes were for-gotten, but now there is a revival of interest in them; women's pages of news-papers give a good deal of space to them, and the west coast magazine *Sunset* helps to keep them alive.

Ways of cooking game vary interestingly from the east to the west in the states. Cow Country cookery has some superb camp fare like Bannock Bread and Buckaroo Spuds—the latter a simple and subtle concoction of water, raw potatoes, and onions which is "all in the cooking."

The Northwest has produced some real epicures, among them Henry Theophilus Finck, for many years the music critic of the New York *Post* who used to take time off from music now and then to write such books as *Girth Control*, or *Food and Flavor*. Mr. Finck, who grew up in the religious-communist community at Aurora, Oregon, has written tender passages recalling the early cookery at Aurora which was good enough to affect the train schedules and bring stopovers a few miles from Portland so that the crew could have such community prepared dishes as "chicken cooked in garlic water, smoked venison hams, pies too deep to believe."

Some of Mr. Finck's pleasantest memories are of the Oregon apples, and he says that they were in such demand in the south that in 1853 four bushels sold in San Francisco for $500, and the following year forty bushels brought $2500 in the same market. It might be an upstate New Yorker talking thus instead of an old-time Oregonian:

"Of course we had the luscious Gravensteins—winesaps, excellent Newton pippins; with other favorites of our time, like Baldwins and greenings. We doted on white winter pearmains and on the russets, both golden and Roxbury which, alas, have become so scarce. We had green Newtons which were even more juicy than the yellow. What has become of them and what of the mealy bellflowers, and the unique western seek-no-further and others worth perpetuating? There were rambos, too; and you can never get them now. . . ."

Remembering the plight of the growers in the Wenatchee Valley one ponders these words of Mr. Finck's: "You may not believe it, but it is a positive fact that we never needed to spray against pernicious insects and we never had it plowed [the land]. No need of these things."

The first apple tree in Oregon is still supposed to stand on the site of old Fort Vancouver, although skeptics doubt the tale that the seeds came from England well over a hundred years ago in the dress suit pocket of a visiting dignitary of the Hudson's Bay Company. During the fruit course at a London dinner a beautiful young lady put them there and when, months later, the gentleman got to Vancouver he remembered them. John McLoughlin's able Scotch gardener planted the seeds and they grew.

CHAPTER III

The Jumping-off Place

From its very beginning American pioneering has been characterized by the development of small colonies—outside the main stream of social consciousness—where people could come together to work out what seemed to them a better way of life. Brook Farm, Harmony, Oneida, Bethel are familiar names to most students of American social development. Colonies of a similar nature established in the Pacific Northwest have received little attention from historians; though actually such communities as Aurora, Oregon; Home, Glennis, the Port Angeles Co-operative, Freeland and Burley, Washington, presented in their day an economic and social challenge perhaps not as imposing but certainly quite as real as the challenge today of Grand Coulee and Bonneville.

It is apparently true that the Socialist Party of America undertook to select one state and to plant colonies there which would furnish final demonstration of the superiority of Socialism over other ways of life. The state the party selected for the experiment in the early nineties was Washington; in part because of the amount of cheap land available, the phenomenal rise of a great industry, lumber; and also perhaps for other less materialistic reasons.

In the yellowing files of the old newspaper published in the Freeland colony, which flourished for some years in Skagit County, the editor has this to say: "If in a country where pea vines grow as large as trees, clams weigh four pounds, grass grows nine feet high and fish worms look like snakes, Socialism can't successfully get a foothold there must be something wrong with the Socialist brand of seed."

The Freeland colony failed; so did the colony at Aurora, and the one at Burley and the one at Glennis, apparently because of human weaknesses blocking abstract idealisms. The editor of the Freeland newspaper finds an explanation: "The underlying cause has been the indisputable fact that as Socialists most of us were pulled before we were ripe. We thought we had raised Socialism to a science before we had mastered the alphabet, and furthermore we did not analyze our own natures to discover how much of the old competitive, murderous, individualistic spirit yet lingered there."

There are members of the "Anarchist" colony still living in their village of Home across the Sound from Tacoma. In this community which flourished at the end of the nineteenth century complete independence of conduct was allowed all members so long as there was no interference with any other's life. All views were tolerated and anyone might use Liberty Hall to air his views provided only that he permitted courteous questioning from the audience. A Harvard Phi Beta Kappa, grandson of the author of *America*, was a leader in the community. Free love was said to be practiced; a professor with a long beard wore women's skirts because he found them more comfortable; and people bathed nude—until reported to the authorities. The colony paper *Discontent, the Mother of Progress* became in time *The Agitator*, and under both names drew the fire of pulpit, press, and women's clubs. Once a United States Marshal came to Home to arrest the editors of *Discontent*. With true Tolstoian Christianity, which the colony practiced, he was met at the wharf with great courtesy, taken to one of the homes for an excellent dinner, then made the guest of honor at a dance at Liberty Hall. The next day he presumably placed his hospitable charges under arrest pending their trial.

Stewart Holbrook, who did a series of articles on this colony for the Portland *Oregonian* a few years ago, reported that some of the colonists had significant remarks to make about their experiences. One said: "The stuff we printed in *Discontent* wouldn't raise an eyebrow today."

The village barber said that the colony had offered him whatever he could have asked: ". . . a decent living in good times as well as bad; plenty to read; excellent neighbors; and more freedom than I have ever seen elsewhere. I don't think there is much else in life."

The kind of plan for living which promises a citizen full individual freedom—so long as he does not actively interfere with the life of any other community member—is pretty well out of fashion in the world today; but the spirit which animated this way of life is very much alive in parts of the Pacific Northwest where old-timers and their easygoing liberal notions still dominate a community.

The early pioneers in the Northwest have given written evidence that they were conscious of the potentially important destiny of this last outpost. Within recent years there has been a singular reawakening of this sense of destiny. The citizen of the Pacific Northwest is beginning to ask pertinent questions. One hears them everywhere—the same ones; from small town newspaper editors, farmers, ranchers, little businessmen, big businessmen, doctors and lawyers and teachers and housewives. Men who love the streams and the green uncluttered countryside speak worriedly of Pittsburgh, want to know whether the Pacific Northwest must sacrifice its green beauty and look on helplessly while its streams are polluted with new industries seeking cheap power. People vote for and then stand around and question Public Utility Districts. They remind one another that local waterworks have never been as well run under public ownership as they were under Old Mr. X.

This discrepancy between majority votes and apparently general opinion is one of the factors which make Pacific Northwest politics an engrossing, if slightly mystifying, study. In the years when Oregon Klan activity was at its height the voters put in a Jewish governor. Oregon won fame as the first state to adopt that highly democratic form of procedure, the Initiative and Referendum, but then, as Richard Neuberger has said, the citizens used their power "to authorize new county jails and regulate the sale of oleomargarine." Worse, the people of Oregon once adopted, by a substantial majority, a measure to close all religious and private schools—a law later declared unconstitutional by the United States Supreme Court. All of which brings thinking people to puzzled head-shaking and the question as to whether—observing Oregon's almost forty years of experience with direct legislation—Americans are yet educated to accept civic responsibility to its fullest extent.

Symbolic of growing awareness of the fate line of the Pacific Northwest are the number of regional planning councils and regional resource boards which have come into prominence in the last few years. Their publications range from small booklets entitled *Pacific Northwest Chemiurgic Conference* to *Caravans to the Northwest*, a book made possible by Rockefeller money, graphically setting forth with the aid of pictures and a concise text the hopes and the dangers of the immediate future.

Browsing behind the somewhat formidable title of the report on the chemiurgic conference one comes upon material offering, not a specific answer, but surely a general one, to some of the questions people are asking one another in this rich land:

"If our sunshine and our soil produce more than we can eat or sell abroad then we must turn them into other articles that may be for non-food necessities, or for the enjoyment of life. For example, after we have drunk all the milk and eaten all the soybeans that our stomachs can accommodate, we may use the surplus milk and beans for a casein glue for plywood which in the Northwest has become one of our great industries.

". . . We have great forests of trees . . . of which more than ten million tons of wood are annually wasted. We have vast potential hydro-energy from rain, snow and ice at high elevations. We have to work with twenty million bushels of wheat a year, ten million boxes of apples that are unmarketed, ten million bushels of cull potatoes; and millions of acres of unused fertile land challenge us.

". . . There is adventure to it as thrilling as there was for those early pioneers a hundred years ago. They were wresting a living from the soil in the shape of food itself, directly. We are doing that same thing, but indirectly as well as directly."

Many Pacific Northwest forest resources, outside wood itself, have been left quite untouched. Pine needle oil, selling for several dollars a pound in

New York, comes from Europe—this in the face of tons of pine needles rotting on the Pacific slopes. Western hemlock, rich in tannin, has not been developed commercially. The oils from the myrtle and the madrona have not been studied for their uses—although from a little herb man in Spokane who provides us with our kitchen rosemary, thyme, peppermint, and savory, I bought recently a small vial of perfume made from the concentrated essence of myrtle, which has a charming fresh and woodsy scent. This may be a small beginning in a new field.

The Pacific Northwest is really just starting the manufacture of wood derivatives, a field extensively exploited in Europe—particularly in Germany—and to some extent in the eastern United States.

"It is not for lack of forest products that it is not a great industry here. . . . The material left in the woods after logging amounts to around 6,000,000 cords of material, cord-wood size and larger. This amounts to nearly 20 percent of the original stand. . . . In addition . . . there is an average of about 5,000 feet per acre left as trees which will be wind blown or destroyed in the usual slashing fire."

Besides the potential products that may be developed from what now amounts to waste in the lumber field, the Pacific Northwest is also exceptionally rich in chromium, manganese, tungsten, phosphates, aluminum—and there is the cheap power available now for their fullest development.

Hope for the Pacific Northwest lies in its relatively late development. Just as all America took so naturally to the advantages of the industrial age—because it was young enough not to have to throw over the established old to make way for the new—so the Pacific Northwest, coming late to that transition from the use of "natural" resources to manufactured or scientific products, has a chance to develop more rationally than older sections of the country. Will she do it rationally?

"Between 1935 and 1940 there have arrived in the Pacific Northwest more families than could be accommodated on farms in the immense Columbia River Basin, even after it is fully developed." This is from the Northwest Regional Council's Book, *Caravans to the Northwest*.

What does such a startling statement imply? That if this section of

America is adequately to meet the challenge which circumstances have flung at it people will have to fulfill to the utmost their capacities as men. If this population growth is to be a source of strength, people in the Northwest are going to have to think very hard and very clearly and act on what they think.

According to regional planning council reports these two states, Oregon and Washington, should not worry about an influx of new blood. They should indeed be pleased about it—if they can assimilate it—for Oregon is third from the top in the declining birth rate of this country and Washington is fifth. Already one envisions these two hardy frontier states growing softer and softer with the enervating effects of a population overpoweringly middle-aged or aged. From this fate the Northwest may, it is pointed out, escape in the nick of time, by accepting the freshening effect of new immigration.

These new immigrants are not being greeted with open arms and shouts of joy from the communities into which they are moving. In the summer of 1940 we tried in vain to get from the Chamber of Commerce in Grants Pass, Oregon, some information about a new colony from the Dust Bowl, via California, which was moving into this part of the state. There was an ominous and markedly cold silence on the whole matter. We finally decided that this taciturnity was quite as interesting as any possible facts we could accumulate on the new arrivals.

The Northwesterner says: "We've already got more unemployed now than we can handle." He does not know the statistics on it, usually, and perhaps it is just as well. They are a bit on the gloomy side. Add to the figure of sustained unemployment the dark facts about seasonal unemployment—always a factor in any consideration of Pacific Northwest economy, since the region is built up on too few major industries—and you have a picture either hopeless or challenging, depending on your general outlook.

The Pacific Northwest has a migrant problem every year with the ripening of pears and apples, hops, cherries, peas, loganberries, strawberries, beans, and sugar beets, and all the other perishable farm products which must be harvested in a hurry. At this time some eighty thousand people move into the harvest areas and work ten hours a day until the crop is exhausted. Their grotesque shack-towns of canvas, tin, tarpaper, wooden boxes, and homemade trailers have long been a familiar sight to people in the fruit and berry districts where owners do not always provide cabins for workers. The government is now building a few camps for migratory laborers. I have seen them near Vale in Oregon and in the apple valley of the Wenatchee in Washington. There are not enough of them, of course, and they do not really solve the problem of the migratory worker, for this is certainly no way of life for a man, his wife, and his growing children. But at least they do provide sanitation and decent living conditions, and constitute far less of a health threat to a community than acreage given over to rugged individualism as expressed in tin can and tar paper down along the railroad tracks—like the eyesores one sees when going in and out of proud Seattle, seated on the comfortable plush of a pullman.

Average citizens find it hard to realize that the migrant's way of life could hardly produce glowing examples of the more standard virtues any more than it could produce such signs of health as a straight spine and good teeth. But before one gets too impatient with these same average people like the small grower-owners, one must take a look at their side of the budget and note the sharp decline in market prices and the rising scale of wages which many men—coming to the end of years of hard work and denial—must now face. There is not as unthinking and hearty optimism here as one might imagine with the present war threat booming both coast and inland areas. People have not yet completely forgotten the aftermath of depression and the dark picture of waste following on the hurried timber slaughter and over-expansion in agriculture and mining which the last war brought about.

Certainly whatever the ultimate part that these Pacific Northwest states play in the big American drama, they have a chance through the development of such purely contemporary activities as regional research and regional planning to see their best direction. Once having seen it they then need the will to take it. Too much praise cannot be given to such research activities, and yet it seems a striking oversight that nothing is mentioned anywhere, among Plans with a capital P, for keeping alive activities to feed man's spirit as well as his body in a possibly approaching Dark Age. There is waste of human material quite as appalling as the waste in lumber operations. When will there be a survey made of cultural trends in the Pacific Northwest, of the rise and fall of such enterprises as the State Theatre of Washington which carried Shakespeare and Chekhov and the work of modern playwrights to high schools which had never seen a play? Why has the Washington State Library been so miserably understaffed and underfinanced? How has the state of Oregon created such an unfortunate reputation of late years in the field of education by the long-drawn-out disgraceful bickerings between the State College at Corvallis and the University at Eugene?

Often in talking with rural or small town people who still live close to the major experiences of human life—birth and death seen in the seasons, in their livestock and in their own homes, with children born in the upstairs bedroom and grandparents dying in a room off the dining room—one encounters a wholesome and uplifting philosophy. It might be a good thing, these people ruminate gently, for this country to be really hard up against it. Not just the Pacific Northwest, but all of America.

There is a kind of isolationism in their viewpoint, but its roots strike deeper than that overused and unexamined word might imply. These roots lie in a belief that out of hardship, privation, suffering, there grow cooperation, ingenuity, and brotherhood. We'll have to stick together and tighten our belts, is the general idea. Not: you tighten your belt, fellow, you're just a vagrant! But: all of us, standing together!

Here is a last echo of the kind of fellowship and sharing that characterized community life here in the days of the pioneer when the death of a villager truly taught those remaining "for whom the bell tolled," since the church bell numbered the years of the dead man's span and all living men stood at attention to heed the slow strokes and honor thus the passing of a comrade.

Those vanished times of the pioneer were times of faith and testing. So are these. Essentially the basic problems have changed very little. They are still: how best can I, a human being, live the good life; have work, adequately rewarded; enough leisure to prevent my becoming a senseless robot; the satisfaction of knowing that my children will have health and the hope also of employment. Above all how can the lives of all of us have a measure of those extras which lift man above the plane of the animal: good books and the chance to read them; good music and the chance to make and hear it; painting and architecture and sculpture expressive of our times; and the education to understand our times and its natural expression?

The Pacific Northwest is still pioneering. It has just begun to see its problems and to seek its final answers. Since it represents the last geographic reach of the American continent the graph which shows its growth and its setbacks and its final achievement will be as significant for America as the flowering and decline of New England. The present problems of the Pacific Northwest spring from America as it is today, but the answers this section of the country still has a chance to find may well determine the America of tomorrow.

Reading List

Applegate, Jesse: *Recollections of My Boyhood*. Chicago: Printed for the
Caxton Club; 1934.

Binns, Archie: *The Laurels Are Cut Down* (novel). Reynal & Hitchcock, 1937.

——: *The Land Is Bright* (novel). Charles Scribner's Sons, 1939.

——: *Mighty Mountain* (novel). Charles Scribner's Sons, 1940.

——: Northwest Gateway, The Story of the Port of Seattle. Doubleday, Doran
& Company, 1941.

Carey, Charles H.: *A General History of Oregon*. 2 vols. Portland:
Metropolitan Press; 1935.

Carr, Mary Jane: *Young Mac of Fort Vancouver* (juvenile). The Thomas Y.
Crowell Company, 1940.

Clarke, S. A.: *Pioneer Days of Oregon History*. 2 vols. New York: Burr Printing
House; 1905. Portland: J. K. Gill.

Cox, Ross: *Adventures on the Columbia River*. J. & J. Harper, 1832.

Davenport, Homer: *The Country Boy* (the story of his early life in Oregon).
New York: G. W. Dillingham; 1910.

Davis, H. L.: *Honey in the Horn* (novel). Harper & Brothers, 1935.

Drury, Clifford Merrill: *Marcus Whitman, M.D., Pioneer and Martyr*.
Caxton Printers, 1937.

——: *Elkanah and Mary Walker.* Caxton Printers, 1940.

Dye, Eva Emery: *Conquest, The True Story of Lewis and Clark* (fictionized history). Chicago, 1902; Portland, 1938.

——: *McLoughlin and Old Oregon* (fictionized history). Chicago: A. C. McClurg & Company, 1913; Portland, 1938.

Eaton, Jeanette: *Narcissa Whitman, Pioneer of Oregon* (juvenile). Harcourt, Brace & Company, 1941.

Ernst, Alice Henson: *High Country* (plays). Metropolitan Press, 1935.

Fee, Chester: *Chief Joseph, The Biography of a Great Indian.* Wilson-Erickson, 1936.

Fuller, George W.: *A History of the Pacific Northwest.* Alfred A. Knopf, 1938.

Goddard, P. L.: *Indians of the Northwest Coast.* American Museum Press, 1924.

Hicks, Granville: *John Reed.* The Macmillan Company, 1936.

Holbrook, Stewart: *Holy Old Mackinaw.* The Macmillan Company, 1938.

Hosmer, Paul: *Now We're Loggin'.* Portland: Metropolitan Press, 1930.

Irving, Washington: *Astoria.*

Jones, Nard: *Swift Flows the River* (novel). Dodd, Mead & Company, 1940.

Judson, Katharine Berry: *Myths and Legends of the Pacific Northwest.* Chicago: A. C. McClurg & Company, 1910.

——: *Early Days in Old Oregon.* Chicago: A. C. McClurg & Company, 1916.

Leighton, Caroline: *Life at Puget Sound, 1865–1881.* Boston: Lee & Shepard; New York: Charles T. Dillingham; 1884.

McKay, Allis: *They Came to a River* (novel). The Macmillan Company, 1941.

Meany, Edmond: *History of the State of Washington.* The Macmillan Company, 1927.

Meeker, Ezra: *Pioneer Reminiscences of Puget Sound and the Tragedy of Leschi.* Seattle: Lowman & Hanford; 1905.

Monroe, Anne Shannon: *Feelin' Fine.* Doubleday, Doran & Company, 1930.

Montgomery, Richard Gill: *The Whiteheaded Eagle, John McLoughlin, Builder of an Empire.* The Macmillan Company, 1935.

Neuberger, Richard Lewis: *Our Promised Land.* The Macmillan Company, 1938.

Parrish, Philip: *Before the Covered Wagon*. Portland: The Metropolitan Press, 1931.

Powers, Alfred: *History of Oregon Literature*. Portland: The Metropolitan Press; 1935.

Shephard, Esther: *Paul Bunyan*. Harcourt, Brace & Company, 1941.

Stevens, James: *Paul Bunyan Legends*. Alfred A. Knopf, 1925.

——: *Homer in the Sagebrush*. Alfred A. Knopf, 1928.

Swan, James: *The Northwest Coast, or Three Years' Residence in Washington Territory*. Harper & Brothers, 1857.

Turney, Ida Virginia: *Paul Bunyan Comes West*. Houghton Mifflin Company, 1928.

Walkinshaw, Robert: *On Puget Sound*. G. P. Putnam's Sons, 1929.

Watts, Roberta Frye: *Four Wagons West*. Portland: The Metropolitan Press, 1935.

Whiteley, Opal: *The Story of Opal, the Journal of an Understanding Heart*. Atlantic Monthly Press, 1920.

Wilkinson, Marguerite: *The Dingbat of Arcady* (a boat trip down the Willamette). The Macmillan Company, 1922.

Winthrop, Theodore: *The Canoe and the Saddle*. Boston: J. R. Osgood, 1875; Tacoma: J. H. Williams, 1913.

Wood, C. E. S.: *Heavenly Discourse*. Vanguard Press, 1928.

——: *A Book of Tales, being some myths of the North American Indians*. Vanguard Press, 1929.

——: *The Poet in the Desert* (poetry). Vanguard Press, 1929.

Note from the Publisher

Graphic Arts Books has chosen to bring to a new generation of readers *Farthest Reach: Oregon and Washington* by Nancy Wilson Ross. The author was born in Washington State and educated in Oregon, and although she was well-traveled and lived abroad, she never lost her enthusiastic appreciation for the landscape and the people of the Pacific Northwest. *Farthest Reach* was first published in 1941, on the cusp of the Second World War but also a time when it was still possible for Ms. Ross to interview some of the earliest nonnative settlers in the Oregon Territory. So not only her background but the period during which she wrote provide a unique and valuable perspective on the culture and character of this part of the world, where "nature is inescapable."

As *Farthest Reach* is an historic document (Ms. Ross died in 1986), we have decided against making any revisions to the text. In the introduction to the book, Ms. Ross asserts that the treatment of minorities and Native Americans by the white settlers was often shameful but elsewhere in the text she does occasionally use terms for various races or ethnicities common to her era that will regrettably cause offense to some readers, and for that we sincerely apologize.

CPSIA information can be obtained at www.ICGtesting.com
Printed in the USA
BVOW01s0853170315

392039BV00005B/13/P